INVESTING IN THE STRUCTURAL TRANSFORMATION

Investing in the Structural Transformation

2024 European Public Investment Outlook

Edited by Floriana Cerniglia and Francesco Saraceno

All external links were active at the time of publication unless otherwise stated and have been archived via the Internet Archive Wayback Machine at https://archive.org/web

Digital material and resources associated with this volume are available at https://doi.org/10.11647/OBP.0434#resources

ISBN Paperback: 978-1-80511-438-3
ISBN Hardback: 978-1-80511-439-0
ISBN Digital (PDF): 978-1-80511-440-6
ISBN Digital ebook (EPUB): 978-1-80511-441-3
ISBN DIGITAL ebook (HTML): 978-1-80511-442-0
DOI: 10.11647/OBP.0434

Cover image: photo by Martin Sanchez (2023), https://unsplash.com/photos/a-large-metal-structure-with-a-clock-on-top-of-it-N5YFJ9s1Sew

Cover design: Jeevanjot Kaur Nagpal

Contents

PART II—CHALLENGES

List of Figures

List of Tables

Acknowledgements

The *Outlook* is the result of a joint effort by several economists belonging to a wide range of academic institutions and policy institutes; each writes in their own personal capacity.

The work was coordinated by Floriana Cerniglia and Francesco Saraceno with logistical and financial support by CRANEC—Centro di ricerche in analisi economica e sviluppo economico internazionale, Università Cattolica del Sacro Cuore—Milano; and OFCE-SciencesPo Paris.

The authors are affiliated with the following institutions:

- Bennett Institute for Public Policy, University of Cambridge
- Brussels School of Governance (BSoG) at the Vrije Universiteit Brussel (VUB) (Brussels, Belgium)
- Caisse des Dépôts et Consignations—CDC (France)
- CRANEC, Centro di ricerche in analisi economica e sviluppo economico Internazionale, Università Cattolica del Sacro Cuore (Milan, Italy)
- European Commission
- European Investment Bank—EIB (Luxembourg)
- European Long Term Investor Association—ELTI (Brusells, Belgium)
- European Trade Union Institute (ETUI) (Brussels, Belgium)
- Georgetown University (Washington, DC)
- Instituto Valenciano de Investigaciones Económicas—IVIE (València, Spain)
- International Monetary Fund (IMF)
- La Fabrique de l'Industrie (Paris, France)
- Luiss Institute for European Analysis and Policy—LEAP, Università Luiss Guido Carli (Rome, Italy)
- Macroeconomic Policy Institute—IMK (Dusseldorf, Germany)
- Observatoire français des conjonctures économiques, OFCE—SciencesPo (Paris, France)
- Paris School of International Affairs—PSIA, Sciences Po, Paris (Paris, France)

- Policy Crossover Center Vienna (Vienna, Austria)
- Technology and Industrialization for Development Centre, University of Oxford
- Universidad Autónoma de Madrid (Madrid, Spain)
- Universidad Complutense de Madrid (Madrid, Spain).
- Università Sapienza Roma (Rome, Italy)
- Università di Parma (Parma, Italy)
- Vienna University of Economics (Vienna, Austria)

As this *European Public Investment Outlook* goes to print, we want to express our gratitude to those who made our work possible: first and foremost, to all the chapter authors who enthusiastically provided this instalment with high-quality contributions; they also simplified our job as editors by (generally!) respecting the deadlines and responding to our queries. The result is a collective volume that has a consistent message throughout.

We also sincerely thank Alberto Quadrio Curzio, President of CRANEC, and Xavier Ragot, President of OFCE-Sciences Po, for their constant support and encouragement. Their help was essential in securing financial and logistical support and, even more importantly, in putting the issue of public investment at the centre of their respective institutions' scientific projects.

Our thanks also go to Giovanni Barbieri from CRANEC for his efficient and painstaking and patient editing of the fifth instalment of the *European Public Investment Outlook*. Thanks are also due to Micaela Tavasani from CRANEC for her proofreading. Last but not least, our gratitude goes to Alessandra Tosi, of Open Book Publishers, who smoothly managed the refereeing process, and who believed in and supported our project since it began in 2020. The editorial team at Open Book Publishers once again moved swiftly and efficiently to ensure a timely publication of the *Outlook*.

Floriana Cerniglia
Francesco Saraceno

Preface

Alberto Quadrio Curzio and Xavier Ragot

Investing in the Structural Transformation: 2024 European Public Investment Outlook continues the remarkable effort to keep public investment at the centre of the European policy debate. The European election results came to confirm that the political polarization of many countries is making policy cooperation increasingly difficult, in a very complicated geopolitical environment.

We concluded the preface to the 2023 *European Public Investment Outlook*, devoted to the financing of public investment, with the statement that "One after the other, the chapters of this *Outlook* argue convincingly that while the issue of fiscal sustainability should not be neglected, it should never be in the way of maintaining, and scaling up the effort to steer the structural transformation of our economies". The 2024 instalment of the report takes it from there and explores possible paths for pushing the transformation of the European Union in an ecologically and socially sustainable and productive economy.

As with the previous four volumes of the *Outlook*, Floriana Cerniglia and Francesco Saraceno have brought together an impressive roster of contributors, consolidating the cooperation between our institutions (CRANEC, Milan and OFCE-SciencesPo, Paris) and continuing in the creation of a network of European researchers working on the topic of public investment.

The *European Public Investment Outlook* has been published yearly since 2020, in an ever-changing economic and geopolitical environment. Yet, as different as the macroeconomic conditions can be, the need for public policies to support growth and structural transformation, notably public investment and industrial policies remains constant over time. The current volume is published when Europe seems finally to be aware of the structural productivity and growth gap that has opened between the EU, on one side, and the United States and emerging economies, on the other side. The Draghi report was presented just a few weeks before the publication of this volume, when the chapters were already written, and yet the authors of these chapters offer interesting insights on how to respond to the challenges identified by the former President of the European Central Bank.

 https://doi.org/10.11647/OBP.0434.00

We commend the effort by the editors of the *Outlook* to renew every year the collaboration between our institutions and to keep alive the attention of policy makers and economists on the topic of public investment, especially at a juncture when the temptation of fiscal consolidation is strong, and risks jeopardizing our common future.

Professors Cerniglia and Saraceno, through these instalments, have introduced an important innovation supported by a group of outstanding scholars who contributed to the various chapters. To all we express our appreciation for their generous and qualified support to the progress of Europe.

Introduction

Floriana Cerniglia[1] *and Francesco Saraceno*[2]

Investing in the Structural Transformation is the fifth *European Public Investment Outlook*. The multifaceted impact of the changing global scenario on Europe and its Member States is the Ariadne's thread that runs through this *Outlook* which focuses on industrial policy. At the end of 2024 the European economy is, once again, at a crossroads. While many European Union governments are engaging in more or less draconian fiscal consolidation plans to bring down public debt, the publication of the Draghi (2024) report on productivity in September 2024 has highlighted a completely different set of priorities. The report's starting point is the diagnosis of an increasingly evident growth gap that has been opening between the EU and its main competitors (mainly the United States and China)—a gap that the former European Central Bank (ECB) president rightly attributes to a chronic stagnation of productivity growth, for large and small countries alike.

Furthermore, the report highlights what has been apparent to most economists and practitioners for at least half a decade, but is only now gaining the attention of the media and policy makers: boosting productivity requires a more efficient organization of the European economy, most notably concerning the single market. And, of course, the layers of regulation and constraints that have accumulated over the past decades have become a drag on growth and need to be reorganized and rationalized. In short, it goes without saying that boosting productivity is not just a question of resources. Nevertheless, the Draghi report is unambiguous about this, it is impossible to imagine that the digital and green transition, and making up for the lost ground in terms of productivity and growth, can be implemented without massive investment (Cerniglia and Saraceno 2022). The team working on the Draghi report quantified these resources in around €800 billion per year (around 5% of EU GDP), of which more than half would have to come from public investment (for numbers in a similar ball park, see Baccianti 2022). The existing evidence, in fact, quite robustly points to the fact that public investment crowds-in private capital. This happens, on one side by providing a stable macroeconomic environment; and on the

1 CRANEC—Università Cattolica del Sacro Cuore (Milan).
2 Observatoire Français des Conjonctures Economiques (OFCE) Sciences Po and Luiss Institute for European Analysis and Policy (LEAP)

 https://doi.org/10.11647/OBP.0434.01

other side by increasing the expected profitability of private investment; the crowding-in effect is even larger when uncertainty is higher, so, typically during periods of structural transformation like the one that lies ahead for the European and the world economies (Durand et al. 2021).

The sequence of crises that has shaken the world and European economies since 2008 has belied the faith in the markets' ability to converge to the natural equilibrium that characterized the consensus in macroeconomics before the Global Financial Crisis. The long period of supposed "Great Moderation", characterized by stable growth and inflation, led some economists to speak somewhat imprudently of the end of history.[3] However, this period actually fostered growing inequality and financial fragility, issues which, when they eventually emerged into the light of day during the Global Financial Crisis, exposed the inability of markets to allocate resources efficiently and to integrate long-term constraints such as environmental and social sustainability into their behaviour (Saraceno 2023).

The long overdue "Rethinking Macroeconomics" process (Blanchard 2016) set in motion by the crises is not over yet, and it is unclear whether a new consensus will emerge. However, the repeated, evident inability of markets to coordinate on stable and satisfactory equilibria suggests that, in the future, theoretical models will foresee a role for economic policy in pursuing socially desirable outcomes. Depending on the circumstances, this can be accomplished by supporting markets, guiding them, and sometimes even replacing or counteracting them.

In particular, since 2008 a prominent role has been assumed by fiscal policies, that had been relegated by the pre-crisis consensus to a closet: first, during the Global Financial Crisis, with "standard" Keynesian policies to support aggregate demand. Then, with the attempt to pull the economy out of the chronic demand shortage that characterized advanced economies since the early 2000s (the *secular stagnation hypothesis*, see Platzer and Peruffo 2022 and Holston et al. 2023). Again, with the renewed attention paid to the importance of global public goods (e.g. health care, social protection, education; see Buti et al. 2023, Hemerijck et al. 2020), to avoid economic and social collapse during the COVID-19 pandemic. Last, but certainly not least, with the return in force of industrial policy and public investment: to cope in the short term with the disarticulation of the world economy induced by the pandemic, by inflation, and by repeated geopolitical shocks; and to facilitate and guide, in the long term, the ecological and digital transitions (Buti et al. 2023; Cerniglia and Saraceno 2022). It is interesting to observe, as a side note, how this return of fiscal policy largely eludes the dichotomy taught to students of economics between structural policies for the supply

3 "My thesis in this lecture is that macroeconomics in this original sense has succeeded: Its central problem of depression prevention has been solved, for all practical purposes, and has in fact been solved for many decades. There remain important gains in welfare from better fiscal policies, but I argue that these are gains from providing people with better incentives to work and to save, not from better fine-tuning of spending flows" (Lucas 2003: 1).

side and monetary and fiscal policies for the demand side: industrial policies, as well as the policies protecting consumers and businesses adopted first during the pandemic and then during the inflationary episode, which could be defined as "expansionary fiscal policies for the supply side", require a new economic theory that has yet to be elaborated (Blot et al. 2024).

Fiscal policy for the supply side, which is relevant for the topic of the current issue of the *European Public Investment Outlook,* also involves investment in that it contributes to shaping the economy in the long run. Mazzucato's (2013) "Entrepreneurial State" has a role in fostering innovation and productivity growth that goes well beyond the standard compensating for market failures. The State, according to Mazzucato, has some features which private enterprises, including venture capitalists, do not have. First, it is patient, in the sense that it can wait long periods of time before reaping the returns for investment. Second, it does not maximize profit, but social welfare; third, even if Mazzucato does not mention it explicitly, it has deep pockets, and capacity to raise debt (Cerniglia et al. 2023). Because of these features, the State, according to Mazzucato, does much more than the simple standard tasks of tackling market failures (like providing public goods, or standard Keynesian aggregate demand support). In fact, it provides the economy with the essential task of exploring possibilities that markets would *never* explore, even absent market failures.

Thus, industrial policy cannot be reduced to simply enabling markets, for example by levelling the playing field and by eliminating or at least reducing rents and market power (which is the doctrine that prevailed within the European Commission in the past); nor can it be reduced to fostering the creation of large oligopolistic conglomerates to compete for market shares.[4] Industrial policy rather needs to be a multidimensional strategy to favour structural transformation and reduce bottlenecks in strategic sectors, facilitating the creative destruction process that reallocates resources from low-productivity activities to sectors that are strategic for geopolitical reasons, and/ or for managing the green and digital transitions. This approach is spelled out by K. Aiginger in Chapter 6, which discusses the need for a new industrial policy for the green transition. Aiginger critiques past industrial policies—whether sectoral (French) or horizontal (German)—and examines their relevance in today's context. The chapter advocates for a modern industrial policy that transcends traditional boundaries between manufacturing and services and is tailored to diverse economic and regional contexts. Emphasizing resilience, sustainability, and inclusivity, this policy must align with societal needs and the Sustainable Development Goals (SDGs), rather than focusing solely on GDP growth. It also stresses the importance of international cooperation over protectionism. While populist movements may push for nationalistic approaches, the chapter argues for a globally oriented policy driven by education, green innovation, and societal well-being to address the profound

4 It is reassuring, in this sense, that the Draghi report emphasizes productivity rather than competitiveness, rejecting the idea that growth is a zero-sum game.

transformations of the twenty-first century. R. Cherif, F. Hasanov, and X. Li develop Chapter 7 along similar lines, discussing what this new industrial policy should look like in the European context. The authors note that problems for EU countries are not limited to the so called "peripheral" countries: since the 2008 Great Financial Crisis, the core countries have been losing their competitive edge in the global market for sophisticated industries such as electronics and green transportation and power technologies. Meanwhile, the peripheral European countries have been slowing down and in the pre-crisis period have mostly channelled their investment into non-tradable industries, concentrating their resources in low productivity and low skill activities. For the EU, the implication at the macroeconomic level is the appearance of dislocating forces: the faltering of the engine of growth, internal trade imbalances, and a convergence slowdown (if not reversal). The lessons of the so-called "Asian miracles" and the earlier European growth experience suggest reigniting business dynamism by spurring innovation, scaling up, and production in sophisticated industries, reorienting the engines of growth of peripheral economies toward exports to the European and global markets and linking up with complex value chains, and changing the mindset of the European institutions from a focus on government failures to tackling market failures in sophisticated sectors with resources steered toward them.

The other chapters of the 2024 *European Public Investment Outlook* deal with specific sectors that are particularly relevant in the current juncture and reinforce the point that industrial policy needs to resort to a multiplicity of instruments in order to address the challenges of structural transformation.

A recurring theme in the *Outlook* is the need for European public goods, much explored by P. Guerrieri and P. C. Padoan (Chapter 8). They focus on the role of economic security in European industrial policy and explore the vulnerabilities and strengths of the EU's industrial and technological strategies, emphasizing the need for deeper European integration and more robust governance to meet these challenges, which require stronger EU-level governance and financial resources for European public goods. A more integrated European defence is obviously another European public good; in Chapter 9, A. Cepparulo and P. Pasimeni examine the significant shift in European security since 2022, characterized by increased and more integrated defence spending. Using new data, the authors analyse the composition and evolution of defence spending in the EU, as well as the distribution of responsibilities across the multi-level governance system. The aim of the authors is to explore how the institutional evolution of EU defence policy is striving to achieve greater convergence of foreign policy objectives and potentially concentrate defence spending at the supranational level. Chapters 10 and 11 focus on two current weaknesses of the European economy. D. Guarascio and A. Simonazzi in Chapter 10 provide an assessment of the vulnerability of the automotive industry. The authors then assess whether the German development model remains viable and outline what might be the essential elements for an effective European industrial policy for sustainable mobility.

Chapter 11 by S. Barbier and H. von Glasenapp attempts to delineate the challenges of the financial framework for the next long-term EU budget. To accelerate the EU's transformation, the authors advocate for mixed public and private financing, a recommendation that also emerges from the Draghi report. The European budget will have to rely on four pillars: prioritize and plan, activate expenditure, decentralize implementation, and strengthen steering. It is on this basis that Europe will be able to finance its investment needs and achieve the structural transformation necessary to maintain and develop its long-term competitiveness within the framework of a new European Competitiveness Pact.

As with the previous instalments, *Investing in the Structural Transformation: 2024 European Public Investment Outlook* includes a first part that details the challenges for public investment and industrial policy in Europe and in its largest countries followed by in-depth country reports for the EU's four largest economies (France, Germany, Italy, and Spain). In Chapter 1, A. Brasili et al. note that while public investment has increased in recent years, there is a need for better coordination and coherence in three key areas: European Public Goods (EPGs), national policy coordination, and funding in the current global context of strained multilateralism and globalization due to constantly shifting geopolitical developments, climate change, the COVID-19 pandemic, energy crises, and the demand for strategic autonomy.

Individual countries face specific challenges, such as import dependency and technological backwardness, which require tailored solutions. Chapter 2, by V. Charlet, M. Plane, and F. Saraceno first traces the long-term evolution of public investment in France, noting how, while comparatively high with respect to other advanced economies, the public capital stock and the general government net wealth have been steadily decreasing since the crisis of 2008. After the COVID-19 shock, despite the 2021 "Plan de Relance" of the 2022 "Build the France of 2030" program, public investment remained surprisingly flat. The chapter then shows how the objectives of French industrial policies have evolved in the recent past. The Lisbon strategy was centred on boosting productivity through innovation and climbing the value-added ladder. The response to the crisis of 2008 marks a first change, with a strong emphasis on price competitiveness and cost reduction (mostly through tax reductions for corporations). Since the early days of the pandemic, then, the notion of "industrial sovereignty" has very quickly eclipsed that of competitiveness, with policies aimed at reindustrialization, especially in strategic sectors. The chapter concludes that these frequent changes signal an excessive short-termism of French policy makers, incompatible with managing long-term structural transformation.

In Chapter 3, K. Rietzler and A. Watt, describe the challenges for Germany caused by a persistent underfunding of public investment. The grim scenario has been exacerbated by the Federal Constitutional Court's ruling declaring unconstitutional the transfer of unused pandemic-related funds to the Climate and Transformation Fund (KTF), which is already underfunded. The renewed application of the debt brake in 2023 has further increased fiscal constraints, risking Germany's ability to meet critical infrastructure and climate transformation needs.

Chapter 4, by G. Barbieri, F. Cerniglia, and F. Mosconi, shows how for a country like Italy—the EU's second largest manufacturer with a strong export vocation—the European perspective is the natural framework for shaping industrial policy. The authors attempt to illustrate what (and if) an industrial policy direction can be traced in the Italian National Recovery and Resilience Plan (NRRP), looking at the so-called "Mission 1" (i.e., Competitiveness) and "Mission4" (i.e., Education and Research). This includes also the strengthening (with investments and reforms) of the Special Economic Zones (SEZs) established in 2017.

Chapter 5 by I. Álvarez and Jorge Uxó provides an assessment of the overall public investment trends for Spain, showing that the COVID-19 pandemic marked a significant shift, with renewed fiscal stimulus and Next Generation EU funds enabling an industrial transformation strategy focused on key sectors with high potential and multiplier effects.

The 2024 *European Public Investment Outlook* examines the crucial need for a robust European industrial policy that effectively addresses pressing challenges such as the green transition, economic security, and the imperative to invest in key strategic sectors, including defence and the automotive industry. This issue of the *Outlook* embraces a multidimensional definition of industrial policy, and advocates for public investment to be a key component of such a structural strategy to build a modern and resilient European Union economy. The chapter authors highlight the need for this new approach to industrial policy to be tailored to an evolving global context. This includes effectively addressing climate change, geopolitical instability, and changing societal needs.

All issues of the *Outlook* emphasize the critical need for improved coordination, effective policies, and addressing challenges such as economic vulnerabilities, defence, and sustainable mobility. A robust EU industrial policy is essential for sustainable growth, economic security, and recovery.

Moreover, *Investing in the Structural Transformation* links with the 2023 issue of the *Outlook* (Cerniglia et al. 2023), dedicated to the constraints posed by high public debt, by offering some proposals on sustaining structural investment financing beyond the year 2027. It further underscores the urgent need for a coordinated, effective, and sustainable approach to public investment and industrial policy in Europe to ensure long-term prosperity and address the complexities of the twenty-first century.

References

Baccianti, C. (2022) "The Public Spending Needs of Reaching the EU's Climate Targets", in F. Cerniglia and F. Saraceno (eds), *Greening Europe: 2022 European Public Investment Outlook*. Cambridge: Open Book Publishers, pp. 107–128, https://doi.org/10.11647/OBP.0328.08

Blanchard, O. J. (2016) "Rethinking Macro Policy: Progress or Confusion?", in O. J. Blanchard et al. (eds), *Progress and Confusion: The State of Macroeconomic Policy*, pp. 287–290. Cambridge, MA: MIT Press.

Blot, C., J. Créel, H. Kempf, S. Levasseur, X. Ragot, and F. Saraceno (2024) "Sailing in All Weather Conditions the Next 25 Years: Challenges for the Euro", Paper Presented at the European Parliament ECON Committee Monetary Dialogue, February, https://www.europarl.europa.eu/thinktank/en/document/IPOL_STU(2024)747835

Buti, M., A. Coloccia, and M. Messori (2023) "European Public Goods", in Cerniglia F. et al. (eds), *Financing Investment in Times of High Public Debt: 2023 European Public Investment Outlook*. Cambridge: Open Book Publishers, pp. 191–200, https://doi.org/10.11647/obp.0386.11

Cerniglia, F., and F. Saraceno (eds) (2022) *Greening Europe: 2022 European Public Investment Outlook Greening Europe: 2022 European Public Investment Outlook*. Cambridge: Open Book Publishers. https://books.openbookpublishers.com/10.11647/obp.0328/

Cerniglia, F., F. Saraceno, and A. Watt (eds) (2023) *Financing Investment in Times of High Public Debt: 2023 European Public Investment Outlook Financing Investment in Times of High Public Debt*. Cambridge: Open Book Publishers.: https://books.openbookpublishers.com/10.11647/obp.0386/

Draghi, M. (2024) *The Future of European Competitiveness*. Brussels: European Commission, https://commission.europa.eu/document/download/97e481fd-2dc3-412d-be4c-f152a8232961_en

Durand, L., R. Espinoza, W. Gbohoui, and M. Sy (2021) "Crowding In-Out of Public Investment", in F. Cerniglia and F. Saraceno (eds), *The Great Reset: 2021 European Public Investment Outlook*. Cambridge: Open Book Publishers, pp. 107–126, https://doi.org/10.11647/obp.0280.07

Hemerijck, A., M. Mazzucato, and E. Reviglio (2020) "Social Investment and Infrastructure", in F. Cerniglia and F. Saraceno (eds), *A European Public Investment Outlook*. Cambridge: Open Book Publishers, pp. 115–134, https://doi.org/10.11647/OBP.0222.07

Holston, K., T. Laubach, and J. C. Williams (2023) "Measuring the Natural Rate of Interest after COVID-19", *Federal Reserve Bank of New York Staff Report* 1063 (June), https://www.newyorkfed.org/medialibrary/media/research/staff_reports/sr1063.pdf

Lucas, R. E. (2003) "Macroeconomic Priorities", *American Economic Review* 93(1): 1–14.

Mazzucato, M. (2013) *The Entrepreneurial State*. London: Anthem Press.

Platzer, J., and M. Peruffo (2022) "Secular Drivers of the Natural Rate of Interest in the United States: A Quantitative Evaluation", *IMF Working Papers* 2022(030), https://www.imf.org/en/Publications/WP/Issues/2022/02/11/Secular-Drivers-of-the-Natural-Rate-of-Interest-in-the-United-States-A-Quantitative-512755

Saraceno, F. (2023) *Oltre Le Banche Centrali. Inflazione, Distribuzione e Politiche Economiche*. Rome: Luiss University Press.

PART I—STATE OF THE ART

1. Public Investment and Industrial Policy: A Case for More European Union Coordination

Andrea Brasili,[1] *Tuna Dökmeci,*[2] *Atanas Kolev,*[3] *Debora Revoltella,*[4] *Jochen Schanz,*[5] *Annamaria Tueske,*[6] *and Wouter Van Der Wielen*[7]

Europe needs more investment. Speeding up the climate transition and relaunching EU innovation capabilities require special efforts. Coupled with strategic autonomy and the need to secure stable and clean energy sources, these issues highlight the increasing importance of European public goods (EPGs) and policies that extend beyond national boundaries, as they involve externalities and network effects. However, Europe's current institutional structure and mechanisms may struggle to meet this challenge. This essay examines public investment trends in the EU, arguing that while public investments have increased, greater coordination and coherence are needed. Three critical axes are identified: the provision of EPGs, policy coordination at national levels, and sufficient funding. Improving the coordination of public investment, particularly in research and development (R&D) and the climate transition, is key to unlocking Europe's full potential. This chapter emphasizes the importance of initiatives like Important Projects of Common European Interest (IPCEIs) in fostering collaboration across countries and sectors, but argues for expanded and more integrated efforts moving forward.

1 European Investment Bank (EIB).
2 European University Institute (EUI).
3 EIB.
4 EIB.
5 EIB.
6 EIB.
7 EIB.

 https://doi.org/10.11647/OBP.0434.02

1.1 Introduction

Europe needs more investment. This simple truth has become something of an imperative or, to put it in Draghi's words, an existential challenge. Two valuable reports on Europe were released between spring and late summer: Enrico Letta's report on the single market (2024) and Mario Draghi's report on European Union (EU) competitiveness (2024). Both highlight the need for a quantum leap in European integration. From a global perspective, recent years have highlighted the urgency of accelerating the climate transition, the need to be prepared for health emergencies, the quest for strategic autonomy, and the importance of securing a reliable and clean energy supply. In addition, Europe should strive to maintain or regain its ability to generate innovations and be at the forefront of technological progress. Draghi's report suggests the need to mobilize public and private resources to generate the required additional investments (the EU investment share should increase from 22% of GDP to around 27%), given that the public sector cannot undertake the entire effort and the private sector does not have strong enough incentives. The message has been clearly perceived by the European Commission (EC), with Ursula Von der Leyen, in her presentation speech after the election for her second mandate (2024), saying : "Europe needs more investment from farming to industry, from digital to strategic technologies but also more investment in people and their skills. This mandate has to be the time of investment". The recipe for generating this large public-private effort should be carefully designed. However it is worthwhile to remember that each of the five major topics mentioned by Von der Leyen above highlights the growing role of public goods and public policy as they all involve externalities and network effects (i.e., they share features like generating spillovers and economies of scale) (Buti, Coloccia, and Messori 2023).

A few months prior to the outbreak of the COVID-19 pandemic, Jean Pisani-Ferry and Clemens Fuest argued for the growing need to centrally supply European public goods (EPGs) in a report for the German and French ministries of finance (2019).[8] This need has been clearly stated in Draghi's report as well.[9] However, there are risks regarding the current institutional setting's ability to speed up the provision of EPGs and embedding them in a coherent strategy. As Draghi pointed out in a recent lecture (Draghi 2023): "... as it stands, Europe's institutional construct is not well suited to carry out these transitions—as a comparison with the US reveals. Here, we are seeing a new focus on so-called 'statecraft,' where federal spending, regulatory changes, and tax incentives align to pursue US strategic goals".

---

8 The need for European strategic investments in this area was also emphasized in the recent white paper of the Belgian Presidency of the Council of the European Union (Demertzis, Pinkus, and Ruer 2024).

9 "To maximise productivity, some joint funding for investment in key European public goods, such as breakthrough innovation, will be necessary. At the same time, there are other public goods identified in this report—such as defence spending or cross-border grids—that will be undersupplied without common action" (Draghi 2024: 14).

The existence of a strategy to tackle these issues and the coherence of the design of policies at the different institutional levels may constitute a crucial challenge in the coming years for the EU. In fact, public policies and public investment choices should be integrated into a broader vision, including industrial policies, in order to stimulate the needed response in private investment. There are at least three different axes along which the EU should explicitly clarify and measure its ambitions in designing strategies and policies. The first is the provision of expenditures related to EPGs, where the EU may lack political willingness or capability to enforce. An example here is the choices in terms of support for basic R&D in the field of energy, such as nuclear fusion. This is a field in which economies of scale may be decisive. The second axis is the degree of coordination of policies that are left to the national level, like the choices regarding energy efficiency in buildings or incentives and support to climate adaptation expenditures: an insufficient coordination may well result in an inefficient use of resources. The third is the level of funding provided that may be insufficient also at the national level.

In what follows, we show the recent evolution of public investments in the EU from this perspective. Following the overview of recent trends in public investment (public investment is growing, based on aggregate numbers), we move on to highlight where actions seem to fall short of what is needed along the three suggested axes.

1.2 The Ongoing Post-pandemic Increase in Government Investment

The uptake in EU government investment that started in 2017 and accelerated in 2020 has continued in 2023. Nominal government investment increased by about 15% in the EU, comfortably outpacing inflation in the same year (Fig. 1.1). The increase spread across the EU but was particularly strong in Central and Eastern Europe (37%) and in Southern Europe (21%).

The increase in government investment also exceeded that of GDP. The government investment rate, the ratio of government investment to GDP, increased by 0.25% to 3.5%. In the case of Central and Eastern Europe, the government investment rate increased by nearly a full percentage point to 5% of GDP.

High inflation in 2022 along with costly fiscal packages to compensate households and businesses for the massive increase in energy prices meant that real government investment stagnated in the EU (EIB 2024). In 2023, inflation decreased significantly, while nominal government investment recorded its highest annual increase over the past 30 years. This allowed real government investment to grow by 10% in the EU. This increase is even more impressive in Southern Europe (19%) and Central and Eastern Europe (27%).

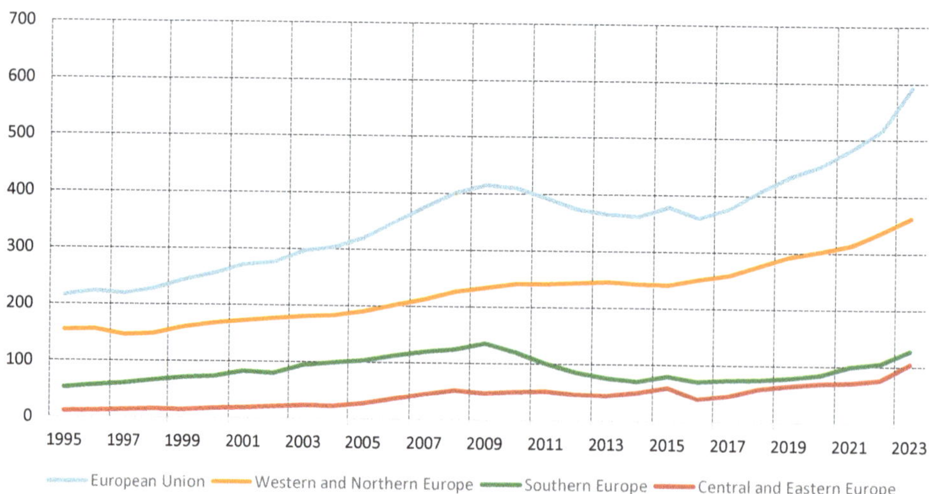

Fig. 1.1 Gross fixed capital formation of the general government (EUR billion). *Source*: Eurostat and EIB staff calculations. *Notes*: Western and Northern Europe includes Austria, Belgium, Denmark, Finland, France, Germany, Luxembourg, Netherlands, and Sweden. Southern Europe includes Cyprus, Greece, Italy, Spain, Malta, and Portugal. Central, and Eastern Europe includes Bulgaria, Croatia, Czech Republic, Estonia, Hungary, Latvia, Lithuania, Poland, Romania, Slovakia and Slovenia.

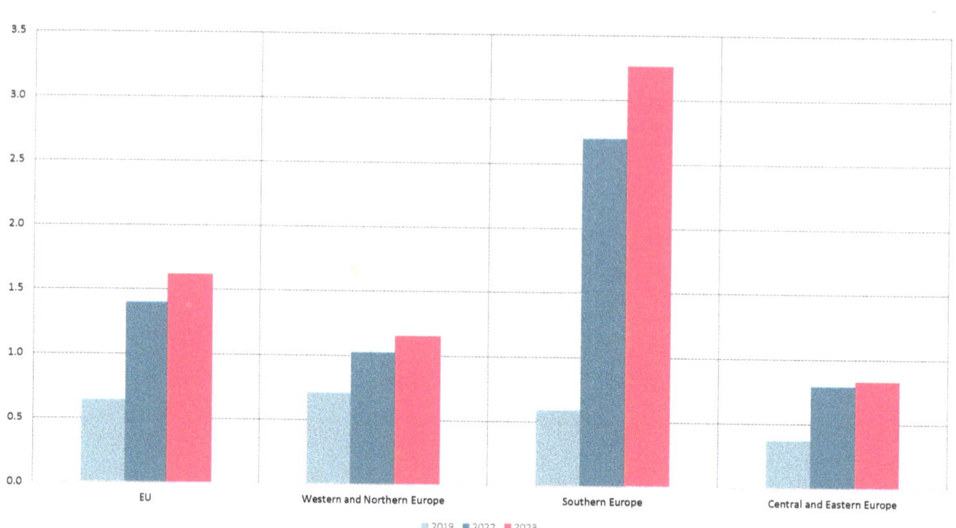

Fig. 1.2 Investment subsidies of the general government (% GDP) *Source*: Eurostat and EIB staff calculations. *Notes*: For definition of the country groups on the chart, please see the notes to Fig. 1.1.

The strong push in government investment in 2023 was accompanied by an extraordinary increase in general government investment grants. Following the outbreak of the COVID-19 pandemic and helped by funds from the Recovery and Resilience Facility (RRF) (cf. EIB 2024), European governments have significantly increased the allocation of investment grants to stimulate investment (Fig. 1.2). In 2023 investment grants payable by the general government increased by 1 percentage point of GDP relative to their level before the pandemic, which constitutes a three-fold increase. While the increase happened across the EU, it was most significant in Southern Europe. There, investment grants jumped six-fold, compared to their level before the pandemic to 3.2% of GDP, exceeding the size of government investment (3.1%).

Local governments accounted for about two-thirds of the increase in the investment of the general government in the European Union, driven mostly by developments in Western, Northern and Southern Europe. In Central and Eastern Europe, local governments accounted for some 40% of the increase in general government investment. In these countries, the share of local government investment is also lower, thereby explaining to some extent the lower contribution. Investment subsidies, on the other hand, increased almost entirely due to increasing expenditure on investment subsidies by central governments.

Given the changes in the EU fiscal framework, this year we cannot rely on the information that Member States provide in terms of their plans on public investment and subsidies for the next years. However, the EC spring forecasts include a projection for these variables[10] that shows a further increase in 2024–2025. Public investment as a ratio to GDP is projected to increase by another 0.1% per year, reaching 3.7% in 2025, the highest level since 2009–2010 (when the ratio was mechanically inflated by the drop in GDP). As shown in last year's *Outlook* (Cerniglia, Saraceno, and Watt 2023), there is a substantial contribution of RRF financed expenditures to this increase. While it is not possible to update this picture with new information, it is useful to show the RRF's role graphically (see Figure 1.4). By contrast, the aggregate "other capital expenditures" is projected to decline after the peak hit in 2023. Figure 1.3 raises two questions: what will happen after the expiration of the RRF in 2026, and what is the role and nature of investment subsidies?

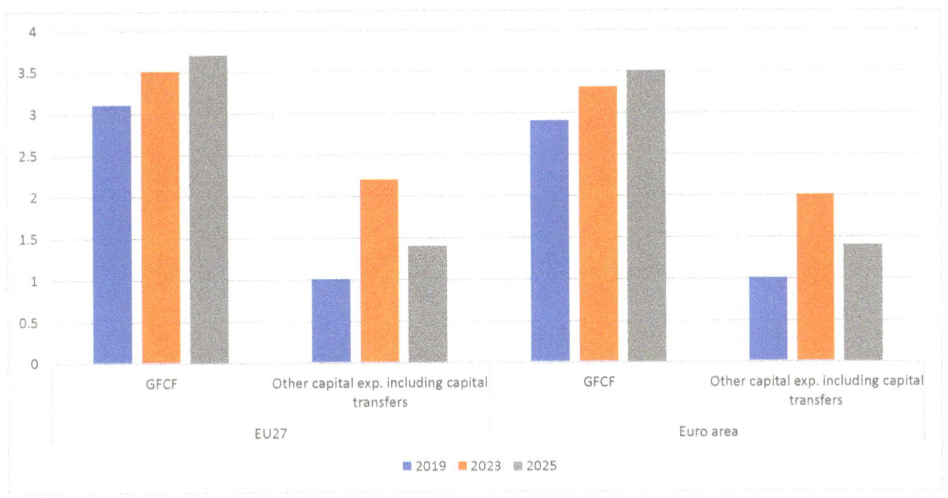

Fig. 1.3 GFCF and other capital expenditures as projected by EC (% GDP). *Source*: AMECO online database.

10 Actually, the projected variables include public investment and other capital expenditures, such as capital transfers, which represent a slightly broader category than the investment subsidies shown in Figure 1.2.

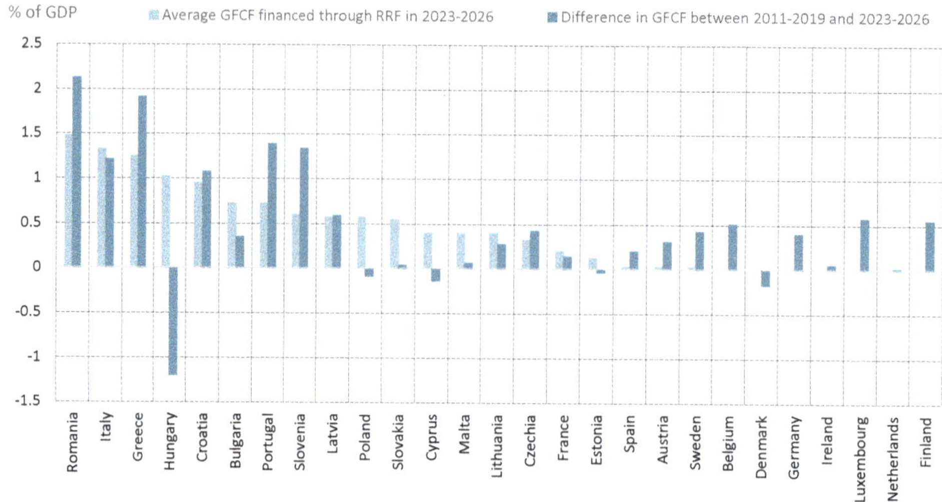

Fig. 1.4 The role of RRF in supporting the acceleration of public investment, 2023–2026. *Source*: Authors' calculations based on Member States' Stability and Convergence Programs.

Looking at the COFOG[11] categories of public investment expenditures, there is no evidence of trends or changes in the aggregate EU27 figures. While the "Economic affairs" category accounts for one third of the expenditures (almost stable with respect to 2001) there are some declines in the share of investment devoted to "Environmental protection" and "Housing and community amenities", and an increase in "General public services". The portion devoted to R&D (that is distributed across all the other categories in Eurostat data, here is re-aggregated) has grown till 2016 (to represent 10% of the whole public investment) and declined slightly thereafter.

Table 1.1 Public investment by categories (COFOG). *Source*: Authors' calculations on Eurostat data.

	General public services	Defence	Public order and safety	Economic affairs	Environmental protection	Housing and community amenities	Recreation, culture, and religion	Education	Social protection	R&D
2001	15.0	9.2	3.6	33.9	6.2	7.0	6.0	10.5	2.0	8.3
2002	16.1	9.4	3.7	34.2	6.0	7.1	6.1	11.3	–0.7	8.7
2003	14.9	8.8	3.5	34.6	5.7	6.7	5.9	10.6	2.3	8.5
2004	14.8	8.7	3.0	35.7	5.6	6.3	6.1	10.4	2.2	8.3
2005	14.7	7.4	3.2	36.4	5.8	6.5	6.1	10.3	2.2	8.6
2006	15.3	7.4	3.3	35.6	6.2	6.7	6.2	10.2	2.2	8.1

11 Classification of the Functions of Government (COFOG).

	General public services	Defence	Public order and safety	Economic affairs	Environmental protection	Housing and community amenities	Recreation, culture, and religion	Education	Social protection	R&D
2007	15.4	7.1	3.4	35.6	6.0	7.0	6.2	10.0	2.5	7.9
2008	15.3	7.1	3.2	36.2	5.8	6.7	6.2	10.0	2.5	7.7
2009	16.0	7.2	3.2	35.1	5.7	7.1	6.0	10.2	2.8	8.1
2010	15.0	7.5	3.3	36.4	5.6	5.8	6.2	11.0	2.3	8.5
2011	15.8	7.3	3.0	36.1	5.8	5.2	5.9	10.9	2.6	9.0
2012	17.4	6.9	2.9	35.6	5.8	5.0	5.7	10.5	2.5	9.0
2013	17.9	6.7	3.0	34.6	5.9	5.1	6.1	10.8	2.5	9.5
2014	18.4	5.8	2.9	34.9	5.7	5.0	6.0	11.1	2.5	9.4
2015	18.0	6.8	3.1	35.2	5.6	4.9	5.6	11.0	2.5	9.4
2016	18.8	8.3	3.1	34.0	5.0	4.5	5.5	10.7	3.0	10.0
2017	18.6	8.2	3.1	35.0	4.7	4.3	5.8	10.7	2.6	9.7
2018	18.2	7.6	3.2	35.2	4.8	4.6	6.3	10.9	2.4	9.4
2019	18.2	7.4	3.2	34.2	5.0	5.3	6.2	11.3	2.5	9.2
2020	18.2	8.0	3.5	34.1	4.7	4.6	5.8	11.3	2.4	9.0
2021	17.8	8.4	3.5	34.1	4.6	4.7	5.9	11.3	2.3	9.1
2022	17.5	8.9	3.8	33.3	4.9	5.1	5.8	11.5	2.3	8.8

1.3 EU Public Goods and Public Investments: A Bird's-eye View

The provision of public goods at the EU level has higher value than at the national level, when there are increasing returns to scale in their "production" and when they generate positive spillovers. However, these advantages should not be outweighed by the factors that instead point to a "local" advantage—such as the existence of information asymmetries (between the central and the local governments), differences in preferences, democratic control, and jurisdictional competition—which may give advantage to national and local authorities instead. The discussion on EPGs is often centred around the climate transition, the digital transition, health-related issues, strategic autonomy, and R&D. In a paper prepared for the EU Parliament, Charles Wyplosz (2024) argues that among these, the ones that qualify for a centralized financing and provision, according to the fiscal-federalism literature, are climate and R&D. We will focus on these two issues in the remainder of this chapter.

Knowledge and knowledge diffusion (and hence R&D) constitute the best possible example of an EPG, as the motivations to keep its organisation/implementation/expenditures decentralized are minimal, while its contributions in terms of spillover/increasing returns to scale are large. In addition, the climate transition and its needs add a particular context to this: in a number of fields related to emissions control and carbon neutrality, there are still many competing technologies, and the technological breakthroughs which will determine the new technological trajectories are not yet here. Hence, there is an additional premium in R&D investment.

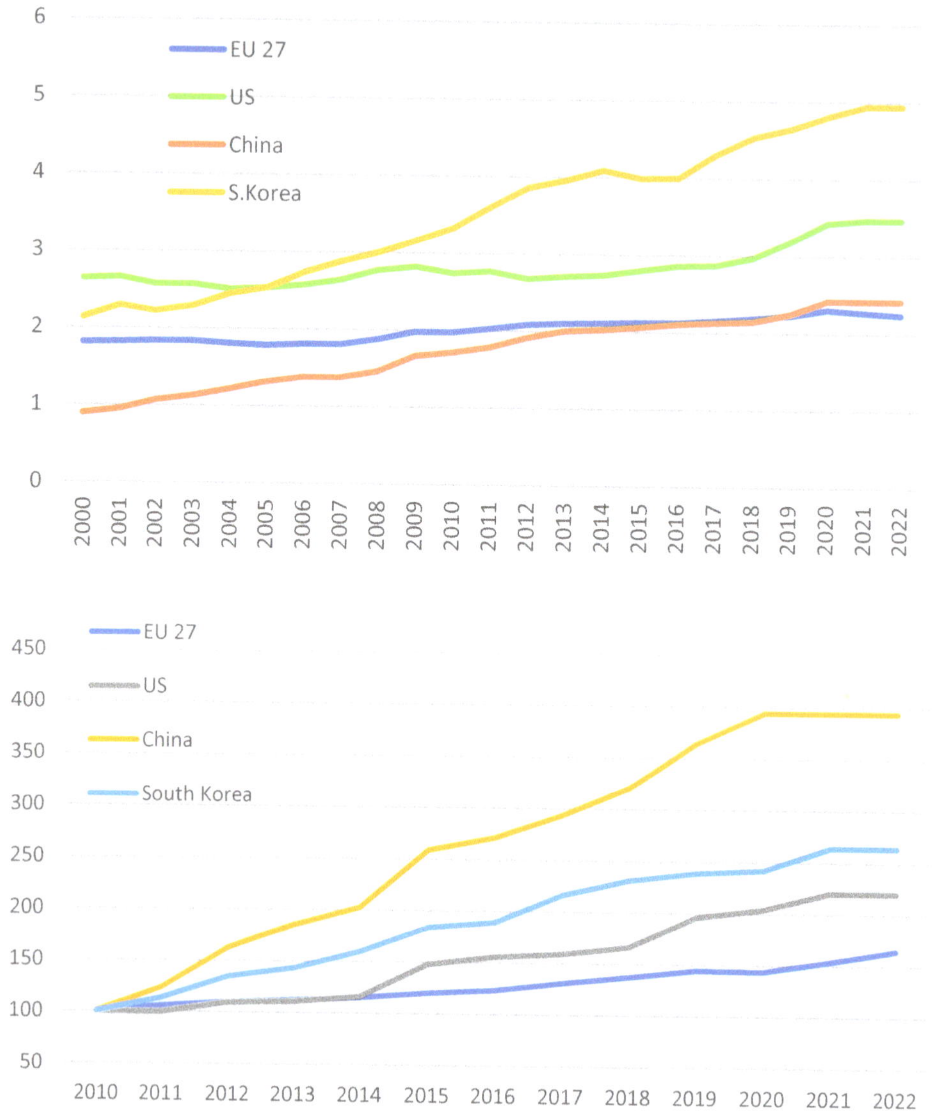

Fig. 1.5 R&D expenditures as (a) a share of GDP (above) and (b) in nominal value fixing 2010=100 (below). *Source*: Authors' calculations on Eurostat.

By looking at Eurostat data on R&D investment at all levels, it becomes evident that the EU has fallen behind the other most technologically advanced economies in the first two decades of the twenty-first century. Figure 1.5 shows total spending in R&D (by government, universities, and private sector) as a proportion of GDP. We observe a sharp and steady increase in R&D investment in South Korea (to close to 5% of GDP) and in China (2.41% of GDP), surpassing the EU starting from less than 1% of GDP in 2000. While the increase in the United States was more limited compared to China and South Korea, it was still larger than that of the EU, rising from 2.6% to 3.46%, thereby widening the gap between the US and the EU. In Japan, the increase in the ratio of R&D to GDP was similar to that in the EU (from 2.86% to 3.34%), but starting from a notably higher level. The gap in aggregate R&D spending between the EU and these economies is mainly driven by differences in business sector R&D, rather than government R&D spending. The sum of government spending and higher education institutions spending varies in a narrow range, from 0.57% for China to 0.93% for South Korea. The EU ranks second with public R&D expenditures of 0.73%.

It must be noted that growth rates are significantly more important than shares. Expressing the expenditures as a share of GDP hides part of the dynamics. Because GDP did not grow that much in the EU, particularly when compared with the countries under consideration, with the exception of Japan. Fixing the total amount of R&D spending at 100 in 2010,[12] the amount spent in the EU was 164 in 2022. In the US, it was 220, 263 in South Korea, and a notable 393 in China.

For some countries in the European Union, expenditures on R&D represent quite a large amount as a proportion of GDP. Denmark, Germany, Austria, Finland, and Sweden have total expenditures in R&D that are close to or above 3% of GDP, and for all of them the public share (government plus higher education institutions) is close to or above 1%. However, the R&D expenditure in these countries grew more slowly than global peers.

R&D policy for the climate transition should resemble the efforts made in the US with the DARPA agency. The gist of this single agency approach is to finance and monitor a large portfolio of research proposals via a typical bottom-up project selection method.[13] In Europe, R&D financing is still largely national and run by a large number of national institutions and universities. Horizon Europe is the program that regroups the majority of the EU funds for R&D and it amounts to €95.5 billion in the Multiannual Financial Framework (MFF) 2021–2027, compared to around €115 billion per annum spent in total in the EU, according to Eurostat. Furthermore, while the European Research Council highlights the merits of a bottom-up approach, Horizon Europe is a top-down exercise. To reap the benefits of R&D investment, the features that justify its classification as an EPG should be emphasized. IPCEI (Important Projects of Common European Interest) and STEP (Strategic Technologies for Europe Platform) are correctly designed to amplify cross-border coordination. It is interesting to put these actions in perspective within the general framework of the EU policy.

12 Some noise due to fluctuations in nominal exchange rates is included here; however, this should not significantly alter the overall picture.

13 Here credit is due to Wyplosz (2024) for these descriptions.

A comprehensive analysis by Antonin Bergeaud (2024) on the developments of EU productivity studies the insufficient presence of EU firms among global champions in breakthrough technologies and concludes that misallocation of R&D resources can occur. This was the result of US firms entering earlier "new" sectors that were "contiguous" to those of their operations. This was aided by more developed financial markets, with higher capacity to provide risk capital. In addition, European leading research universities are not well connected to European businesses and created breakthrough knowledge does not transform easily into business opportunities. Furthermore, R&D programmes are not designed to improve the connection between businesses and research universities. Hence, R&D is not generating the same kind of spillovers in comparison to the US. The role of R&D and innovation has been emphasized by Letta in his report on the single market (2024: 7): "the fifth freedom entails embedding research and innovation drivers at the core of the Single Market, thereby fostering an ecosystem where knowledge diffusion propels both economic vitality, societal advancement and cultural enlightenment". He also proposes the creation of an EU stock exchange for Deep Tech, emphasizing that the scale and scope of public interventions, financial markets, and innovative ecosystems must be pan-European.

1.4 European Public Investment in Action: Implementing RRF for the Green Climate Pillar and R&D

With total disbursement close to €240 billion, RRF constitutes the largest coordinated effort put in place by the European Union to support recovery after COVID-19. It is aimed at steering this recovery towards the EU strategic goals of green and digital transitions by requiring that climate and digital projects should represent at least 37% and 20% of the total envelope. This is further reinforced by a governance of the whole plan that gives a large role to the European Commission.

As of 2024, the shares of climate and digital objectives in the projects presented by Member States surpassed the requested minimum shares and amount to 42% and 26%. The disbursed amounts, however, are smaller. The total amount disbursed for the green pillar is about €36 billion, representing 18% of the disbursed total. The RRF scoreboard also contains the list of the 100 largest disbursements for each country. The list falls slightly short of 2700, because three countries presented shorter lists. The total disbursed amount in this list is €160 billion out of the 240 disbursed, a notable portion.

It is interesting that among the 2400 projects, 410 include the words research, innovation, or R&D in the description, with a total of €48 billion. Among those, the part that can be considered as subsidies or investment incentives for firms (mainly for small firms) is represented by 120 measures with a total amount of less than €1 billion. Note also that the measures included in IPCEI are only seven, for a total amount of €0.7 billion.

1.5 European Policy in Action: State Aid for Climate Action and R&D

The RRF was designed as a response to the negative demand shock the economy experienced during the COVID-19 pandemic. However, it has goals beyond mere recovery, aiming to increase investments in digitalization and the green transition. It can therefore be considered a form of active industrial policy with strong EU impetus. A substantial part of industrial policy in Europe, however, remains state aid, which national authorities allocate to firms following the guidelines set out by the European Commission.

One can define industrial policy as a set of measures or policies influencing industries vertically or horizontally to increase domestic production capacity and maintain competitiveness at the international level. State aid rules, managed by Directorate-General Competition in the European Commission, were conceived as the best way to generate a level playing field in which competitive forces in a wider internal market could stimulate and push EU firms to the technological frontier. It must be said that this approach is defined "by subtraction".[14] In recent years, however, state aid rules were adapted to the changed circumstances.

The State Aid Scoreboard, managed and released by the EC, includes not only support financed by the Member States and allocated to national firms, but also the EU funds that are distributed by local authorities in the Member States.[15] Table 1.2 highlights the total amount of funds that are channelled to firms in each Member State, together with the fraction of the total that is financed by the European Union. Our intention here is not to analyze the whole state aid data, but the resources that are dedicated to the two themes that may be considered the clearer example of EPGs, namely R&D and green transition.

Table 1.2 State aid in 2022 (million Euro) and amount co-financed. *Source*: EC state aid scoreboard.

	Total State Aid	Of which EU co-financed	Share
Austria	6517.8	240.2	3.7%
Belgium	5692.0	340.1	6.0%

14 On the website of the European Commission it is stated that "the Treaty generally prohibits State aid unless it is justified by reasons of general economic development" (https://competition-policy.ec.europa.eu/state-aid_en).

15 P. Nicolaides, in the document "State Aid and EU Funding" requested by the Policy Department on Budgetary Affairs of the EU Parliament, clarifies that "...EU funds channeled through the managing authorities of Member States become state resources and can constitute state aid if all the other criteria of Article 107(1) are satisfied" (2018: 5).

	Total State Aid	Of which EU co-financed	Share
Bulgaria	867.9	108.6	12.5%
Cyprus	149.5	33.9	22.7%
Czechia	3962.6	584.4	14.7%
Germany	73669.6	982.8	1.3%
Denmark	5302.4	104.9	2.0%
Spain	17124.4	1900	11.1%
Estonia	331.3	72.3	21.8%
Finland	17124.4	354.9	2.1%
France	44793.8	4000	8.9%
Greece	2846.6	278.7	9.8%
Croatia	570.9	196.9	34.5%
Hungary	3526.2	373.4	10.6%
Ireland	1583.0	201.8	12.7%
Italy	27607.0	3500	12.7%
Lithuania	764.3	279.1	36.5%
Luxembourg	515.8	42.2	8.2%
Latvia	391.7	86.3	22.0%
Malta	259.1	6.4	2.5%
Netherlands	9922.7	195	2.0%
Poland	6069.9	598.3	9.9%
Portugal	2303.5	681	29.6%
Romania	4189.0	681.4	16.3%
Slovakia	970.1	460.6	47.5%
Slovenia	483.0	91.4	18.9%
Sweden	5028.7	201.5	4.0%

The need to involve and stimulate private investment is always a key objective of economic policy. The European Commission defined a "European industrial strategy"[16] in 2020, before reviewing and updating it afterwards to adjust it to new economic realities.[17] The 2023 State Aid Scoreboard report describes the interventions

16 European Commission (2020).
17 European Commission (2021).

that were implemented regarding R&D and Climate. In 2022, the "R&D&I" (Research, Development, and Innovation) framework[18] and the General Block Exemption Regulation were modified to facilitate the adoption of supporting actions by Member States. In 2022, the sum of all the state aid devoted to this theme was €12.7 billion, that represented a significant drop with respect to 2021 (€19.3 billion) even though it represents the second highest value in history (in 2019 the total was €9.2 billion). The 2023 Scoreboard outlines the larger supporting measures that gained the approval (for example, €1.5 billion in France to a company aiming at developing solid state batteries). Then, the report also describes the portion of these aids that were provided in the context of the IPCEIs. There are seven approved IPCEIs (two in microelectronics, two for EV batteries, two focused on hydrogen for energy-intensive sectors, and one for cloud computing) that in principle should receive support for a total of €27.9 billion from the involved Member States and possibly unlock much more in private investment. However, in 2022, they totalled just above €1 billion (i.e., around 8.2% of the total resources earmarked for R&D).

On climate transition, in 2022, the European Commission released new Guidelines on State Aid for Climate, Environmental Protection, and Energy (CEEAG) to facilitate the implementation of supporting measures by Member States. To illustrate, the report highlights the approved scheme for decarbonizing the production of energy intensive sectors in Slovakia (€1 billion) and in Germany (€4 billion), and the Danish project to roll-out Carbon Capture and Storage (CCS) technologies.

To take a closer look at the state expenditure on these areas, we analyze the state aid awarded to businesses for R&D&I and environmental protection. Our analysis is based on data from the Transparency Award Module (TAM), covering state aid awarded to firms in thirteen European countries.[19] Due to reporting thresholds, our data include mostly large aid packages. We focus on aid awarded between 2017 and 2019, using firm-level balance sheet data from Orbis spanning 2012 to 2021.

Overall, environmental protection, energy efficiency, R&D&I, and regional development are the main objectives under which governments award large sums of aid to businesses. Firms that receive R&D&I aid tend to invest more than prior to the aid award and are more likely to be large firms. These factors do not matter as much for the probability of receiving environmental aid. R&D&I aid shows a clearer sectoral component, with scientific research, and manufacturing of transport, chemicals, basic metals, computers, and pharmaceuticals being top recipient sectors. Manufacturing industries are also more likely to receive state aid for environmental protection and energy efficiency, however the degree of discrimination among sectors seems to be much less pronounced for this type of aid.

18 European Commission (2022).

19 Belgium, Denmark, Estonia, Finland, France, Croatia, Hungary, Ireland, Italy, the Netherlands, Portugal, and Sweden.

We examine the impact of national government support for R&D&I and green transition, by using a generalized difference-in-differences approach in which we control for firm fixed effects and year effects. We observe positive effects on firm net investment rates for both types of aid. Figures 1.6 and 1.7 below show the dynamic effects of the aid received on firm investment relative to the control group for each year relative to the year of aid reception.

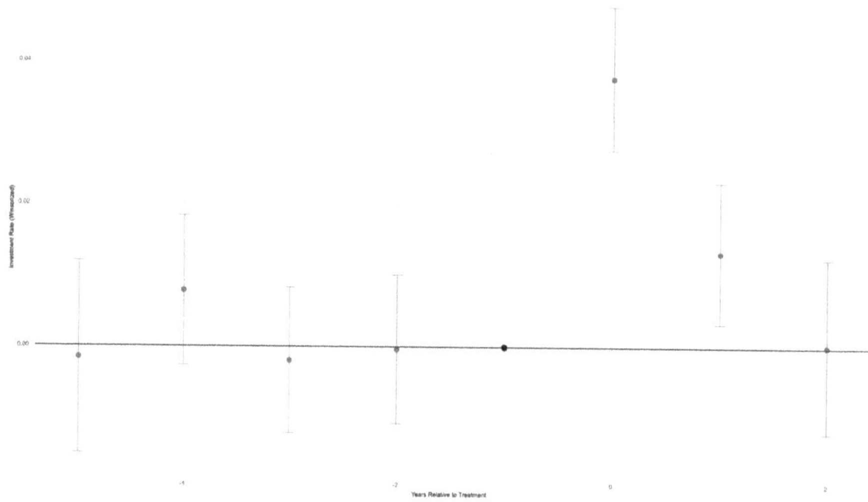

Fig. 1.6 Dynamic effects of state aid award on firm investment, for firms receiving aid related to R&D&I. *Source*: EIB staff calculations on EC—State Aid TAM data.

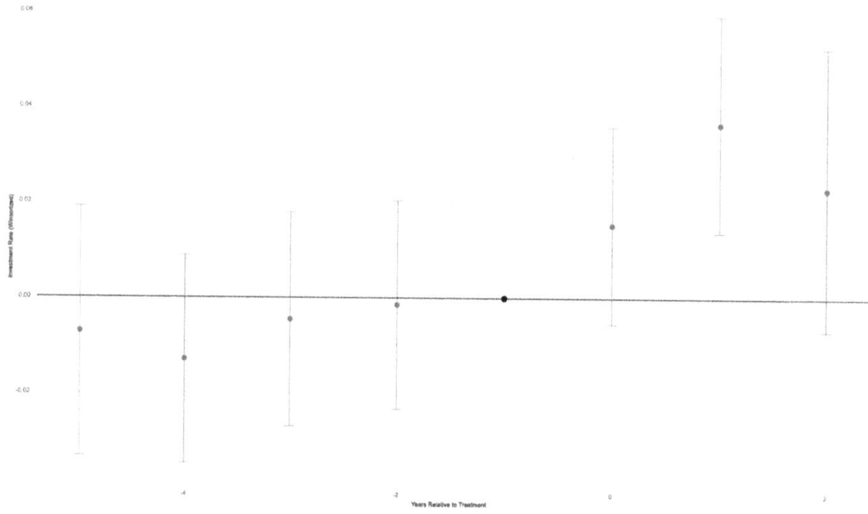

Fig. 1.7 Dynamic effects of state aid award on firm investment, for firms receiving aid related to environmental protection and energy efficiency. *Source*: EIB staff calculations on EC—State Aid TAM data.

While there are no significant differences in investment trends prior to aid reception, firms receiving aid significantly invest more in the following years. Our results suggest that aid given for environmental protection and green transition leads to an increase in investment rates. For environmental aid, we see a gradually increasing but more sustained effect. There may be two reasons for this. First, an important share of environmental aid is given for investment in greener and more energy-efficient means of production. Second, even if this type of aid does not have firm investment as a primary goal, it may generate other positive effects on firm performance that eventually lead the firm to be in a better position to carry out investments. R&D&I aid shows a stronger immediate impact that is visible for the first two years only, with firms potentially investing for specific projects.

These reduced-form results point to positive effects of state aid on firm investment, with different objectives exhibiting different effects. At the same time, they do not allow us to assess the optimality of the allocation of state aid across projects and firms, nor on the type of financing instruments used. Government aid should ideally target projects and enterprises that are most promising in terms of social value creation, but that are too risky to be financed in the absence of the state participation. It is important to choose the most appropriate tools in order to minimize the tax burden of the aid. A cost-effective, key role of governments is enabling coordination among market participants whose investment and R&D&I effort decisions depend on those of other firms (Aiginger and Rodrik 2020).

1.6 Conclusion and Prospects

Public investment has been growing as a share of GDP in the last years in Europe and it is likely to continue to grow at least until the expiration of the RRF in 2026. The COVID-19 pandemic and the energy crisis gave a boost to public investment and created a renewed appreciation for industrial policies both in political debate and in academic circles. Still, while the momentum is there for reshaping the European industrial policy, it is not clear how the Union will move after the expiration of the RRF. Note that, as clearly stated in Draghi's report, issuing more common debt to finance joint investment projects would also help the integration of the EU capital market. With Member States facing challenges to lower public debt to respect the fiscal rules of the Union, as well as the political climate, it may not be an easy task to increase public funds to speed up the green and digital transitions, and heavily invest in R&D. However, there are potential gains to be unlocked simply through a better use of available funds. A bird's-eye tour of the clearer examples of European public goods such as R&D and climate transition suggests that there are significant opportunities that can be realized through enhanced coordination and greater coherence between EU and national public investment decisions. Exploiting the full potential of the European research and production networks, and coordinating efforts, is essential to reap maximum benefits while minimizing costs. IPCEIs are commendable examples of how governments can come together to coordinate actions between firms and institutes that invest at different stages of a technology, as well as between firms headquartered in different countries. However, they constitute only a small share of the industrial policies and public investment carried out in the EU, most of which is channelled via national authorities. There needs to be continuous investment in and reaffirmation of such projects. Given that externalities and spillovers are the core justifications for public investment and industrial policies, it is necessary and logical to take them into account in their entirety on a European scale.

References

Buti M., A. Coloccia, and M. Messori (2023) "European Public Goods", June 9, *CEPR*, https://cepr.org/voxeu/columns/european-public-goods

Bergeaud, A. (2024) "The Past Present and Future of EU Productivity", Prepared for the ECB Central Banking Forum, July 2024, https://www.ecb.europa.eu/pub/pdf/sintra/ecb.forumcentbankpub2024_Bergeaud_paper.en.pdf

Cerniglia, F., F. Saraceno, and A. Watt (eds) (2023) *Financing Investment in Times of High Public Debt: 2023 European Public Investment Outlook*. Cambridge: Open Book Publishers, https://doi.org/10.11647/OBP.0386

Demertzis, M., D. Pinkus, and N. Ruer (2024) "Accelerating Strategic Investment in the European Union beyond 2026", Bruegel Report, January 24, https://www.bruegel.org/system/files/2024-01/Report%2001%202024.pdf

Draghi, M. (2023) "The Next Flight of the Bumblebee: The Path to Common Fiscal Policy in the Eurozone", 15th Annual Feldstein Lecture at the NBER Summer Institute 2023 in Cambridge, October 10, *NBER*, https://www.nber.org/reporter/2023number3/next-flight-bumblebee-path-common-fiscal-policy-eurozone

Draghi, M. (2024) *The Future of European Competitiveness*. Brussels: European Commission, https://commission.europa.eu/document/download/97e481fd-2dc3-412d-be4c-f152a8232961_en

European Commission (2020) "A New Industrial Strategy for Europe", COM(2020) 102, March 10, https://eur-lex.europa.eu/legal-content/EN/TXT/PDF/?uri=CELEX:52020DC0102

European Commission (2021) "Updating the 2020 New Industrial Strategy: Building a stronger Single Market for Europe's recovery", SWD(2021) 352, May 5, https://eur-lex.europa.eu/legal-content/EN/TXT/?uri=CELEX%3A52021SC0352

European Commission (2022) "Framework for State Aid for Research and Development and Innovation", 2022/C 414/01, October 28, https://eur-lex.europa.eu/legal-content/EN/TXT/HTML/?uri=OJ%3AC%3A2022%3A414%3AFULL#:~:text=This%20Framework%20provides%20guidance%20on,)(c)%20of%20the%20Treaty.

Fuest, C., and J. Pisani-Ferry (2019) "A Primer on Developing European Public Goods (A Report to Ministers Bruno Le Maire and Olaf Scholz)", November 3, https://www.bruegel.org/sites/default/files/wp-content/uploads/2019/11/European-public-goods-primer.pdf

Letta, E. (2024) *Much More Than a Market*, https://www.consilium.europa.eu/media/ny3j24sm/much-more-than-a-market-report-by-enrico-letta.pdf

Nicolaides, P. (2018) "State Aid and EU Funding: Are They Compatible?", In-Depth Analysis Requested by the CONT Committee, Policy Department for Budgetary Affairs, April, https://www.europarl.europa.eu/cmsdata/142819/Briefing_State%20Aid%20and%20EU%20funding_Final.pdf

Wyplosz, C. (2024) "Which European Public Goods?", IPOL | Economic Governance and EMU Scrutiny Unit, March, https://www.europarl.europa.eu/RegData/etudes/IDAN/2024/755722/IPOL_IDA(2024)755722_EN.pdf

Von der Leyen, U. (2024) "Statement at the European Parliament Plenary by President Ursula von der Leyen, Candidate for a Second Mandate 2024–2029", *European Commission*, https://ec.europa.eu/commission/presscorner/detail/ov/STATEMENT_24_3871

2. Public Investment and Industrial Policy in France

Vincent Charlet,[1] *Mathieu Plane,*[2] *and Francesco Saraceno*[3]

This chapter first traces the long-term evolution of public investment in France, noting how this is mostly channelled through local governments and how, while comparatively high with respect to other advanced economies, the public capital stock and the general government net wealth have been steadily decreasing since the Global Financial Crisis of 2008. After the COVID-19 shock, despite the 2021 "Plan de Relance" and the 2022 "Build the France of 2030" program, public investment has remained surprisingly flat. The chapter then discusses the recent evolutions in French industrial policy objectives. The Lisbon Strategy was centred on boosting productivity through innovation and climbing the value-added ladder. The response to the crisis of 2008 marks a first change, with a strong emphasis on price competitiveness and cost reduction (including through corporate tax reduction). Since the early days of the pandemics, then, the notion of "industrial sovereignty" has very quickly eclipsed that of competitiveness, with policies aimed at reindustrialization especially in strategic sectors. The chapter concludes that these frequent changes indicate an excessive short-term focus among French policy makers, incompatible with managing long-term structural transformation.

2.1 The Historical Evolution of Public Investment

From the end of the 1940s until today, public investment in France has gone through different phases. After a long period of sustained growth during the 1960s (5.6% of GDP on average; see Figure 2.1), it remained at a relatively high level during the 1970s and 1980s (5% of GDP on average) until the mid-1990s. The first break took

1 Fabrique de l'industrie.
2 Observatoire Français des Conjonctures Economiques (OFCE) Sciences Po.
3 Observatoire Français des Conjonctures Economiques (OFCE) Sciences Po and Luiss Institute for European Analysis and Policy (LEAP).

 https://doi.org/10.11647/OBP.0434.03

place during the 1990s, a period during which priority was given to reducing the public deficit to meet the Maastricht criteria and join the euro. During this time, public investment fell to an average of 4.4% of GDP from the mid-1990s to the mid-2010s, when a second break occurred. Following the sovereign debt crisis, the fiscal stance turned restrictive, and a substantial part of the fiscal adjustment was achieved by reducing capital expenditure. Indeed, the reduction of public investment during that period has contributed to almost a third of fiscal consolidation, even though investment represented only 6% of public expenditure. The share of public investment to GDP from 2015 to 2018 fell to under 4% on average and, during this period, reached its lowest level since the beginning of the 1950s. A recovery in public investment began in the two years before the COVID-19 crisis, with an increase of nearly 12% between the end of 2017 and the end of 2019. This shift was linked to the cycle of municipal elections and the government's desire to preserve investment within the framework of the targeted budget contract with local governments. It is also important to note that public investment remains mainly the responsibility of local authorities (around 53% of the total in 2023, see Figure 2.1) even though local public expenditure barely represents 20% of total public expenditure.[4]

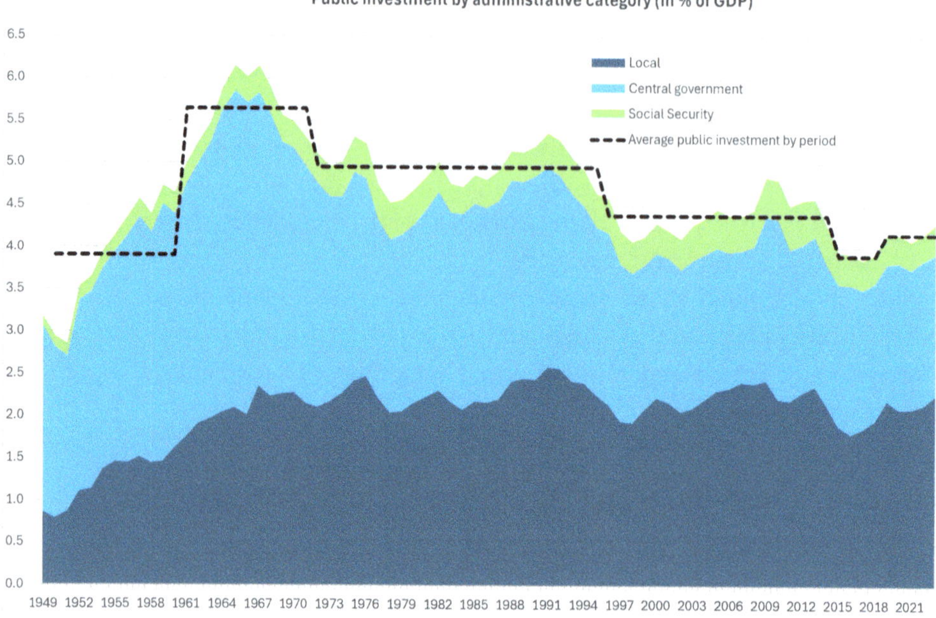

Fig. 2.1 Public investment by administrative category in % of GDP. *Source*: Insee.

4 The Central government and the Social security represent respectively 36% and 45% of total public expenditure.

2.2 The Public Investment Dynamics since the COVID-19 Crisis

Due to the nature of the political cycle, a partial reversal in public investment was to be expected after the municipal elections of 2017. Nevertheless, the drop observed in 2020 is out of proportion with that observed in previous cycles and is a result of the pandemic. Indeed, the COVID-19 crisis (most notably, the first lockdown, in the Spring of 2020) led to a drop of 12% in public investment in the first half of 2020. By comparison, the two strongest bi-annual decreases observed in the previous four decades were between 4% and 5%.

From the second semester of 2020, however, public investment nearly returned to the pre-COVID-19 level (-3% at the end of the year 2020 with respect to the end of 2019), despite the second lockdown in November and December 2020 (Fig. 2.2). In addition, the government voted in September 2020 for a hundred-billion-euro recovery plan ("Le Plan de Relance", see Plane and Saraceno 2021), partially financed (€40 billion) with funding from the Next Generation EU program. The "Plan de Relance" includes a section on public infrastructure, with particular emphasis on the thermal renovation of public buildings, with increased planned investment from the beginning of 2021. The plan allocated resources as follows: €30 billion for Ecological Transition (energy-efficient building renovations, development of renewable energies, green mobility, sustainable agriculture), €34 billion for Competitiveness and Sovereignty (reduction of production taxes, support for research and innovation, industrial relocation), and €36 billion for Social and Territorial Cohesion (employment and training, support for local authorities, and support for struggling sectors).

Moreover, a new investment plan, "Build the France of 2030", was announced in October 2021.[5] With a budget of €54 billion, this plan is intended to meet long-term challenges, particularly those related to the green transition, through massive investment to help the technological champions of tomorrow to emerge and to support the transitions of French sectors of excellence: energy, automotive, aeronautics, and space. "Build the France of 2030" identifies public investment as central to the revival and strengthening of the economy as well as to the structural transformation required by the green transition. The main goals of "Build the France of 2030" are organized around several strategic pillars: €8 billion for energy and ecological transition, €4 billion for future transport, €7 billion for health and biotechnologies, €6 billion for digital and intelligent technologies, €2 billion for sustainable agro-food sector, and €2 billion for training and skills development. Despite these major announcements to revive the economy, particularly through investment policy, public investment has remained surprisingly flat, with even a drop of more than -2% between the end of 2020 and mid-2022. In fact, it has only reached its pre-COVID-19 level more than three years after the start of the crisis. By contrast, it took only five quarters for GDP and only

5 The "Build the France of 2030" plan, worth €54 billion over five years, aims to develop industrial competitiveness and the technologies of the future.

one year for private investment (Fig. 2.2). Private investment was very dynamic over this period, which suggests that the Recovery Plan was more focused on supporting business investment than on public infrastructure. Since the second half of 2022, public investment has been more dynamic than private investment and GDP. In the second quarter of 2024 it is 5% above its pre-COVID-19 level while GDP is only 4% above.

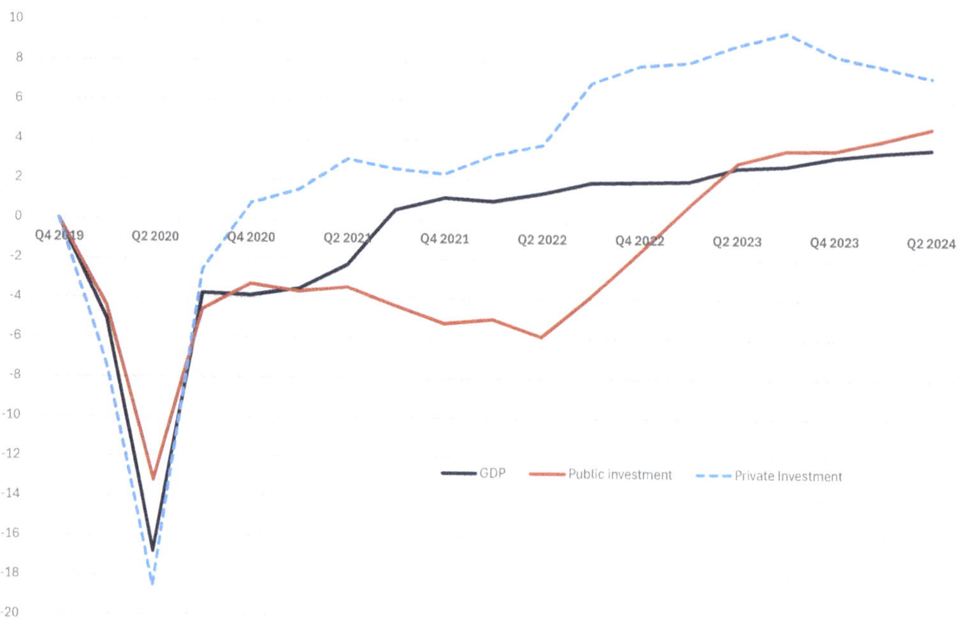

Fig. 2.2 Public/Private investment and GDP (0 = 2019q4, in %, volume). *Source*: Insee.

2.3 Net Investment Increases but the Pace of Public Capital Accumulation is Still Low

The gross investment dynamics need to be complemented with an analysis of net flows of fixed assets (net investment) to better assess the dynamics of the capital stock (excluding the effects of revaluation of the existing stock). Thus, if gross investment is larger (smaller) than the depreciation of capital (consumption of fixed capital, CFC, in national-accounts nomenclature), then net investment increases (decreases), and the stock of capital increases (decreases).

From the late 1970s to the first half of the 1990s, France's general government net investment was strong, averaging more than 1% of GDP per year (Fig. 2.3). It even experienced a strong boom over the period 1987–1992, averaging above 1.4% of GDP per year. From 1993 to 1998, general government net investment declined sharply, reaching 0.5% of GDP in 1998, which amounted to a decrease of more than 1 point of GDP over the space of seven years. This decline, as was the case in other European countries, was mostly due to the effort to meet the Maastricht criteria in the run-up to the adoption of the euro: the cyclically adjusted deficit for France decreased from 4.6% of GDP in 1993 to 1.8% in 1998, and investment was the main adjustment variable. Net investment recovered in the next phase, then fluctuated between 0.7% and 1.1% of GDP over the 2000–2010 period, without ever returning to the level observed during the 1980s and the first half of the 1990s. Since 2011 and the Global Financial Crisis, net investment has been at its lowest level since the late 1970s, when wealth accounts were introduced.

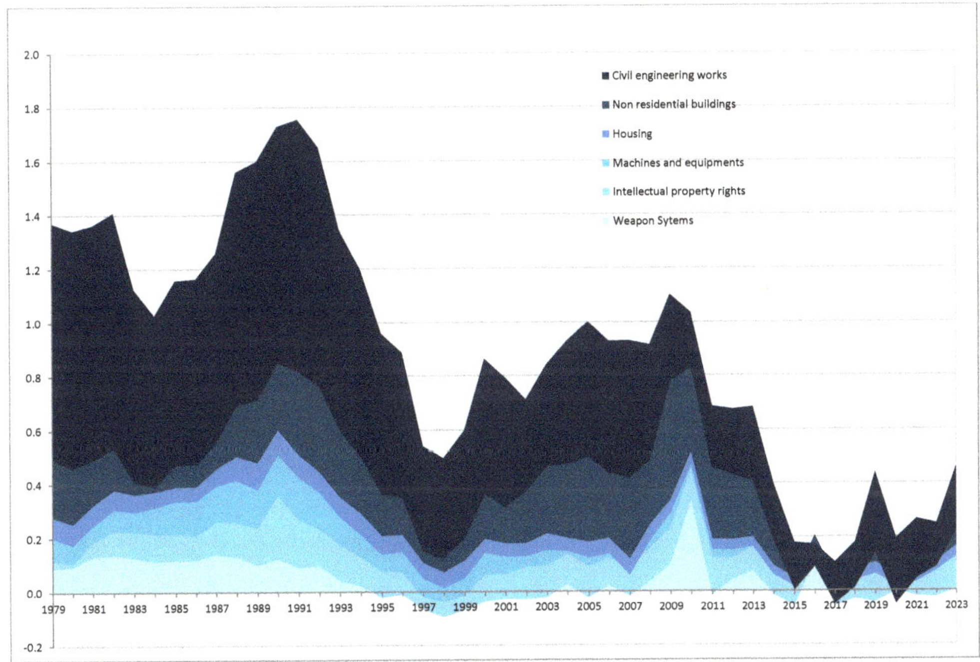

Fig. 2.3 Net General Government Investment by Component as a % of GDP. *Source*: Insee.

To sum up, during the period 2015–2018, France spent about 0.7 percentage points (pp) of GDP (about €20 billion per year in 2023 euros) less on net investment than it did during the period 2000–2010, and 1.6 pp (approximately €45 billion per year in constant 2023 euros) less than during the period 1990–1992. The necessary amount of additional public investment per year to achieve carbon neutrality in 2050 would have to be the level of the early 1990s.[6] Public investment has been gradually recovering since 2019 and has been accentuated by the COVID-19 crisis and the implementation of the recovery plan and "Build the France of 2030". Over the last five years, net investment

6 According to the Pisani-Ferry Mahfouz (2023) report, the need for additional financing in 2030 for the energy transition to meet our climate commitments would represent €67 billion per year, of which €34 billion would be public investment (1.2 pp of GDP).

by public administrations increased on average by 0.4 point of GDP per year, i.e. a rate twice as high as that of the years 2015–2018. Although improving, this rate of investment remains well below what was achieved before 2013 and the turning point in fiscal austerity. The fiscal adjustment program for €60 billion recently announced by the Prime Minister, which does not spare investment incentives and transfers to local authorities, risks undermining the slight recovery in public investment observed in recent years.

The picture that emerges from the analysis of stocks and flows is rather consistent with the previous analysis and gives two main messages. The first is that, in France, public investment and the stock of capital have been largely affected by the budgetary cycle. In the two significant phases of fiscal consolidation—the run-up to adopting the euro in the 1990s and the aftermath of the sovereign debt crisis—investment was strongly reduced (see also Bubbico et al. 2020). Especially in the latter case, net investment turned close to zero for all levels of government, thus stopping the increase of the stock of capital. The second message that emerges, specifically from the analysis of stocks, is that, despite these trends in investment, the capital stock in France remains significant (and larger than in other countries). As a result, one might ask, then, whether the effort of consolidation and the disproportionate burden that it has placed on public investment has led to more sustainable public finances.

It is interesting to look at the evolution of non-financial assets' net flows in relation to primary net financial flow (financial assets–financial liabilities–interest expenses), which we consider here as a proxy of the net worth. This reveals the existence of two sub-periods in the past three decades: the first sub-period, which runs from 1996 to 2008, can be seen as one in which the additional public net financial debt (excluding interest expense) was more than offset by the net accumulation of non-financial assets, leading to a positive net worth. This indicates that the general government stock of wealth increased in value over this period, even abstracting from price effects. The second sub-period, which runs from 2009 to 2022, displays a new pattern in which the net financial debt increase is no longer offset by an increase in public non-financial capital, generating a sharp deterioration in government net worth. In summary, during the period of strong public debt accumulation, there was a corresponding disinvestment in public assets, which ultimately led to a sharp reduction of the net asset value of public administration.

The economic and financial crisis led to a sharp increase in public debt. Fiscal consolidation began to be implemented in 2011. On one hand, it partly reduced new financial commitments; on the other, it has been more than offset by a reduction in the net accumulation of non-financial assets. This is yet-further proof that the burden of fiscal consolidation was disproportionately laid on the shoulders of public investment. The sharp reduction in net worth, therefore, casts doubt on the effectiveness of fiscal consolidation in strengthening the public-finances outlook for France.

2.4 General Government Net Wealth: Still Positive but a Strong Decrease Since 2008

What is referred to as "public capital" covers a wide variety of assets, such as land, residential buildings, ports, dams, and roads. It also includes intellectual property rights. It is necessary to break down the "wealth of the State" into these different components to understand its dynamics, considering that price (most notably land prices) and volume effects may play a significant role in explaining the evolution of the different components and of aggregate figures.

We use public data from the French National Statistical office (Insee) national accounts; our analysis covers the period 1978–2022. Insee reports the consolidated level (general government) and its components, distinguishing between the central government, local governments, social-security administrations, and other government agencies.

In 2022, the consolidated public sector had a positive net wealth, despite the negative impact of the COVID-19 crisis (Table 2.1). Total assets held represented 167% of GDP, of which 103% was for non-financial assets. Financial liabilities totalled 134% of GDP.[7] The net worth in 2022 was, therefore, 33% of GDP, which corresponds to €12,700 per capita.

Table 2.1 Decomposition of general government net wealth. *Source*: Insee and authors' calculations.

	As a % of GDP			In euros per head
	1978	2007	2022	2022
Non-financial assets	60.8	90.4	102.9	39 920
Financial assets	27.6	52.6	64.0	24 820
Financial liabilities	33.7	84.9	134.2	52 040
Net worth	54.7	58.1	32.7	12 700

After reaching a record level in 2007 (58% of GDP), the net worth has lost 25 points of GDP in the space of fifteen years. The reasons for this sharp drop are to be found on the net financial liabilities (debt) side, which increased substantially while non-

7 The difference between Maastricht debt and the financial liabilities of public administration is significant, as these two concepts are used in different accounting and economic contexts, although both relate to public debt. Maastricht debt includes the financial commitments of public administrations in the form of debt securities (bonds), loans (bank loans, credits), and deposits (debts to depositors) but commercial debts (unpaid bills, arrears) and financial derivatives (such as swaps) are not included in this definition but are included in financial liabilities.

financial assets only increased slightly (see Figure 2.4).

This net worth is unevenly distributed among different levels of government. Indeed, it is very positive for local administrations (72% of GDP in 2022), very negative for the central government (-57% of GDP in 2022), and slightly positive for social-security administrations and other government agencies (8% and 10%, respectively). Broadly speaking, the central government—which runs recurrent deficits—has accumulated debt; low-debt local governments hold non-financial assets, be they land, buildings, or civil-engineering works. With the economic and financial crisis from 2008 onwards, the net worth of the central government deteriorated considerably as public deficits and debt increased. On the other hand, the net worth of local governments remained high and relatively stable over the same period due to a stable value of non-financial assets and of their debt.

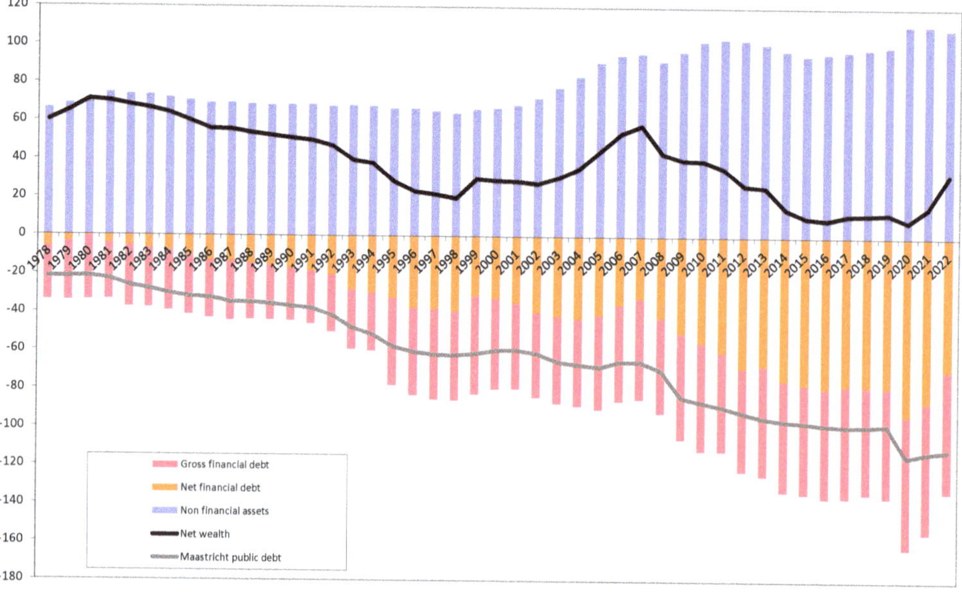

Fig. 2.4 Evolution of general government net wealth as a percentage of GDP. *Source*: Insee.

Online resources for Figs. 2.1–2.4 are available at https://hdl.handle.net/20.500.12434/de2539b0

2.5. Industrial Policies in France: A Perspective

2.5.1 A "Preference for the Present" More Marked than Ever

From the outbreak of the COVID-19 crisis in March 2020 until the legislative elections of July 1, 2024, the economic policy of French governments has been dominated by an explicit desire to support the industrial sector and to contribute to the reindustrialization of the country. This is even more noticeable considering that, from 2000 to the *subprime* crisis in 2008, France was committed with its European partners to the Lisbon Strategy: then, the aim was for the EU to become "the most competitive knowledge-based economy in the world". In other words, it was tacitly assumed (and accepted) by policy makers, who sought remedies to revive flagging growth and productivity in Europe, that low value-added manufacturing activities were going to migrate to other countries and that Europe's salvation laid in innovation and moving up in the value-added ladder. Hence the imperative to increase the national R&D effort to 3% of GDP. Not only has this objective not been achieved, but the indicator has even stagnated at 2.2% of GDP since 2000, with both public and private investment in R&D remaining below their target.

Then came the 2008 crisis. Admittedly, in terms of public investment, the main response imagined by President Sarkozy was to undertake a "major loan" to finance "investments for the future": this approach was therefore still part of the "Lisbon" logic oriented towards specialization in high value-added sectors and developing new knowledge. But very quickly the focus shifted, and for the entire decade of the 2010s (and beyond), industrial policy was dominated by a new imperative: "restoring competitiveness", the key concept of the report submitted to the Prime Minister Jean-Marc Ayrault in 2012 by Louis Gallois, former CEO of Airbus Group. The business world and public officials, at that time, no longer spoke of innovation, research or technological breakthroughs. On the contrary, they focused mainly on the effects on immediate competitiveness to be expected from reduction in costs. First, the massive reductions in employers' social contributions granted by the government, which went from €26 billion in 2012 to €53 billion in 2018 (mainly to absorb unskilled unemployment but also to boost the price competitiveness of exporting companies); second, the reduction in production taxes by several governments in the past decade and the public support for the modernization of industrial sectors. In a sentence, even when it was about promoting new technologies, the focal point of industrial policies was no longer in the research laboratories but returned to the workshops and factories. The shared view was that thanks to the positive effects of labour costs moderation on cost competitiveness, businesses could invest in the upgrading of their productive apparatus. In other words, the State decided to support industry *hic et nunc* and seemed to have given up on the target of 3% of GDP in R&D, as if the development of the technologies of the future had become a less pressing emergency.

A new crisis, COVID-19, a new upheaval. Since the early days of the lockdown, in 2020, the notion of "industrial sovereignty" has very quickly eclipsed that of competitiveness. It is worth looking into this term, which in the current context has little to do with economics. The notion of "industrial sovereignty" appeared in the public debate after the response to the pandemic shock brought the economy to a standstill. Soon after that, the Russian invasion of Ukraine (which has considerably strained European energy supplies) and other traumatic events, such as the shortage of semiconductors during the recovery from the pandemics, also marked the spirits as confirmations that a political shift was necessary and urgent. Well beyond France, the "preference for the present" shaped policy responses to these crises, with a risk of giving excessive importance to their contingent causes, and of introducing biases in the subsequent recovery plans. In a tense international context, between China's uncooperative state capitalism and the uninhibited protectionism of the United States, today we have reached a point where, to use the expression of a business leader, "politics has taken over".[8] In the United States, the Inflation Reduction Act (IRA) was introduced in August 2022 (White House 2023). The plan, which mobilizes almost $1400 billion in a variety of instruments including subsidies and tax incentives over ten years, is less a green transition policy than an industrial policy with several objectives: sovereignty, energy transition and catching up on infrastructure and all the physical assets in the United States. Europe's response arrived only in February 2024, too late and too little, in the form of a very watered-down version of the European sovereignty fund proposed in 2022 by Ursula Von der Leyen (2022) during her State of the Union to support certain critical technologies: the Strategic Technologies for Europe Platforms (STEP). STEPs will leverage funding in support of critical technologies under existing EU programs and funds, up to €10 billion (European Commission 2023)—no comparison with the US budget. The most frequently stated objective of French policy makers is that of increasing the share of manufacturing value added in the economy by two or even five points of GDP, thanks to a plurality of public interventions: (a) ring-fencing of one of the most generous research tax credits in the world (€7.2 billion in 2021, of which around 60% mechanically benefits the industrial sector); (b) support for the reindustrialization of territories (€2 billion committed over three years by various public operators as part of the "Territoires d'industrie" operation); (c) state aids to promote the decarbonization of industrial processes (for example via €850 million in aid for the decarbonization of ArcelorMittal's steel sites) and the establishment of giga-factories in the field of batteries (€1.5 billion in subsidies for ProLogium, €659 million for Verkor, among others) and so on.

Today, in Washington and Brussels as well as in Paris, there is no hesitation in considering or even calling for bold and interventionist industrial policies, driven by short-term political gains even when their long-term economic effectiveness

8 This quote is attributed to Pierre-André de Chalendar, when he was president of Saint-Gobain.

remains uncertain. Paradoxically, this attitude presents two different and even quite independent starting points: a logical premise (Chinese industrial and environmental dumping and its effects on the American attitude, that call for a response from the EU) and a chronological beginning (the COVID-19 shock, which has propelled to the top of the political agenda the need to ensure "strategic autonomy" in the access to critical goods, from with masks and paracetamol to energy and semiconductors). The fact remains that, since 2020, a growing number of economists have joined their voices to those of business leaders, calling for the protection of European industry from global competition that is increasingly seen as unfair. Whether the "trade aggression' first came from the United States (for several decarbonized industries such as low-carbon steel or green hydrogen for example, subsidized by the Inflation Reduction Act, see Blot et al. 2024), or came from China and triggered an American response (electric vehicles, photovoltaic panels, sovereign ambitions over Taiwan and its semiconductor industry), the conclusion is always formulated in the same terms: the European Union would be very "naïve" (this is the recurring term) not to protect its industry from a flood of Chinese and American imports. Not to mention the need for our continent to diversify its supplies of critical materials (lithium, rare earths, etc.) to succeed in its low-carbon transition while, once again, getting rid of dependence from China. We can see how this doctrine of public intervention differs from the two previous ones: it is no longer a question of betting on market mechanisms and free competition, nor of conditioning state aid to the broad objective of innovation, but rather of adopting a logic of capacity. There is no doubt that the COVID-19 crisis and the rise in international tensions have constituted an unprecedented framework within which the rethinking of industrial policies has taken place, but one cannot help but note that this new, widespread, doctrine has not yet been the subject of an in-depth examination of its effectiveness.

2.5.2 A Geological Stack of Public Investment Policies

In the ministerial titles and the formulation of the government's strategic priorities, this substitution of competitiveness by sovereignty is total. Such a semantic shift is also in tune with the international environment: Chinese dumping, colossal fiscal spending in the United States, promises of industrial and energy independence by the pro-Brexit advocates in the United Kingdom, and affirmation of an objective of industrial sovereignty in Korea... The French goal of supporting "industrial sovereignty" is in the spirit of the times.

However, it remains contradictory in the sense that, on the ground, more precisely in the details of the policy mix currently active in France, the public investment channels from these different eras coexist, like fossils of different ages imprisoned in their respective geological layers. Thus, from the "Lisbon" period, France has retained the measures to support technology and certain disruptive innovations, a strong encouragement for public-private cooperation and business creation in the additional credits for public research, the already mentioned research tax credit, competitiveness clusters to promote innovation in the territories, etc. From the following period of "cost competitiveness", we already mentioned the massive reductions in employer social contributions, which today are higher than ever (almost €74 billion in 2022), the gradual reduction of production taxes, which benefits above all medium-sized enterprises, and the support for firms in their effort to upgrade to 4.0 solutions. Finally, the "sovereignty" phase is exemplified by the already mentioned "Build the France of 2030" investment programme which emphasizes targeted, top-down, State aids (in particular the decarbonization of the main greenhouse gas emitting sites, the revival of defence programs, support for supply security strategies, etc.).

2.5.3 A Strong Point: A Refocusing of Strategic Decision-Making

From what precedes, it is clear that French industrial policies are currently at the service of a plurality of objectives, stemming from layers of very different visions of "market failures" that justify public investment. And yet, the business world—that loves nothing more than predictability—today does not seem particularly critical of this panoply of interventions. There are several reasons for this. The first, obvious one, is that the rise of a political narrative of protecting the industrial sector has given economic actors a positive image of the role they play for the economy as a whole and specifically in certain regions. The fact that the public investment programs are piling up in a somewhat disorderly manner is not enough to obliterate the (correct) impression among businesses that there is growing attention paid to their daily difficulties and survival conditions. A second explanation is that, amid this plurality of financing tools, a few emerge in a central, visible position and quite close to the central government. Thus, the General Secretariat for Investment (*Secrétariat général pour l'investissement*, SGPI) stands out as the major player in charge of coordinating several strategic investment channels, as part of the "Build the France of 2030" programme. Additionally, the powerful Caisse des Dépôts (CDC) is increasingly attentive to the fate of industry within the context of its investment projects for territorial development and infrastructures. This is where the French government has some fiscal space to finance priority investments (apart from defence), beyond the mechanical renewal of the commitments made by the ministries and other dedicated agencies. Powerful operators with a good public image, such as Bpifrance, the Banque des territoires (a subsidiary of CDC) and Ademe[9] are in fact the armed wings of CDC and SGPI in terms of industrial policy. For example, the Banque des territoires plans to spend more than

9 Bpifrance is the French public bank dedicated to venture investment (reindustrialization, green transition, Deep Tech...). The "Banque des territoires" is its counterpart dedicated to public investment in regions (infrastructures, sustainable mobility, ICT equipment...). The Ademe is the national agency devoted to energy transition and savings.

€1 billion to reindustrialization over 2023–2027 period, financing "turnkey" plants and industrial projects. All in all, since 2020, the Banque des territoires has provided €1.2 billion in equity financing for 260 projects, including 40 new plants (Charlet 2024).

Finally, a third reason why the business world does not seem concerned with a somewhat chaotic set of interventions may be that, in the current economic and geopolitical environment, what is perceived by businesses as the most urgent need is a properly functioning framework for doing business: managing energy prices and production ramp-ups (gas, carbon-free electricity and hydrogen, etc.), adapting human capital and skills to the new needs and attracting talents, securing the supply of critical assets, guaranteeing access to land resources that seem increasingly scarce as conflicts and environmental constraints become more important, economic and geopolitical stabilizing of global supply chains, and so on. These are the concerns that top the list of businesses surveyed: not the fiscal aid to support price competitiveness nor the technological sources of non-price competitiveness.

2.6 Conclusion. A Lack of Readability, Reflecting a Lack of Doctrine

The main weakness of France's industrial policies today is not a "simple" problem of disorderly accumulation of policies but, more fundamentally, a lack of doctrine. The common belief that industry must be supported through ad hoc public investments has certainly gained momentum, but it has also become more cacophonous. It does not seem excessive to conclude that French policy makers no longer know what they are looking for in this area: is it a question of raising industrial employment to the point of "reindustrializing the country"? Of restoring the competitiveness of businesses to stop the deterioration of the trade deficit? Of supporting the development of innovations, green or not, which will prepare tomorrow's industrial activity? To put an end to the widening of economic gaps between territories? To defend France's place in a turbulent geopolitical environment...? All these goals—and others—are explicitly mentioned at the same time, sometimes even accompanied by sets of key performance indicators.

Realistic policies inherently require balancing multiple objectives; but it must be acknowledged that these objectives can only be partially achieved, a concession that is not often voiced these days. It is undeniable that the deindustrialization of developed countries has led to several disastrous collateral effects; however, it is far more doubtful that the resources currently available for public policies are sufficient to fully address them. As it stands, a great deal of emphasis is therefore placed on industrial policies, but no one knows how to measure whether success will be possible in a few years; time, which may seem problematic in an unstable political climate, when there is, more than ever, the need for clarity.

References

Blot, C., J. Créel, H. Kempf, S. Levasseur, X. Ragot, and F. Saraceno (2024) "Sailing in All Weather Conditions the Next 25 Years: Challenges for the Euro", Paper Prepared for the European Parliament ECON Committee Monetary Dialogue, February.

Bubbico, R. L., P. B. Brutscher, and D. Revoltella (2020) "Europe Needs More Public Investment", in F. Cerniglia and F. Saraceno (eds), *A European Public Investment Outlook*. Cambridge, UK: Open Book Publishers, pp. 17–32, https://doi.org/10.11647/OBP.0222.01

Charlet, V. (2024) *Ce que l'industrie attend des banques*. Paris: Presses des Mines.

European Commission (2023) "EU Budget: Commission Proposes Strategic Technologies for Europe Platform (STEP) to Support European Leadership on Critical Technologies", *European Commission*.

Pisani-Ferry, J., and S. Mahfouz (2023) "Les Incidences Économiques de l'action Pour Le Climat", May 22, *France Strategie, Rapport à La Première Ministre*, https://www.strategie.gouv.fr/publications/incidences-economiques-de-laction-climat

Plane, M., and F. Saraceno (2021) "From Fiscal Consolidation to the Plan de Relance', in F. Cerniglia et al. (eds), *The Great Reset—2021 European Public Investment Outlook*. Cambridge, UK: Open Book Publishers, pp. 33–46, https://doi.org/10.11647/OBP.0280.02

Von der Leyen, U. (2022) "State of the Union", 14 September, *European Commission*, https://state-of-the-union.ec.europa.eu/state-union-2022_en

White House (2023) *Building a Clean Energy Economy: A Guidebook to the Inflation Reduction Act's Investments in Clean Energy and Climate Action*. Washington, DC: The White House, https://www.whitehouse.gov/wp-content/uploads/2022/12/Inflation-Reduction-Act-Guidebook.pdf

3. Germany: Additional Investment Needs Require Reform of the Debt Brake

Katja Rietzler[1] *and Andrew Watt*[2]

In recent quarters, German public investment has increased slightly in real terms. However, this development is driven largely by special effects such as the reclassification of public transport companies and increased military spending. Additional investment needs are estimated to be as high as 1.4% of GDP, and cannot be met without a substantial reform of the debt brake. Economists have recently come up with numerous reform proposals, but there is still no political majority for a reform. While European fiscal rules do not require much fiscal tightening in Germany, they do constrain the use of credit to finance the necessary additional public investment. Instead of a big push, the more likely scenario is continued incremental progress, or "muddling through".

3.1 Introduction

Insufficient public investment has been an issue in Germany for years (Dullien et al. 2020; Rietzler and Watt 2021 2022; Rietzler et al. 2023). With the Federal Constitutional Court's ruling in November 2023, which came just as last year's *European Public Investment Outlook* was being finalized, a boost to German public investment has become much more difficult. The court ruled that the transfer of €60 billion of unused credit authorizations to deal with the pandemic to the climate and transformation fund (KTF) was unconstitutional and thus void. A direct consequence of the court ruling was that the KTF lost about two-thirds of its reserves. In 2024, additional funding to cover feed-in tariffs for electricity from renewable sources will come from the reallocation of funds originally budgeted for the subsidization of new production sites of computer chips. With the break-up of the government, it is unclear whether the feed-in tariffs will in future be funded from the core budget as planned. The KTF

1 Macroeconomic Policy Institute (IMK).
2 European Trade Union Institute (ETUI).

 https://doi.org/10.11647/OBP.0434.04

might have to rely solely on current revenue from carbon pricing to support a wide variety of transformative investment from hydrogen networks to energy-efficient home refurbishment. The "climate allowance" to mitigate the social impact of carbon pricing, which was promised in the coalition agreement, has become extremely unlikely.

The court ruling has implications beyond the KTF. It also affects other off-budget funds, e.g., for rebuilding the infrastructure destroyed in the flooding of summer 2021 (Sondervermögen "Aufbauhilfe 2021") or the economic stabilization fund, which was intended to subsidize electricity network fees that have increased due to the need for grid investments to enable the expansion of renewable electricity. Any such expenditure will now have to come from the core federal budget, increasing the fiscal pressure. At the same time, some off-budget operations to finance decarbonization investment at the level of the federal states are now equally under threat. The off-budget fund to finance the modernization of the armed forces (Sondervermögen "Bundeswehr") remains unaffected by the court ruling, because it was established via an amendment to the constitution, requiring a two-thirds majority in both houses of parliament (Bundestag and Bundesrat).

This worsening of the fiscal room for manoeuvre has been exacerbated by high uncertainty due to permanent disagreement in the government and its eventual break-up. This comes at a time when substantial additional investment needs have been identified. In an update of their prominent study of 2019 (Bardt et al. 2019), the IMK and the IW Köln estimate the required additional spending for general government investment and investment grants at almost €600 billion over ten years (Dullien et al. 2024b). We discuss the estimated additional spending needs below.

3.2 Recent Developments in Public Investment

After a pronounced decline in 2021 and 2022 and stagnation in early 2023, real government gross fixed capital formation has risen somewhat since the second half of 2023, but still has not regained the peak of 2020. There has been a marked increase of investment into machinery and equipment, while construction investment fluctuated around a slightly positive trend, and the decline in other investment (mostly intellectual property) seems to have stopped (Fig. 3.1).

There are two main drivers behind the strong increase in investment into machinery and equipment: increased military spending from the extrabudgetary armed forces fund (Sondervermögen "Bundeswehr") and investment into vehicles for local transport at the state and municipal levels. With the introduction of the heavily subsidized "Deutschland-Ticket", a Germany-wide local transport ticket, all state-owned local transport companies were reclassified into the government sector—increasing public investment. Under pressure to consolidate the budget, the federal government that introduced the ticket is now increasingly reluctant to provide the necessary funding. Therefore, the ticket price will increase by more than 18% in

2025 and long-term financing remains uncertain, hampering the transition to a more climate-friendly transport system.

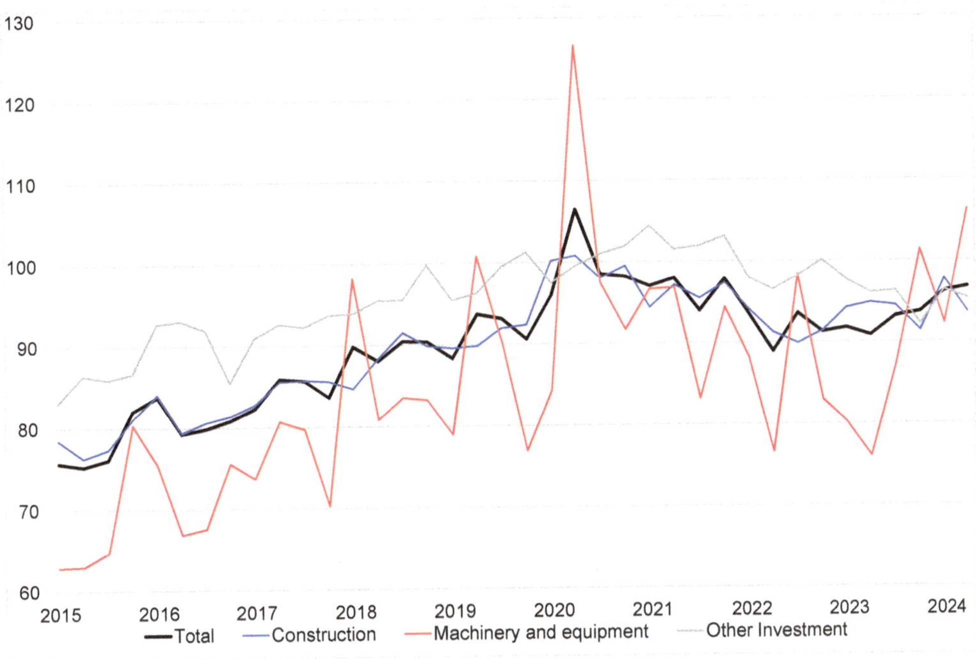

Fig. 3.1 Real government gross fixed capital formation by type (Index: 2020=100). *Source*: Destatis, seasonally and calendar adjusted.

Online resources for Fig. 3.1 are available at https://hdl.handle.net/20.500.12434/19989e57

Looking at government subsectors, the slight upward trend in real investment can be attributed to the federal and municipal levels (Fig. 3.2). Investment at the state level has been weak recently, as the rise of investment into machinery and equipment has been offset by plummeting investment in construction as well as intellectual property. The municipalities, which account for almost 40% of public gross fixed capital formation (down from around 50% in the early 1990s) have sustained a strong expansion of their investment since the end of 2022, despite the massively increased price level of construction activities, which account for more than 80% of municipal investment.

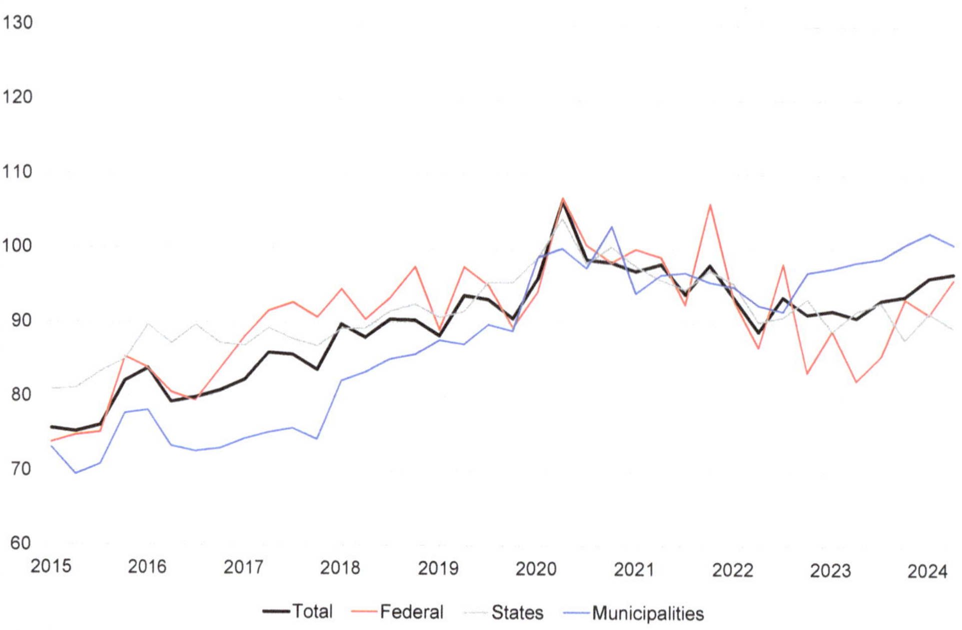

Fig. 3.2 Government gross fixed capital formation by level of government (Index: 2020=100). *Source*: Destatis, national accounts, seasonally and calendar adjusted, adjustment of subsectors by IMK, social security excluded due to negligible amount.

It is unlikely that the relatively strong first half of 2024 marks the beginning of a new upward trend for public investment. At the federal level, much of the additional dynamic comes from defence spending out of a limited extra-budgetary fund (€100 billion over several years). The investment activity of the states is fluctuating at a reduced level. Both federal and state governments are under pressure to comply with the debt brake, which allows very limited credit financing for the federal government and hardly any for the states. The municipalities may not be able to sustain their strong investment activity due to rising pressure from increased wage costs and high social spending, while expected tax revenues have just been revised further downwards for all levels of government (BMF 2024b). A recent survey among municipalities with more than two thousand inhabitants reports an increasingly pessimistic outlook. They suffer both from a lack of funds and non-financial barriers to investment such as excessive bureaucracy, limited capacity of construction firms, and insufficient staff (Scheller and Raffer 2024). According to this survey the investment backlog of the municipalities rose further to a total of €186.1 billion in 2023 despite sustained efforts.

An additional problem is the persistence of regional disparities in public investment. Since 2011, when regional data for the whole government sector became available, Bavaria, Baden-Württemberg, and Saxony consistently showed investment per capita above the German average, whereas in North Rhine-Westphalia, Saarland, Brandenburg, Lower Saxony, and Rhineland-Palatinate it has been consistently below average. Regional disparities are therefore widening, as wealthy states can invest in their infrastructure, raising their growth potential, while poorer states are increasingly left behind.

While there has been limited progress in direct public investment, government investment grants to other sectors have skyrocketed in recent years and amounted to €61.1 billion in 2023. Even in real terms, investment grants more than doubled between the first quarter of 2019 and the second quarter of 2024 after having been flat for years (Fig. 3.3). As the figure shows, the evolution of investment grants has lost some momentum in recent quarters. The strong rise reflects, among others, grants from the "Climate and transformation fund" as well as grants by municipalities to local businesses.

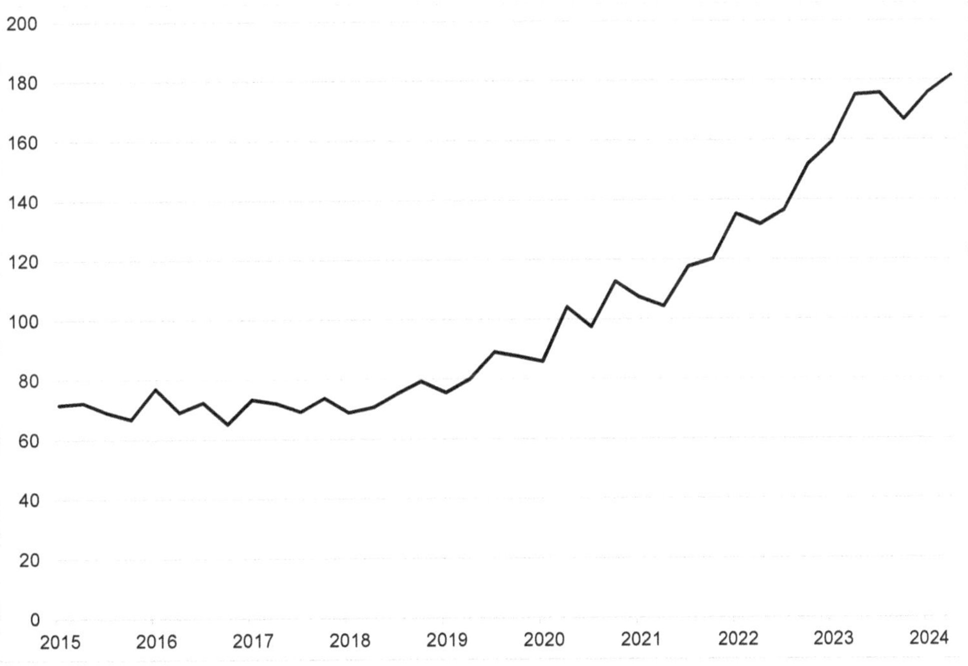

Fig. 3.3 Real Government Investment Grants (Index: 2020=100). *Source*: Destatis, national accounts, price adjustment (deflator of gross fixed capital formation) and seasonal adjustment by IMK.

Online resources for Figs. 3.2 and 3.3 are available at https://hdl.handle.net/20.500.12434/3f72f28e

Cross-country comparisons of public investment need to be treated with caution, due to definitional differences (such as how motorways are financed). Still, as the

European Commission notes in its spring economic forecast (European Commission 2024a: 46), Germany has recorded one of the smallest percentage-point increases in public investment (as a share of GDP) of all EU Member States between 2019 and the forecast for 2024. At under 3%, its investment-to-GDP ratio is now the second lowest in the EU after Ireland, having been overtaken by several countries, in particular, southern and eastern European countries.

In part, this is because these countries have benefited from financing from the Recovery and Resilience Facility (RRF) and other EU funds to a much greater extent than Germany. As previous editions of the *EPIO* have emphasized, the RRF plays only a marginal role for Germany, contributing €28 billion over six years. On top of this, there have been delays in the originally scheduled payment of tranches from the RRF because planned milestones have not been (fully) reached (Bundesrechnungshof 2023: 12 ff.). Apart from the initial so-called "pre-financing" that was made available, Germany has submitted only one payment request (as of July 2024). The European Commission in its European Semester report on Germany described the implementation of the RRF as "significantly delayed" (European Commission 2024b: 29).

3.3 Additional Public Investment Needs Remain High

It is true, of course, that there is no simple and generally agreed basis for determining the necessary or the optimal size of the public capital stock, and thus the gap compared to its current level. Yet orders of magnitude can be derived from coupling cost estimates with political commitments to achieve certain goals (such as reducing delays in rail transport) and government commitments (such as meeting climate goals). Taking this approach, five years ago a team of researchers produced an estimate—€460 billion over ten years—which has become a reference point in the German public debate (Bardt et al. 2019). This analysis has recently been updated (Dullien et al. 2024b) and its findings are summarized here.

The revised estimates were necessary to take account of substantial changes since the first analysis. These relate, on the one hand, to the costs in nominal terms of the investments and to legal or other changes that place additional demands on the extent or urgency of transformation. Set against these forces pushing up the investment bill are those investment projects that have, in the meantime, been completed.

Clearly, the inflationary shock of 2022/2023 has increased the (nominal) cost of any given project, whereby it is not so much consumer prices, but rather construction that is decisive: the index of construction costs is roughly 40% higher than in 2019. The tightening of national and European environmental (especially decarbonization) standards and targets, and the impact of the war in Ukraine on energy supply—which demands a faster rollout of renewable energy—and a population boost—with more than one million Ukrainians migrating to Germany since 2022—have substantially increased the investment need. As in 2019, estimates of investment needs were taken from the literature and adjusted for price increases where necessary or actual investment if data are available. Unlike in 2019, current operational spending (e.g., for running kindergartens) is not included in the 2024 study.

The offsetting impact of the projects implemented during the last five years is generally rather modest, so that the ten-year public investment need is now assessed to be just under €600 billion, around one third higher—in nominal terms—than five years ago. While nominal GDP has also increased significantly, €60 billion per year presents a substantial, but far from overwhelming, 1.4% of 2024 estimated GDP. However, this amount is additional to the capital spending that is actually planned.

As in Bardt et al. (2019), the focus is on the investment needed to ensure the modernization of the economy towards a green growth model. This is one reason for why military investment requirements—however important they may be from a political perspective—have not been taken into account. Dullien et al. (2024b) offers an assessment of the order of magnitude of current investment needs, without providing an exhaustive list.

Table 3.1 summarizes the main areas of required spending. Publicly financed decarbonization measures and improvements to infrastructure at local government level, including local public transport, account for a little more than one-third of total spending needs each. Around 10% of the total, €60 billion, would be required to develop the rail network. Sums just under €40 billion each are estimated to be required for education (especially university buildings),[3] public support for housing construction and refurbishment, and for trunk roads and motorways. As the federal government has made good progress in the expansion of the broadband and 5G networks in recent years, and more investment is foreseen in budget planning, no additional investment need remains in this field.

Table 3.1 Required spending for Public Investment and Government Investment Grants, in € billions, over ten years, 2024 prices. *Source*: Dullien et al. 2024b. Table 1, own translation.

Measure	Investment need
Infrastructure at local government level	
Local government infrastructure	177.2
Expansion of public transport	28.5
Education	
All-day schooling	6.7

3 The estimated investment backlog for school buildings is included in local infrastructure.

Renewal of tertiary education facilities	34.7
Housing	
Public sector share	36.8
Long-distance transport infrastructure	
Rail network	59.5
Road/motorway network	39
Climate mitigation and adjustment	
Decarbonization (public sector share)	200
Local government adjustment measures	13.2
Total	595.7

These estimates are referred to by the European Commission in its Country Report for Germany, where, among other policies, higher public investment is called for (European Commission 2024b: 10).

3.4 Increasing Pressure to Reform the Debt Brake

As mentioned above, following the Federal Constitutional Court's ruling in November 2023 on the second federal budget amendment of 2021, which declared the federal government's reserve operations in extrabudgetary funds unconstitutional, it has increasingly become obvious that it is impossible to comply with the debt brake, while simultaneously integrating more than one million refugees into German society and the labour market, and investing enough into the green transformation of the economy and the modernization of German infrastructure. Apart from being problematic on theoretical grounds, tax-financing of the needed investment is a political non-starter, particularly as the conservatives (CDU and CSU) who lead in the polls favour tax cuts.

In the wake of the COVID-19 pandemic, there have been repeated reform proposals for the debt brake (e.g. Braun 2021; Deutsche Bundesbank 2022), but the reform debate did not gain traction until after the court ruling in November 2023. Since then, prominent economists have come forward with various proposals.

The five-person Council of Economic Experts, although characterized by frequent differences of opinion and minority votes, issued a unanimous proposal to increase the scope for structural deficits up to the limit of the Stability and Growth Pact of 1.5%

of GDP—from 0.35% for the federal government and 0% for the state governments, if the debt-to-GDP ratio is low (i.e., below the Maastricht reference value of 60%). Thus, this approach would not help to enable immediate credit-financed investment, as Germany's debt-to-GDP ratio was 62.9% at the end of 2023. In addition, the Council of Economic Experts demands that the cyclical adjustment method should be made less procyclical and a transition period should be allowed for after severe crises (SVR 2024). A group of three leading economists proposed an amendment to the constitution to establish a public investment fund exempted from the debt brake. Like the fund for the armed forces and all other substantial reforms of the debt brake this would require a two-thirds majority in both houses of parliament (Fuest et al. 2024). Economists at the IW Köln propose a transformation fund along the lines of the fund for the army to finance the decarbonization of the economy (Hüther 2024; Hentze and Kauder 2024). The IMK argues in favour of a golden rule of public investment, as it works in the long term and ensures that additional debt is used for investment. It is also more transparent than enabling yet another off-budget fund (Dullien et al. 2024a).

Several proposals made before the court ruling have also received renewed attention, such as the reform concept of the Deutsche Bundesbank (2022). Its main focus is an improvement to the cyclical adjustment method that would tackle forecast errors, but includes a number of other reform proposals that would widen fiscal room for manoeuvre, such as reducing the positive balance in the debt brake's control account[4] instead of directly paying off debt taken up during the COVID-19 and energy crises, or a higher limit for new debt as long as the debt-to-GDP ratio is low. This could be combined with investment requirements. The scientific council of the Ministry of Economy and Climate Protection (Wissenschaftlicher Beirat des BMWK 2023) recommends what it calls "Goldene Regel Plus" (golden rule plus). Under this regime, net investment would be exempted from the debt brake. To prevent policy makers from declaring any spending as investment, an independent institution would have to confirm the investment character of the envisaged spending. This is what the "plus" stands for. Recently, the International Monetary Fund (IMF) has also argued in favour of a higher debt ceiling, a demand it had already made in last year's report on the annual Article IV consultations. According to the IMF, the debt ceiling could be lifted to about 1% of GDP (IMF 2023: 14).

3.5 Scope for More Investment under the Reformed EU Fiscal Rules?

As we have seen the current German national fiscal rules constitute a serious constraint for a meaningful expansion of public investment. Germany is, of course, also bound by European fiscal rules. These have just been reformed and are now to be applied,

4 The debt brake's control account records over- and underperformance during budget execution. There is currently a positive balance of €49.2 bn (BMF 2024a).

following a period in which, in response to the COVID-19 and energy crises, the rules had been suspended. What are the implications of the new European rules for public investment in Germany in the coming years?

As discussed in more detail in the Introduction to this volume, the new rules mark a substantial change (on the following, see Darvas et al. 2024). The main operative indicator is government spending, adjusted for cyclical items (such as unemployment benefits) and any changes to tax policy. Each country is subjected to a debt sustainability analysis (DSA) by the European Commission. On this basis a country-specific path for bringing the debt ratio down to levels considered sustainable is set with a four-year horizon (adjustment period). This can be extended to up to seven years to the extent that countries can show the EU Commission (and, ultimately, their peers on the Council) that their reform and investment programmes are such that they will raise potential output (and thus debt-carrying capacity) or address common EU goals or country-specific recommendations. Importantly, unlike in the national rules, the scope to put spending items, such as for the military, in shadow budgets is strictly limited under EU rules.

At the insistence not least of the German government, three so-called safeguards were added out of a fear that the rules would otherwise permit too great a degree of discretion to the Commission, particularly in classifying spending as growth-enhancing investment and thus prolonging the adjustment path. The safeguards are as follows: 1. fiscal adjustment cannot increase during the adjustment period (no backloading); 2. the debt ratio must decline by at least one percentage point a year in countries with a debt ratio above 90% of GDP, and by 0.5 percentage points for those with a debt ratio between 60 and 90% (debt sustainability safeguard); and 3. there must be at least a 0.4 percentage point annual adjustment of the primary structural balance if the structural deficit is currently more than 1.5%, with a four-year adjustment period, or a 0.25 percentage point adjustment for a seven-year period (deficit resilience safeguard). These safeguards risk reintroducing, for high-debt and high-deficit countries, the tendency towards pro-cyclicality and the limits to public investment that the reform sought to overcome. The third safeguard also smuggles the unobservable structural deficit back into the rules, which it had been intended to exclude.

Germany's current situation is that it has a debt ratio (on EU definitions) only just above 60%, a current deficit of 1.6%, and a structural balance within the limits of the deficit resilience safeguard. As a consequence, the DSA-based rule is the constraining factor. According to an analysis by Bruegel (Darvas et al. 2024: 5ff.), based on current EU-Commission economic forecasts (Spring 2024), Germany will need to achieve a structural primary surplus of 0.4% at the end of the four-year adjustment period and just 0.1% if the adjustment is extended. This implies a very modest tightening (around 0.1 percentage points) over the four-year horizon and a broadly neutral stance if the seven-year adjustment is granted. What this means for the recommended push to higher public investment is, on the one hand, that it can be assumed that this would enable the seven-year adjustment period to be claimed and granted. However, the need to maintain the structural balance, more or less, at its current neutral stance implies that any additional public investment would need to be balanced by either spending cuts or tax financed. It is a small comfort that, according to Bruegel's calculations, the fiscal constraint would have been tighter under the recently replaced rules.

In June the European Commission issued its first assessment under the new rules. Germany was not among the twelve countries for which an excessive deficit procedure was opened. The exact fiscal trajectory and adjustment needs communicated to the government have not been made public. However, statements by the former finance minister suggest that they are consistent with the Bruegel analysis, implying a very marginal tightening but no scope for substantially higher public investment, unless they are tax-financed.

All in all, we can conclude that the new rules are an improvement on the older ones, and they will not force Germany into a substantial policy tightening. Although the rules allow for a slightly looser fiscal stance than during most of the past thirty years, they do place tight constraints on a substantial push for higher deficit-financed public investment (Paetz and Watzka 2024).

3.6 Outlook: No Sufficient Majority for Substantial Reform of the Debt Brake

With the decision to reapply the debt brake already in 2023, the federal government unnecessarily used up more than three quarters of the general reserve of €48.2 billion generated from surpluses before the pandemic (BMF 2024a). Otherwise, this would have increased the fiscal space in coming years. The remaining amount is to be spent in 2024, so that, from 2025, the reserve is exhausted. With lower expected tax revenues and high social spending, not least for refugees, there is little room for manoeuvre for any future government. Provisional budget management will further limit the scope until a budget for 2025 is passed. In the current frail economic situation this may be better than outright spending cuts, but it is not sufficient to move Germany forward.

The most probable scenario for the near future is a continued muddling through with no great boost to public investment. While some state leaders of the Christian Democratic Union (currently an opposition party in the federal parliament, but likely to lead the next government) have spoken in favour of reforms to the debt brake, the party leadership is still reluctant. A substantial reform of the debt brake is now ruled out before a new federal government is in place and might not happen at all, as a two-thirds majority would be required in both houses of parliament. Even in the event of a reform, the European fiscal rules continue to impose constraints. Thus, the overall outlook is bleak.

References

Bardt, H., S. Dullien, M. Hüther, and K. Rietzler (2020) "For a Sound Fiscal Policy: Enabling Public Investment", *IMK Report* 152e, March, https://www.imk-boeckler.de/fpdf/HBS-007619/p_imk_report_152e_2020.pdf

Braun, H. (2021). "Das ist der Plan für Deutschland nach Corona", *Handelsblatt*, January 26, https://www.handelsblatt.com/meinung/gastbeitraege/gastkommentar-das-ist-der-plan-fuer-deutschland-nach-corona/26850508.html

Bundesministerium der Finanzen, BMF (2024a) "Vorläufiger Abschluss des Bundeshaushalts 2023", *Monatsbericht des BMF*, January, https://www.bundesfinanzministerium.de/Monatsberichte/2024/01/Inhalte/Kapitel-3-Analysen/3-2-vorlaeufiger-abschluss-bundeshaushalt-2023.html

Bundesministerium der Finanzen, BMF (2024b) "Abweichungen des Ergebnisses der Steuerschätzung Oktober 2024 vom Ergebnis der Steuerschätzung Mai 2024 ", Anlage 2 zu Pressemitteilung 15 des BMF, https://www.bundesfinanzministerium.de/Content/DE/Downloads/Steuern/ergebnis-167-steuerschaetzung-02.pdf?__blob=publicationFile&v=6

Bundesrechnungshof (2023) "Bericht nach § 88 Absatz 2 BHO an das Bundesministerium der Finanzen zur Steuerung und Kontrolle der Umsetzung des Deutschen Aufbau- und Resilienzplans", Bonn, December 8, https://www.bundesrechnungshof.de/SharedDocs/Downloads/DE/Berichte/2024/umsetzung-darp-volltext.pdf?__blob=publicationFile&v=3

Darvas, Z., L. Welslau, and J. Zettelmeyer (2024) "The Implications of the European Union's New Fiscal Rules", *Policy Brief* 10/24, https://www.bruegel.org/system/files/2024-07/PB%2010%202024.pdf

Dullien, S., T. Bauermann, L. Endres, A. Herzog-Stein, K. Rietzler, and S. Tober (2024a) "Schuldenbremse reformieren, Transformation beschleunigen. Wirtschaftspolitische Herausforderungen 2024", *IMK Report* 187, January, https://www.econstor.eu/bitstream/10419/283062/1/p-imk-report-187-2024.pdf

Dullien, S., S. Gerards-Iglesias, M. Hüther, and K. Rietzler (2024b) "Herausforderungen für die Schuldenbremse. Investitionsbedarfe in der Infrastruktur und für die Transformation", *IMK Policy Brief* 168, https://econpapers.repec.org/paper/imkpbrief/168-2024.htm

Dullien, S., E. Jürgens, and S. Watzka (2020c) "Public Investment in Germany: The Need for a Big Push", in F. Cerniglia and F. Saraceno (eds), *A European Public Investment Outlook*. Cambridge: Open Book Publishers, pp. 49–62, https://doi.org/10.11647/obp.0222.03

Deutsche Bundesbank (2022) "Die Schuldenbremse des Bundes: Möglichkeiten einer stabilitätsorientierten Weiterentwicklung", Deutsche Bundesbank, Monatsbericht, April.

European Commission (2024a) "European Economic Forecast Spring 2024', *Institutional Paper* 286, May, https://economy-finance.ec.europa.eu/document/download/c63e0da2-c6d6-4d13-8dcb-646b0d1927a4_en?filename=ip286_en.pdf

European Commission (2024b) "2024 Country Report – Germany", Commission Staff Working Document, SWD(2024) 605, June 19, https://economy-finance.ec.europa.eu/document/download/0826d6c6-4c97-44be-8b9e-1a0b5c4361c8_en?filename=SWD_2024_605_1_EN_Germany.pdf

Fuest, C., M. Hüther, and J. Südekum (2024) "Folgen des Verfassungsurteils: Investitionen schützen. Vorteile eines Sondervermögens", *Frankfurter Allgemeine Zeitung*, January 12, https://www.faz.net/aktuell/wirtschaft/folgen-des-haushaltsurteils-investitionen-schuetzen-19440915.html

Hentze, T., and B. Kauder (2024) "Reformansätze für die Schuldenbremse", *ifo Schnelldienst* 2/2024, 13–15, https://www.ifo.de/DocDL/sd-2024-02-haushaltspolitik-reform-schuldenbremse.pdf

Hüther, M. (2024) "Ein gesamtstaatlicher »Transformations- und Infrastrukturfonds« zur Stabilisierung der Schuldenbremse", *Wirtschaftsdienst* 104(1): 14–20.

International Monetary Fund, IMF (2023) "Germany. Staff Report for the 2023 Article IV Consultation", June 28, *IFO*, https://www.imf.org/-/media/Files/Publications/CR/2023/English/1DEUEA2023001.ashx

Paetz, C., and S. Watzka (2024) "The New Fiscal Rules: Another Round of Austerity for Europe?", *IMK Policy Brief* 176.

Raffer, C., and H. Scheller (2024) *KfW Kommunalpanel 2024*. Frankfurt am Main: Kreditanstalt für Wiederaufbau, https://www.kfw.de/PDF/Download-Center/Konzernthemen/Research/PDF-Dokumente-KfW-Kommunalpanel/KfW-Kommunalpanel-2024.pdf

Rietzler, K., and A. Watt (2021) "Public Investment in Germany: Much More Needs to Be Done", in F. Cerniglia, F. Saraceno, and A. Watt (eds), *The Great Reset: 2021 European Public Investment Outlook*. Cambridge: Open Book Publishers, pp. 47–62, https://doi.org/10.11647/OBP.0280.03

Rietzler, K., and A. Watt (2022) "Public Investment in Germany: Squaring the Circle", in F. Cerniglia and F. Saraceno (eds), *Greening Europe—2022 European Public Investment Outlook*. Cambridge: Open Book Publishers, pp. 41–53, https://doi.org/10.11647/OBP.0328.03

Rietzler, K., A. Watt, and E. Jürgens (2023) "Germany Lacks Political Will to Finance Needed Public-Investment Boost", in F. Cerniglia, F. Saraceno, and A. Watt (eds), *Financing Investment in Times of High Public Debt–2023 European Public Investment Outlook*. Cambridge: Open Book Publishers, pp. 51–68, https://doi.org/10.11647/OBP.0386.03

Sachverständigenrat zur Begutachtung der gesamtwirtschaftlichen Entwicklung, SVR (2024) "Die Schuldenbremse nach dem BVerfG-Urteil: Flexibilität erhöhen – Stabilität wahren", *Policy Brief* 1/2024, https://www.sachverstaendigenrat-wirtschaft.de/fileadmin/dateiablage/PolicyBrief/pb2024/Policy_Brief_2024_01.pdf

Wissenschaftlicher Beirat beim BMWK (2023) *Finanzierung von Staatsaufgaben: Herausforderungen und Empfehlungen für eine nachhaltige Finanzpolitik, Gutachten des Wissenschaftlichen Beirats beim Bundesministerium für Wirtschaft und Klimaschutz (BMWK)*. Berlin: BMWK, https://www.bmwk.de/Redaktion/DE/Publikationen/Ministerium/Veroeffentlichung-Wissenschaftlicher-Beirat/gutachten-wissenschaftlicher-beirat-finanzierung-von-staatsaufgaben.pdf?__blob=publicationFile&v=14

4. Italy, NRRP, and Industrial Policy

Giovanni Barbieri,[1] Floriana Cerniglia,[2] and Franco Mosconi[3]

This chapter assesses the National Recovery and Resilience Plan (NRRP) as an industrial policy tool within the Next Generation EU framework, despite limited explicit reference to an industrial strategy. The NRRP emerges during a unique moment for the European Union (EU), characterized by the suspension of the Stability and Growth Pact and the relaxation of state aid restrictions, which have collectively expanded public intervention opportunities. This marks a significant shift from the post-1990s ideological emphasis on competition over state involvement, particularly in Italy, where reductions in capital expenditure since 2009 have constrained public infrastructure and private investment. This chapter delves into the current landscape highlighting the potential for a more effective approach to industrial strategy using public investment. By focusing on "Mission 1" (Competitiveness) and "Mission 4" (Education and Research), the chapter aims to elucidate the NRRP's industrial policy direction including reinforcing the special economic zones (SEZs) established in 2017.

4.1 Introduction

The National Recovery and Resilience Plan (NRRP), the Italian adaptation of Next Generation EU, can be seen as an important tool of industrial policy, although the expression "industrial policy" is mentioned explicitly only once in the plan. Next Generation EU was launched in an unprecedented context for the EU: the suspension of the Stability and Growth Pact and the ban on "state aid" to firms and companies, one of the cardinal principles on which the European single market rests. These two "derogations" from the previous *status quo* have allowed Member States within the European Union (EU) to glimpse unprecedented room for manoeuvre in public

1 CRANEC—Università Cattolica del Sacro Cuore (Milan).
2 CRANEC—Università Cattolica del Sacro Cuore (Milan).
3 Jean Monnet Chair—Università di Parma.

 https://doi.org/10.11647/OBP.0434.05

intervention and new public policies. Among these, industrial policy certainly deserves a prominent place, as it also plays a very important role in accompanying the structural transformation processes of companies and industries, including innovation, companies' growth, and technological specialization. Throughout Europe, these areas have significantly declined since the 1990s, following a decisive ideological shift prioritizing limited state intervention, relying exclusively on the protection of competition. Italy had also followed this path. As documented in the chapters on Italy in the previous *Outlooks*, the reduction in capital expenditure, especially from 2009 onwards, affected public infrastructure investments and grants to private firms. Certainly, these grants, for many reasons, are not a panacea, and must be used with caution when pursuing an industrial policy. However, there is a very marked difference with the current scenario and what happened in the 1960s and 1970s, both in Italy and in Europe, where industrial structures were created through a combination of public investment and well-defined policies within a clearly structured industrial policy framework. Moreover, the recently reformed Stability and Growth Pact greatly reduces room for fiscal manoeuvring for certain Member States which will have to implement robust fiscal consolidation policies (i.e. Italy and France). This new fiscal scenario will likely impact the effectiveness of European industrial policies as it may distort the output of investment decisions under the Next Generation EU (NGEU) programme which is set in a fundamentally different fiscal regulatory framework.

In this chapter,[4] we attempt to illustrate what (and if) an industrial policy direction can be traced in the Italian NRRP, looking specifically at the so-called "Mission 1" (i.e., Competitiveness) and "Mission 4" (i.e., Education and Research). This includes also strengthening (with investments and reforms) the SEZs established in 2017.

4.2 NRRP and Industrial Policy

4.2.1 A European Perspective

To assess the industrial policy measures in the NGEU (and thus in the Italian NRRP), it is necessary to start from a broader background, i.e., the varying industrial policy visions and perspectives that have emerged in the European Union in recent decades. The topic has been well researched in the economic literature and firmly anchored in an international debate that has been evolving since the very beginning of this century.[5]

Since the dawn of the twenty-first century, industrial policy has undergone a substantial evolution on a global scale. The EU has seen its share of changes in both

4 This chapter is a shorter version of a CRANEC Working Paper (Barbieri, Cerniglia, and Mosconi 2024).

5 Cf. Barbieri Goés and Viesti G. (2024); Mosconi (2015); Pianta, Lucchese, and Nascia (2020); Bianchi and Labory (2016); Andreoni (2017). See also chapters 11 and 12 in Di Tommaso et al. (2024), and Guerrieri and Padoan (2024).

theory and practice in this important area of public policy. The picture of the EU that emerges is one of lights and shadows. Does "manufacturing Europe" need an industrial policy? If so, what kind? The answer to the first question is yes, especially if one considers the current trend towards a "new industrial policy", which differs from the approach that prevailed in the last decades of the twentieth century.[6]

It seems useful to briefly retrace the stages of the evolution of industrial policy as conceived by the EU, mainly due to the driving role played by the European Commission. The Brussels-based approach that has emerged from the early 2000s to the present can be summarized in three phases (Mosconi 2022): (i) the "Integrated approach"; (ii) the "Holistic approach"; (iii) the "Twin transition".[7]

The "Integrated approach" was developed by the Commission between 2002 and 2014, during the presidencies of Romano Prodi and Manuel Barroso. There was, from the institutional and economic stances, the historical Eastern enlargement of the single market towards countries that, in more than one case, boasted significant industrial-manufacturing traditions. The term "integrated" was intended to mean a mix of the traditional horizontal approach (policies for all sectors, e.g., antitrust, deregulation, etc.) and vertical applications (i.e., for individual sectors deemed strategic from a technological point of view). In other words, a set of policies that must consider the specific needs and characteristics of individual industrial sectors and must therefore be applied differently.

As a matter of fact, when President Prodi presented his 2002-Communication (Prodi 2003), he offered an initial list of suitable industrial sectors as a breeding ground for growing so-called "European Champions": (i) biotechnology and life sciences; (ii) information and communication technology (where Italy's leadership position in mobile communication is at great risk in a new standards war); (iii) the so-called "hydrogen economy" (as a means of alternative energy storage and transfer); (iv) defence (the industry remains fragmented, hindered by the absence of political will to build a truly integrated European defence system); (v) European aerospace (which is still caught between civil and security applications).

The Presidential Communications continued in 2005 under the Presidency of José M. Barroso, which took up and developed the concept of an "Integrated approach", linking it more directly to the Lisbon Strategy (European Commission 2005).

The second phase is under the Juncker Presidency (2014–2019). Building from

6 The recent definition offered by Réka Juhász, Nathan Lane, and Dani Rodrik (2023: 216) is an excellent description of the state of the art: "We define industrial policies as those government policies that explicitly target the transformation of the structure of economic activity in pursuit of some public goal [...] The goal is typically to stimulate innovation, productivity, and economic growth. But it could also be to promote climate transition, good jobs, lagging regions, exports or import substitution [...] Since IP targets structural change, a key characteristic is the exercise of choice and discretion by the public authorities: 'we promote X but not Y', though the latter part of this statement is typically left implicit".

7 Details and further discussion on these three approaches are found in Barbieri, Cerniglia, and Mosconi (2024).

President Jean-Claude Junker's State of the Union Address (Junker 2017) and the 2017–Communication (European Commission 2017), there was a move towards a "Holistic approach" to industrial policy, that is, to bring all existing and new initiatives—horizontal and sector-specific—under a single strategy. This approach inspired the document entitled *Industrial Policy Strategy* (European Commission 2017), part of the broader 2017 State of the Union report, which expressly mentioned under the specific sectoral measures (as in the case of space, defence, automotive, and steel) the need for a strong focus on key enabling technologies.

Briefly, the main instruments of this new strategy were: (i) sector-specific measures in key enabling technologies (such as in the steel, space, and defence industries); (ii) green production and clean energy technologies with a special emphasis on the automotive industry and low-emission mobility, as well as looking at missing links in the relevant value chains (investments in batteries were considered of strategic importance); and (iii) improving new technologies' value chains—making them more robust to improve the competitiveness and assets of Europe's manufacturing industry.

Europe is currently in the third stage, which began in 2019. The von der Leyen Presidency set a new tone right from the start, with two speeches delivered to the European Parliament in July and November 2019 emphasizing the central role of the "dual—ecological and digital—transition" (von der Leyen 2019a, 2019b) and the need to strengthen Europe's industrial base and innovation capacity. Moreover, on March 10, 2020, the von der Leyen Commission issued its first industrial policy communication: "A New Industrial Strategy for Europe" (European Commission 2020). Other significant documents include the European Green Deal, which is "Europe's new growth strategy" (European Commission 2019).

To conclude, it emerges that over more than twenty years of deliberation, Brussels has consolidated a new European industrial policy, focusing on technological trajectories, strategic sectors, and a supranational cooperation. To this aim, the industrial alliances[8] and the Important Projects of Common European Interest (IPCEI)[9] appear to be the crucial instruments in this strategy pursued by the European Union which also focuses on public-private partnerships at the EU level. Table 4.1 summarizes the projects launched to date.

8 Industrial alliances are a tool to facilitate stronger cooperation and joint action between all interested partners (see https://single-market-economy.ec.europa.eu/industry/industrial-alliances_en). Since 2017, industrial alliances have been strengthened by European Commission communication, *A New Industrial Strategy for Europe* (European Commission 2020).

9 'Nine of these IPCEIs concern predominantly R&D as well as projects of first industrial deployment. One IPCEI is dedicated to infrastructure. The increasing number of participating Member States and companies shows a positive trend' (see https://competition-policy.ec.europa.eu/state-aid/ipcei/approved-ipceis_en).

Table 4.1 European supranational industrial cooperation *Source*: adapted from the European Commission's website.

Important Projects of Common European Interest (IPCEI)	**European Industrial Alliances**
First on Microelectronics (2018)	Zero-Emission Aviation
First on Batteries (2019)	SMRs (Small Modular Reactors)
Second on Batteries (2021)	Raw Materials
First on Hydrogen (2022)	Solar Photovoltaic Industry
Second on Hydrogen (2022)	Clean Hydrogen
Second on Microelectronics and Communication Technologies (2023)	Battery
Next Generation Cloud Infrastructure and Services (2023)	Circular Plastics
Third Hydrogen (2024)	Industrial Data, Edge and Cloud
Fourth Hydrogen (2024)	Processors and Semiconductors Technologies
Med4Cure (2024)	Renewable and Low-Carbon Fuels Value Chain
	Critical Medicines

4.2.2 The NRRP and Industrial Policy

NGEU and the Italian NRRP, as previously said, have successfully brought public intervention instruments (including for industrial policy) back to the forefront after being largely sidelined over the past thirty years. Italy is the EU's second largest manufacturer with a strong export trend; therefore, this new European perspective deserves special attention.

The new European framework on industrial policy is evolving and is manifesting its influence on all Member States (also via NGEU). The Italian NRRP has clearly incorporated the industrial policy framework that emerges from the NGEU.[10] In our view, the most important industrial policy instruments to be considered in the NRRP

10 The NGEU and NRPP are discussed in Barbieri, Cerniglia, Gori, and Lattarulo (2022).

are the measures dedicated to investment in knowledge.

Needless to say, Italy, in comparison with the other major EU founding countries, has for many years shown the lowest ratio of R&D investment to GDP. Figure 4.1 is self-explanatory.

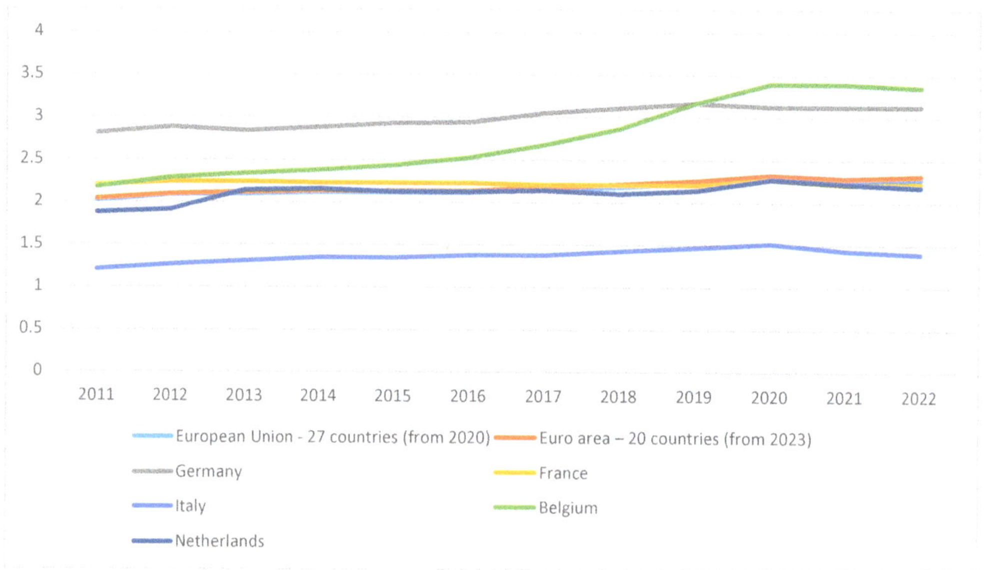

Fig. 4.1 R&D investment (all sectors), %GDP. *Source*: own elaboration based on Eurostat data 2023 (https://ec.europa.eu/eurostat/databrowser/view/tsc00001/default/table?lang=en&category=t_scitech.t_rd).

The NRRP is divided into six "Missions", which in turn are subdivided into sixteen "Components"; all in all, a total of over two hundred funded interventions. Another important NRRP feature is how it is structured around reforms and investments.[11]

The six missions are: 1. Digitization, innovation, competitiveness, culture, and tourism; 2. Green revolution and ecological transition; 3. Infrastructure for sustainable mobility; 4. Education and research; 5. Inclusion and cohesion; and 6. Health. The €194 billion budget is allocated in the plan as follows: 21% for Mission 1; 31% for Mission 2; 13.3% for Mission 3; 16.1% for Mission 4; 10.4% for Mission 5; and 8.2% for Mission 6.[12]

11 On reforms, the primary "horizontal or contextual" ones are the reform of public administration and the justice system. Within this framework, there are also two "enabling reforms": measures to simplify and rationalize legislation and the promotion of competition. Meanwhile, the "sectoral reforms" are contained within the individual missions.

12 Italy's National Recovery and Resilience Plan (NRRP) is worth €235bn: €191.5bn come from the Recovery and Resilience Facility (RRF), €13.5bn from React-EU, and €30.6bn from direct Italian government funding through its Complementary Fund. The National Plan for Complementary Investments (PNC), established by Decree-Law No. 59/2021, is designed to supplement, with national resources, the interventions of the National Recovery and Resilience Plan (NRRP), totalling €30.6 billion for the period 2021 to 2026 (https://www.italiadomani.gov.it/content/sogei-ng/it/it/home.html).

To identify the industrial policy measures, it is necessary to look at the individual components of the plan. Missions can be seen as a first-glance interpretation. It is therefore necessary to read through the components and look at their interconnections. Since our question is what role industrial policy plays in the NRRP, the first thing to mention is that the term industrial policy does not appear often in the text. Indeed, to be accurate, it appears only once, in Component 2 of Mission 1 where funding is provided for the so-called "industrial supply chain and internationalisation policies" (€1.95 billion). The NRRP clearly states that Component 2 of Mission 1 (M1-C2) has the objective of strengthening the competitiveness of the productive system by reinforcing the rate of digitalization, technological innovation and internationalization through a series of complementary interventions. However, it should also be noted that, according to Lucchese and Pianta (2021: 180), "The NRRP envisages various interventions in favour of the production system. The most significant nucleus of measures can be found in two specific Components of the NRRP: Digitisation, Innovation and Competitiveness in the Production System (Mission 1) and From Research to Enterprise (Mission 4)".

Moreover, if industrial policy is considered as a policy aimed at "structural change" in the economy, R&D must be taken into account. Component 2 of Mission 4 (M4-C2) aims to support investments in R&D, promote innovation and the dissemination of technologies, and strengthen skills, fostering the transition to a knowledge-based economy.

The following table offers a picture of the investment measures of the two components considered. The total amount rounds up to €30.4 billion of the total €194 billion NRRP budget, a significant figure in and of itself.

Table 4.2 Key investment measures of Missions 1 and 4. *Source*: Italia Domani (www.italiadomani.gov.it).

M1-C2	M4-C2
Microelectronics innovation and technology	Creating and strengthening "innovation ecosystems", building "territorial R&D leaders"
Industrial supply chain and internationalization policies	Funding of projects submitted by young researchers
Ultra-fast networks—Ultra-wideband and 5G	Introduction of innovative doctorates that meet the innovation needs of companies and promote the recruitment of researchers from companies

Supporting the ecological transition of the production system and strategic supply chains for net zero tech	Introduction of innovative doctorates that meet the innovation needs of companies and promote the recruitment of researchers from companies
Satellite technologies and space economy	Partnerships extended to universities, research centres, companies and funding for basic research projects
4.0 transition	Partnerships extended to universities, research centres, companies and funding for basic research projects
	Research projects of significant national interest—PRIN
	Strengthening research structures and creating R&D "national champions" on *key enabling technologies*

In presenting the missions, components, and investments of the plan in this way, we are not taking a minimalist approach to industrial policy within the NRRP. We are trying to present a view which emphasizes the strategic nature of many instruments; we wish to point out that fostering the process of research and innovation is fundamental in today's industrial policy. In this regard, an interesting perspective is the concept of "technological platforms" (Quadrio Curzio, Silvani, Fortis, and Cerniglia 2023). In other words, looking at the Italian scenario set up by the NRRP, one must consider also the wider European landscape shaped by "European technology platforms" (ETPs). Italy's NRRP represents a great opportunity for the construction of a potentially feasible "platform" (or "network") facility.

Some interventions of the NRRP under the component "From Research to Industry" align with this direction, such as the European KICs (Knowledge and Innovation Communities) networks that unite education, research, and innovation.

Table 4.3 lists the five research facilities and national R&D champions associated with key enabling technologies (KET) and the eleven "Innovation Ecosystems and Territorial R&D Leaders" selected by the Ministry of Universities and Research (MUR) in June 2022.

Table 4.3 The impact of knowledge: centres and ecosystems.[13] *Source*: adapted from MUR (2022).

Five national centres associated with KET	Eleven innovation ecosystems at territorial level
Agritech National Centre	Ecosystem Innovation, digitization and sustainability for the widespread economy in Central Italy
Biodiversity National Centre	TECH4YOU ecosystem
National Centre for Simulation, Computation and High Performance Data Analysis	Ecosystem for Sustainable Transition in Emilia-Romagna
National Centre for Sustainable Mobility	MUSA ecosystem
National Centre for Gene Therapy and Drug Development with RNA Technology	INEST ecosystem
	NODES ecosystem
	RAISE ecosystem
	Roma Tecnopolo ecosystem
	SAMOTHRACE ecosystem
	e.INS ecosystem
	THE ecosystem

These projects suggest that the most relevant technological trajectories of our time are part of the challenge launched with the NRRP. The instruments adopted and the chosen areas of action seem to confirm that, especially through M4-C2, many of the ingredients needed to build true European "platforms" exist. The refinement—now that centres, ecosystems, partnerships, and research infrastructures have been established—must be carried out on the links between the individual "phases". It is a matter of systematizing all those realities that have been financed through the NRRP's calls for proposals in order to create real technological platform models capable of independently surviving beyond the initial public capital funding phase and becoming real "incubators and hubs" of innovation and development (Barbieri and Gahn 2023).

13 The Ministry notes that more than € 4.3 billion were allocated through competitive procedures for these two types of investment, as well as responses to a third Call on 'Research and Technology Infrastructure' (here the number is high, 49).

The NRRP could not (in the drafting phase) and cannot (in the implementation phase) be seen as a complete and exhaustive answer to all Italian bottlenecks (the North-South divide and growth-gap, the low factors productivity and so on) but rather as an extraordinary opportunity to deeply change some of the country's economic and social institutions.[14]

The general picture sketched above through the combination of the interventions—in short—on competitiveness (M1-C2) and industrial research (M4-C2)—should be integrated with other elements, such as the recent measures launched by the Italian government in August 2024: the Transition Plan 5.0. Despite having adequate resources (€6.5 billion), the business community identifies two main shortcomings of the measure: it was introduced too late, leaving little time for companies to prepare their plans, and its procedures are overly complex. Therefore, it cannot be assumed that the success of Industry Plan 4.0 (from 2016/2017 onwards) can be easily replicated.

To complete our overview, we looked at another component of Mission 4 (M4-C1), which refers to "Strengthening the supply of education services: from kindergarten to university". It addresses the issue of educating young people throughout their (potential) educational journey. Quite interestingly, the measure that goes by the name of "Development of the tertiary vocational training system" seeks to strengthen "Higher Technical Institutes for more widespread vocational training". Below is the NRRP description of the objective of this investment, to which €1.5 billion[15] have been allocated:

> Increase the number of ITSs and strengthen their scientific facilities and laboratories also through 4.0 technology while simultaneously investing in teachers' skills. The investment will include the creation of a national digital platform that allows students to find out about job offers for those who obtain their professional qualification.

This investment in Technical and Scientific High Schools (ITS) should be fully valorized, especially to solve the mismatch in the labour market. While there have been positive experiences in some regions (especially Lombardy, Emilia-Romagna, Veneto), there is still a long way to go: the employment rate of young people coming out of ITS is very high and still too few choose this track of post-diploma studies.

To sum up, Italy's gap in terms of investment in knowledge with respect to France and Germany are significant. To bridge this gap, at the very least two strategic lines of action are required. First, complete the NRRP's implementation of everything that concerns R&D measures related to industrial policy. Second, closely related to the first, strengthen the EU's involvement in all the interventions (investments and reforms) envisaged in the crucial missions/components examined here. Moreover, Italian companies participating in the IPCEIs (e.g. STMicroelectronics) and the construction of STPs (starting from centres/ecosystems/partnerships) can be seen as the first steps of Italy-EU intersections that the NRRP aims to stimulate.

---

14 For an insightful discussion on these issues see Viesti (2023).

15 See also the NRRP portal, 'Italia Domani': https://www.italiadomani.gov.it/content/sogei-ng/it/it/il-piano/missioni-NRRP/istruzione-e-ricerca.html

To conclude, science, research, technological innovation, and education may be seen as European public goods. The EU must strengthen them if it intends to play a leading role in the international arena, as was lucidly highlighted by the almost simultaneous publication of the reports edited respectively by Enrico Letta (2024) and Mario Draghi (2024).

4.4 SEZs: An Industrial Policy Bet for the Mezzogiorno

In this context of renewed interest in industrial policy, a significant measure implemented in Italy in recent years is the establishment of SEZs (special economic zones) that have been a widely used industrial policy tool for several decades and in various countries around the world.[16] In Europe, Poland sets the example by establishing its first SEZ in 1995 and now has fourteen SEZs throughout the country.[17] In brief, a SEZ is characterized by: a) a clearly delimited area where a single administration and governance system is envisaged; b) different kinds of benefits for investors physically located within the area; c) the inclusion of "free zones", i.e., areas that have a customs regime that differs from that applied to the rest of the state territory. SEZs should attract more investment by leveraging comparatively advantageous conditions. For this expectation of higher growth in these areas to have a chance of success, they should receive public investment in transport infrastructure. A highly qualified workforce must also be created where specialized SEZs are established.

In Italy, SEZs were introduced as an urgent measure by Decree-Law No. 91/2017, later converted by Law No. 123 of August 3, 2017.[18] Other regulatory interventions have taken place in recent years and between 2018 and 2021, eight SEZs were established (see Table 4.4). The industrial policy vision was linked to the logic of reshoring and the increasing role and integration of logistics within industrial processes. Therefore, the government envisaged one SEZ for each of the TEN-T core ports of Southern Italy.[19]

16 For further discussion and data see Barbieri, Cerniglia, and Mosconi (2024); Nisticò and Prota (2023); Buba and Wong (2017); and Viesti (2024).
17 In Poland, SEZs between 1995 and 2015 attracted investments of €170 billion and created 280,000 new jobs. Cf. PWC (2024).
18 See Coco (2020).
19 See Coco and Lepore (2018).

Table 4.4 SEZs in Italy by year of establishment, surface area, appointment of extraordinary commissioners, post SEZ-NRRP reform. *Source*: Nisticò and Prota (2023) based on data from agenziacoesione.gov.it.

	Typology	**Year of establish-ment**	**Total hectares**	**% of total surface area ZES**	**Commissioner (finalizing appointment decree post SEZ Reform)**
SEZ Calabria	Regional	2018	2,445	10.4	August 2022
SEZ Campania	Regional	2018	5,154	21.9	November 2021
SEZ Adriatica	Interregional (Puglia-Molise)	2019	3,406	14.5	May 2022
SEZ Ionica	Interregional (Puglia-Basilicata)	2019	2,579	11	February 2022
SEZ Abruzzo	Regional	2020	1,703	7.2	October 2021
SEZ Sicilia Occidentale	Regional	2020	1,953	8.3	January 2022
SEZ Sicilia Orientale	Regional	2020	3,627	15.4	December 2021
SEZ Sardegna	Regional	2021	2,659	11.3	August 2022

Various expectations are placed on this industrial policy measure of SEZs because it could serve to bridge the economic and social gap that still separates the South from the more developed areas of the country. Through SEZs, those who invest in the Mezzogiorno could have a great competitive advantage in terms of tax cuts, certain financing, and faster and more streamlined procedures for obtaining authorizations. Companies setting up in SEZs can enjoy higher tax credits than in other areas of southern Italy, with the possibility of reaching (after the latest regulatory interventions) a ceiling of €100 million per investment. The governance strategy is based on the involvement of regional governments that were charged with the task of selecting eligible areas and drafting strategic plans. Each SEZ is originally governed by a committee of members appointed by national government and regional government officials and chaired by the Head of the Port Authority. The minister responsible for the South and territorial cohesion in turn chairs the central SEZs steering committee.

The NRRP has identified SEZs as an important intervention in favour of the Mezzogiorno's economy: it includes investment programs (Mission 5, Component 3)[20] and provides for the reform of normative framework and governance (Decree Law No. 77/2021). The resources earmarked for the SEZs by the NRRP amount to €630 million for infrastructure works and further funding for investments for works in the main ports in southern Italy. The €630 million are broken down by region, implementing entities, and areas of intervention, and can be divided into three categories: a) "last mile" connections, i.e. between ports and industrial areas and the infrastructure and road network forming part of the main transport networks; b) digitalization and enhancement of logistics, green urbanization, energy and environmental efficiency in the back-ports and industrial areas of the SEZs; c) enhancement of the security and resilience of port access infrastructure. It should also be noted that the projects chosen for funding were already available for each region and selected because they were deemed to be more feasible, and executable given the constraints of the NRRP's timetable.

In essence, the interventions planned for SEZs implement a two-stage industrialization policy, i.e. to create an infrastructure that serves to strengthen the industrial production base that SEZs are supposed to promote through tax benefits to enterprises. SEZs are thus given an important role as part of an overall strategy to strengthen and complete the infrastructure and logistics networks for a revitalization of the Mezzogiorno. By connecting the main strategic ports located in southern Italy with the continental transport network, one could leverage the Mediterranean's strategic position globally, thus enhancing its privileged position with respect to the emerging African, Balkan, and Middle Eastern markets.

As previously mentioned, to enhance the SEZs appeal to new enterprises, in addition to the NRRP-funded infrastructure, tax cuts are provided of up to 45% for investments of up to €100 million (the rate varies by company size), provided that the firm invests in and remains in the SEZ for at least seven years. This tax credit was later increased to a maximum of 65% and applied both to the expansion of the company's capital goods and to the purchase of land and real estate. In addition, the 2021 budget law included a 50% tax reduction for up to six tax periods for companies undertaking new economic initiatives in the SEZs. Companies wishing to benefit from the measure will have to meet three requirements: they must not be in a state of liquidation or dissolution, they must maintain their activity in the SEZ, and they must keep the related jobs created for at least ten years. Additional facilities for companies are also envisaged through resources from the Development and Cohesion Fund. The governance structure was simplified as well and each of the eight SEZ was entrusted to a single commissioner with full power of authorization over private investments and procurement for new infrastructure.

20 Labelled "Interventi speciali per la coesione territoriale" (Special interventions for territorial cohesion). https://politichecoesione.governo.it/it/NRRP-e-coesione/la-missione-5-componente-3-del-NRRP-su-interventi-speciali-per-la-coesione-territoriale/

The regulatory framework and SEZ set-up recently experienced an important turnaround: Decree Law No. 124 of September 19, 2023. Minister Fitto used this to abolish the eight existing SEZs and replaced them with a so-called single SEZ that extends over all the regions of southern Italy. A "special" territory of such enormous size has no parallel in any international experience. In essence, two years after Decree Law No. 77/2021, both the governance and the incentive system of a single SEZ have been (re)configured. For 2024, €1.8 billion have been earmarked in the budget law for the 2024 tax credit. However, this is only valid for investments made up to November 2024. Therefore, there have been no tangible economic and entrepreneurial results related to the single SEZ. More generally, an overall vision of industrial policy is still lacking for the Mezzogiorno within which a single SEZ is now being set up that adopts a "sprinkling automatic aid" approach to the entire Mezzogiorno. Any connection with possible strategies for attracting investment in port areas is thus lost. The jury is still out on the effectiveness of such a policy experiment. While the super-charged tax credit attracted a large number of applications (totalling €9 billion in July 2024) it is unlikely that in the short time (up to November 2024) firms will be able to deliver such large investments.

4.5. Conclusion

As we have reported in previous chapters on Italy in past *Outlooks*, Italy's austerity measures between 2009 and 2017 led to a loss of €200 billion in public investment, which is almost equivalent to the NRRP's total budget. Resources coming from the plan might represent a unique opportunity for industrial policy in Italy. While this chapter has explored potential projects, particularly those connected to other industrial policy initiatives, the future beyond 2026 remains uncertain for both Italy and Europe. The Draghi report emphasizes the need for swift action.

Surely, programs such as Next Generation EU and Horizon Europe, as well as cohesion policies, represent important elements of a European industrial policy that can foster the transition to a green economy, support research and innovation in numerous technological fields, and hopefully reduce inequalities. Still, the Multiannual Financial Framework for 2021–2027 foresees the allocation of resources equal to only 1.11% of the EU-27's gross national income. This amount is inadequate to support an effective European industrial policy. As for Italy, it is entirely uncertain what will happen after 2026, even considering the recent Stability and Growth Pact rules that require Italy to undertake significant adjustments to its public finance budgets.

Since the 1990s, neoliberal trends in Italy have consolidated a bipartisan consensus for economic policies favouring austerity and limiting industrial policy intervention, making it challenging to consider the possibility of a national industrial strategy. The neglect of the Southern Question in the political agenda has further widened the North-South gap. The changing global landscape (completely different from that of the 1990s), however, calls for new policies and a more active role for the state.

References

Aiginger, K., and D. Rodrik (2020) "Rebirth of Industrial Policy and an Agenda for the Twenty-First Century", *Journal of Industry, Competition and Trade* 20: 189–207, https://doi.org/10.1007/s10842-019-00322-3

Andreoni, A. (2017) "Strategies for Emerging Technologies and Strategic Sectors: Evidence from OECD Countries and Some Critical Reflections on the Italian Case", *L'Industria. Rivista di Economia e Politica Industriale* 1: 3–14, https://doi.org/10.1430/87136

Barbieri, G., and S. J. Gahn (2023) "Le piattaforme tecno-scientifiche europee: sviluppi recenti in Italia", in A. Quadrio Curzio, A. Silvani, M. Fortis, and F. Cerniglia (eds) (2023) *Le piattaforme tecnico-scientifiche in Europa. Ricerca, economia, innovazione*. Bologna: Il Mulino, Collana Fondazione Edison, pp. 297–318.

Barbieri, G., F. Cerniglia, G. F. Gori, and P. Lattarulo (2022) "NRRP—Italy's Strategic Reform and Investment Programme Sustaining an Ecological Transition", in F. Cerniglia and F. Saraceno (eds), *Greening Europe, European Public Investment Outlook 2022*. Cambridge: Open Book Publishers, pp. 55–70, https://doi.org/10.11647/OBP.0328.04

Barbieri, G., F. Cerniglia, and F. Mosconi (2024) "Italy and Industrial Policy at the Time of the NRRP", *CRANEC Working Paper* 01/2024, https://centridiricerca.unicatt.it/cranec-home-pubblicazioni-22134

Barbieri Goés, M. G., and G. Viesti (2024) "The Revival of Industrial Policy in the EU?", *Review of Political Economy*: 1–25, https://doi.org/10.1080/09538259.2024.2368210

Barbini, M., et al. (2024) "L'anno della crescita differenziata. Le regioni italiane nel 202", *Informazioni Svimez* 4.

Bianchi, P., and S. Labory (2016) *Towards a New Industrial Policy*. Milan: McGraw-Hill Education.

Bratta, B., et al. (2020) "The Impact of Digitalization Policies. Evidence from Italy's Hyper-depreciation of Industry 4.0 Investments", *Ministero dell'Economia e delle Finanze, DF Working Paper* 20, https://www.finanze.gov.it/export/sites/finanze/.galleries/Documenti/Varie/dfwp6-1_ultimo.pdf

Buba, J., and M. D. Wong (2017) *Special Economic Zones: An Operational Review of their Impacts*. Washington, DC: World Bank Group.

Capriati, M., M. Deleidi, and G. Viesti (2022) "Che impatto macroeconomico può avere il PNRR nel Mezzogiorno?", *Menabò* 174, https://eticaeconomia.it/che-impatto-macroeconomico-puo-avere-il-pnrr-nel-mezzogiorno/

Cerniglia, F., and F. Saraceno (eds) (2022) *Greening Europe. 2022 European Public Investment Outlook*. Cambridge: Open Book Publishers, https://doi.org/10.11647/OBP.0328

Cerniglia, F., A. Silvani, and A. Quadrio Curzio (2023) "La ricerca del Centro Cranec dell'Università Cattolica", in A. Quadrio Curzio, A. Silvani, M. Fortis, and F. Cerniglia (eds), *Le piattaforme tecnico-scientifiche in Europa. Ricerca, economia, innovazione*. Bologna: Il Mulino, Collana Fondazione Edison, pp. 263–277.

Chiapperini, C., and G. Viesti (2024) "Il PNRR e i divari territoriali", *Menabò* 210, https://eticaeconomia.it/il-pnrr-e-i-divari-territoriali/

Coco, G. (2020) "Investimenti, disintermediazione, capacità: come superare la retorica delle politiche per il Mezzogiorno", in G. Coco, and C. De Vincenti (eds), *Una questione nazionale. Il Mezzogiorno da "problema" a "opportunità"*. Bologna: Il Mulino, pp. 203-226

Coco, G., and A. Lepore (2018) "Per un nuovo modello di intervento pubblico nel Mezzogiorno", in G. Coco and A. Lepore (eds), *Il risveglio del Mezzogiorno. Nuove politiche per lo sviluppo*. Bari: Laterza, pp. 175-196

Di Tommaso, M. R., L. Rubini, E. Barbieri, and C. Pollio (2024) *Industry Organization and Industrial Policy. Production and Innovation, Development and Public Interest*. Bologna: Il Mulino.

Draghi, M. (2024) *The Future of European Competitiveness*. Brussels: European Commission, https://commission.europa.eu/document/download/97e481fd-2dc3-412d-be4c-f152a8232961_en

European Commission (2005) "Implementing the Community Lisbon Programme: A Policy Framework to Strengthen EU Manufacturing—Towards a More Integrated Approach for Industrial Policy", COM(2005) 464, October 5, https://eur-lex.europa.eu/legal-content/EN/TXT/?uri=celex%3A52005DC0474

European Commission (2012) "A Stronger European Industry for Growth and Economic Recovery Industrial Policy Communication Update", COM(2012) 582, October 10, https://eur-lex.europa.eu/LexUriServ/LexUriServ.do?uri=COM:2012:0582:FIN:EN:PDF

European Commission (2014) "For a European Industrial Renaissance", COM(2014) 14, January 22, https://eur-lex.europa.eu/legal-content/EN/TXT/PDF/?uri=CELEX:52014DC0014&from=ET

European Commission (2017) "Investing in a Smart, Innovative and Sustainable Industry: A Renewed EU Industrial Policy Strategy", COM(2017) 479, September 13, https://eur-lex.europa.eu/resource.html?uri=cellar:c8b9aac5-9861-11e7-b92d-01aa75ed71a1.0001.02/DOC_1&format=PDF

European Commission: Directorate-General for Research and Innovation and M. Mazzucato (2018) *Mission-oriented Research & Innovation in the European Union—A Problem-solving Approach to Fuel Innovation-led Growth*. Brussels: Publications Office, https://data.europa.eu/doi/10.2777/360325

European Commission (2020) "A New Industrial Strategy for Europe", COM(2020) 102, March 10, https://eur-lex.europa.eu/legal-content/EN/TXT/PDF/?uri=CELEX:52020DC0102

European Commission (2021a) "Communication from the Commission. Criteria for the Analysis of the Compatibility with the Internal Market of State Aid to Promote the Execution of Important Projects of Common European Interest", 2021/C 528/02, December 30, https://eur-lex.europa.eu/legal-content/EN/TXT/HTML/?uri=CELEX:52021XC1230(02)

European Commission (2021b) "Communication from the Commission on a New Funding Strategy to Finance NextGenerationEU", COM(2021) 250, April 14, https://commission.europa.eu/document/download/a42a05ab-e656-4cf4-9d0b-b4d2825618ee_en?filename=com2021_250_en_act_part1_v3.pdf

European Commission (2022) "A Chips Act for Europe", COM(2022) 45, February 8, https://eur-lex.europa.eu/legal-content/EN/TXT/HTML/?uri=CELEX%3A52022DC0045#:~:text=The%20EU%20Chips%20Act%20proposes,to%20future%20supply%20chain%20disruptions

Governo Italiano (2021) *Italia Domani: Piano Nazionale di Ripresa e Resilienza*, https://www.italiadomani.gov.it/content/sogei-ng/it/it/home.html

Guerrieri, P., and P. C. Padoan (2024) *Sovereign Europe. An Agenda for Europe in a Fragmented Global Economy*. Brookfield, VT: Edward Elgar.

Jacquemin, A. (1987) *The New Industrial Organization: Market Forces and Strategic Behaviour*. Cambridge, MA: The MIT Press.

Junker, J. C. (2017) "State of the Union Address", Brussels, September 13, https://ec.europa.eu/commission/presscorner/detail/en/SPEECH_17_3165

Juhász, R., N. Lane, and D. Rodrik (2024) "The New Economics of Industrial Policy", *Annual Review of Economics* 16: 213–242, https://doi.org/10.1146/annurev-economics-081023-024638

Letta, E. (2024) *Much More Than a Market*, https://www.consilium.europa.eu/media/ny3j24sm/much-more-than-a-market-report-by-enrico-letta.pdf

Lucchese, M., and M. Pianta (2021) "Il Piano Nazionale di Ripresa e Resilienza in una prospettiva di politica industriale", *Moneta e Credito* 74(294): 177–190.

Ministero dell'Università e della Ricerca (2022) "NRRP, MUR: l'impatto della conoscenza grazie a un nuovo modo di fare ricerca e innovazione", *MUR*, June 26, https://www.mur.gov.it/it/news/martedi-28062022/pnrr-mur-limpatto-della-conoscenza-grazie-un-nuovo-modo-di-fare-ricerca-e

Ministero per gli Affari Europei (2023) "Terza relazione sullo stato di attuazione del Piano Nazionale di Ripresa e Resilienza", June 20, *Italia Domani*, https://www.italiadomani.gov.it/content/sogei-ng/it/it/strumenti/documenti/archivio-documenti/terza-relazione-al-parlamento-sullo-stato-di-attuazione-del-pian.html

Ministero per gli Affari Europei (2024) "Quarta relazione sullo stato di attuazione del Piano Nazionale di Ripresa e Resilienza", https://www.affarieuropei.gov.it/media/7411/iv_relazione_al_parlamento_sezi.pdf

Ministero per gli Affari Europei (2024) "Quinta relazione sullo stato di attuazione del Piano Nazionale di Ripresa e Resilienza", Nota sintetica. https://www.affarieuropei.gov.it/media/7594/quinta_relazione_nota_sintetica.pdf

Mosconi, F. (2015) *The New European Industrial Policy. Global Competitiveness and the Manufacturing Renaissance*. New York: Routledge.

Mosconi, F. (2022) "European Industrial Policy from 2000 to 2020", in J. C. Christophe Defraigne, J. Wouters, E. Traversa, and D. Zurstrassen (eds), *EU Industrial Policy in the Multipolar Economy*. Brookfield, VT: Edward Elgar, pp. 173-209

Nisticò, R., and F. Prota (2023) "Sviluppo industriale per poli? Le zone economiche speciali in Italia e nel NRRP", *Stato e mercato* 2: 227–263, https://dx.doi.org/10.1425/108269

Pianta, M., and M. Lucchese (2020) "Rethinking the European Green Deal: An Industrial Policy for a Just Transition in Europe", *Review of Radical Political Economics* 52(4): 633–641, https://doi.org/10.1177/0486613420938207

Pianta, M., M. Lucchese, and L. Nascia (2020) "The Policy Space for a Novel Industrial Policy in Europe", *Industrial and Corporate Change* 29(3): 779–795, https://doi.org/10.1093/icc/dtz075

Pianta, M. (2021) "La politica industriale al tempo del PNRR", *il Mulino* 2: 152–162, https://doi.org/10.1402/101106

Presidenza del Consiglio dei Ministri (2022) "Seconda relazione istruttoria sul rispetto del vincolo di destinazione alle regioni del Mezzogiorno di almeno il 40 per cento delle risorse allocabili territorialmente", June 30, *Dipartimento per le Politiche di Coesione*, https://politichecoesione.governo.it/media/2954/seconda-relazione-destinazione-mezzogiorno-risorse-pnrr_dati-al-30_06_2022.pdf

Prodi, R. (2003) "Industrial Policy in an Enlarged Europe, Speech Delivered at the Conference Industrial Policy in an Enlarged Europe by the President of the European Commission", Speech Given in Brussels, January 21.

PWC (2024) *Dalle Zone Economiche Speciali regionali e interregionali alla ZES unica*, https://www.pwc.com/it/it/assets/docs/pwc-dalle-ZES-regionali-e-interregionali-alla-ZES-unica.pdf

Quadrio Curzio, A., A. Silvani, M. Fortis, and F. Cerniglia (2023) (eds) *Le piattaforme tecnico-scientifiche in Europa. Ricerca, economia, innovazione*. Bologna: Il Mulino, Collana Fondazione Edison.

Resta, F. (2023) "Università e impresa: dal PNRR nuove reti per la ricerca", in A. Quadrio Curzio A., A. Silvani, and F. Cerniglia (eds), *Le piattaforme tecnico-scientifiche in Europa. Ricerca, economia, innovazione*. Bologna: Il Mulino, Collana Fondazione Edison, pp. 64–75.

Rodrik, D. (2004) "Industrial Policy for the Twenty-First Century", John F. Kennedy School of Government, Cambridge, MA, September, https://drodrik.scholar.harvard.edu/files/dani-rodrik/files/industrial-policy-twenty-first-century.pdf

Viesti, G. (2023) *Riuscirà il PNRR a rilanciare l'Italia*?. Rome: Donzelli editore.

Viesti, G. (2024) "La ZES unica: dal mito alla dura realtà", *Menabò* 208, https://eticaeconomia.it/la-zes-unica-dal-mito-alla-dura-realta/

von der Leyen, U. (2019a) "Speech by President-elect von der Leyen in the European Parliament Plenary on the Occasion of the Presentation of her College of Commissioners and their Programme", Strasbourg, November 27.

von der Leyen, U. (2019b) "A Union that Strives for More. My Agenda for Europe, by Candidate for President of the European Commission 2019–2024", Strasbourg, July 16.

White House (2022) *Inflation Reduction Act Guidebook*. Washington, DC: White House, https://www.whitehouse.gov/cleanenergy/inflation-reduction-act-guidebook/

5. Public Investment and Structural Transformation in Spain

Ignacio Álvarez[1] *and Jorge Uxó*[2]

During the decade of 2010–2019, public investment experienced a profound decline in Spain, because of the fiscal austerity policies implemented during the Great Recession. Even with the recovery of economic growth starting in 2015, public investment did not improve and the net capital stock decreased. The COVID-19 pandemic introduced an important change in trend, with a general turnaround in fiscal policies accompanying the disbursement of Next Generation EU funds. These European Union funds will allow the implementation of an industrial transformation strategy focused on key specific sectors with high pulling power and strong multiplier effects.

5.1 Introduction

For several reasons, public investment is essential to any country's economic and social development. It finances the construction and maintenance of crucial infrastructures such as roads, bridges, hospitals, schools, and transport networks. It stimulates aggregate demand in the short term and economic growth in the medium and long term by increasing the economy's productive capacity. Funding for research and development fosters innovation, technical change, and competitiveness. It can contribute to economic stabilization, particularly during economic recessions, when the private sector withdraws its investment. It helps to reduce regional and social inequalities as economic policy can direct this investment towards essential activities or regions where the private sector does not always invest. Investment in education and health also strengthens human capital, key for productivity development. Also, public investment is a necessary lever to ensure the success of structural transformation processes in modern economies (the transition towards a green economy, the reduction of dependence on fossil fuels, or the progress of digitalization).

1 Universidad Autónoma de Madrid (Madrid, Spain).
2 Universidad Complutense de Madrid (Madrid, Spain).

 https://doi.org/10.11647/OBP.0434.06

Public investment, therefore, plays a vital role in the development of a sound and competitive economy, providing some of the foundations for society's long-term well-being. However, despite this importance, public investment in Spain has experienced a worrying performance over the last decade, with a sustained contraction that has only recently begun to change.

5.2 Trends and Patterns of Public Investment in Spain

In Spain, public investment has experienced a very irregular trajectory over the last few decades, traditionally characterized by pro-cyclical behaviour. From its admission into the European Union in 1986 until the arrival of the Great Recession in late 2007, Spain experienced an intense investment process, always above the European Union (EU) average when measured as a ratio over GDP. However, with the arrival of the Great Recession and austerity policies, public investment fell sharply and remained on the back burner for years.

As we can see in Figure 5.1, from 1986 to 2009, public investment in Spain reached an average of 4.2% of GDP, approximately one percentage point above the European Union average, thus favouring the Spanish economy's convergence with neighbouring countries. However, after the Global Financial Crisis, public investment fell to an average of close to 2% of GDP, one point below the EU average.

Indeed, this remarkable reduction in the investment effort in terms of GDP also translated into a significant cutback in the absolute levels of public investment. As can be seen in Figure 5.2, between 2010 and 2015, Spanish public investment fell by more than 100% (€33 billion), and the recovery of economic growth from 2015 onwards has not even allowed to return to previous levels. Public investment at the end of 2023 was still 40% lower than in 2009 and similar in nominal terms to 2002, two decades earlier.

Public investment was pro-cyclical during the 1980s and early 1990s, growing with the expansion (1986–1991) and shrinking during the subsequent crisis (1992–1993). This pattern repeated in the following decades: public investment participated in the expansionary trend during the real estate boom of 1995–2007 and, although they remained counter-cyclical in the first years of the financial crisis (2008–2009), they finally collapsed from 2010 onwards. Thus, instead of playing a stabilizing role during the Great Recession, the evolution of public investment contributed to deepening the crisis. This pro-cyclical nature of Spanish public investment is related to its use as an adjustment variable by successive governments. It is increased when fiscal resources are available and reduced when they are lacking (Pérez and de Guevara 2024).

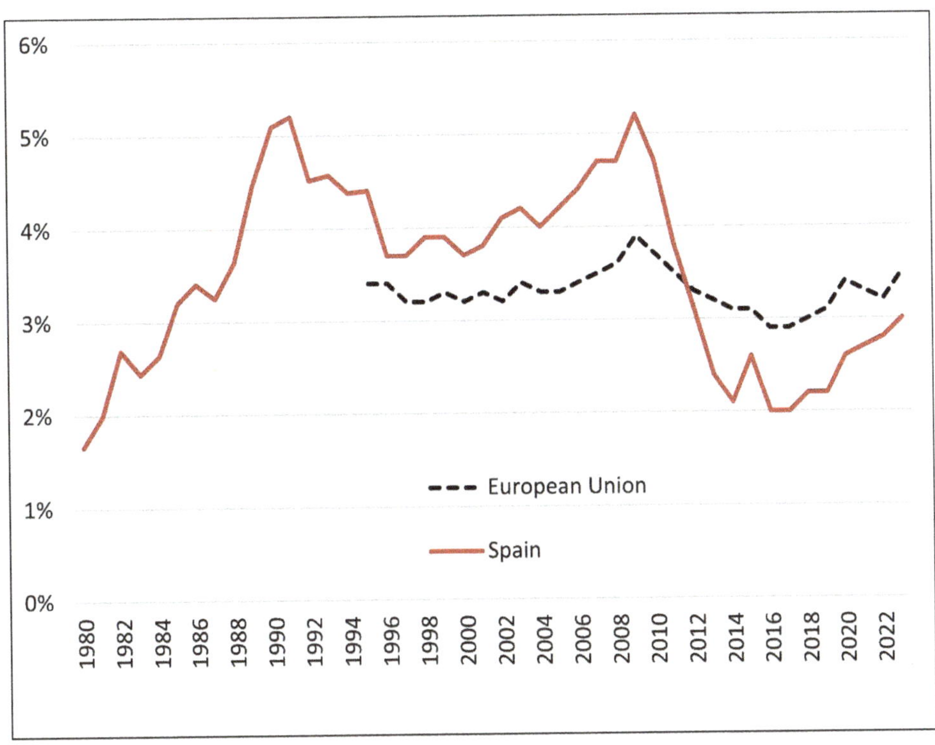

Fig. 5.1 Gross public investment (as a percentage of GDP). *Source*: Spanish National Accounts, National Institute of Statistics (INE) and AMECO.

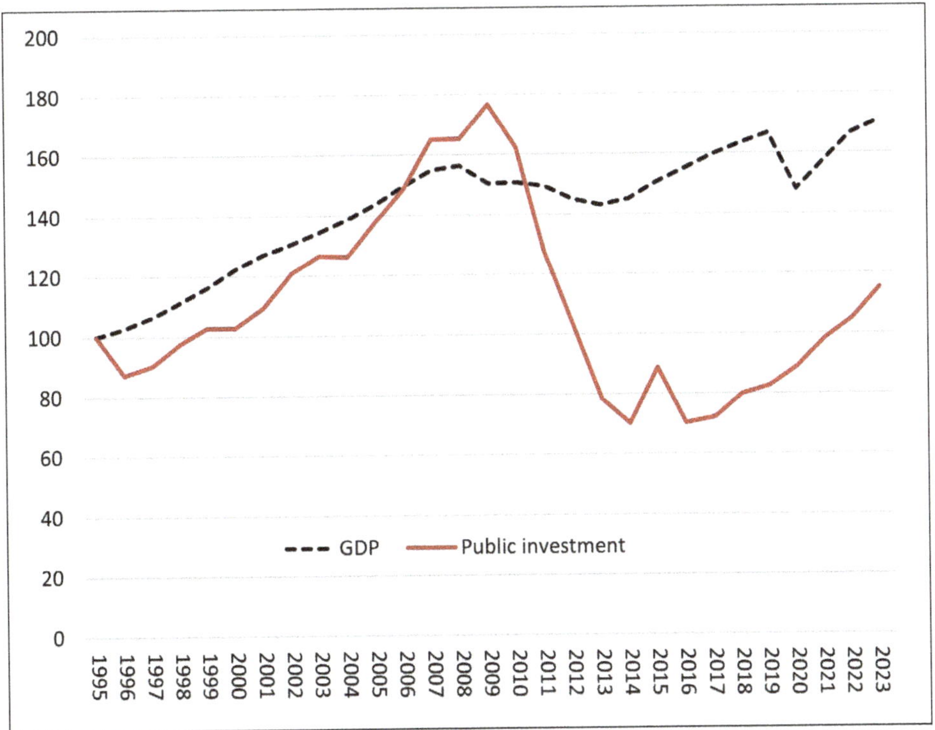

Fig. 5.2 Evolution of gross public investment and GDP in Spain (real, 1995=100). *Source*: AMECO.

The fall in public investment from 2010 onwards was notable both for productive infrastructures (transport, energy, and urban infrastructures) and for social infrastructures (education, health, or social services). They fell sharply from 2010 to 2014 and stagnated considerably in subsequent years (Fig. 5.3).

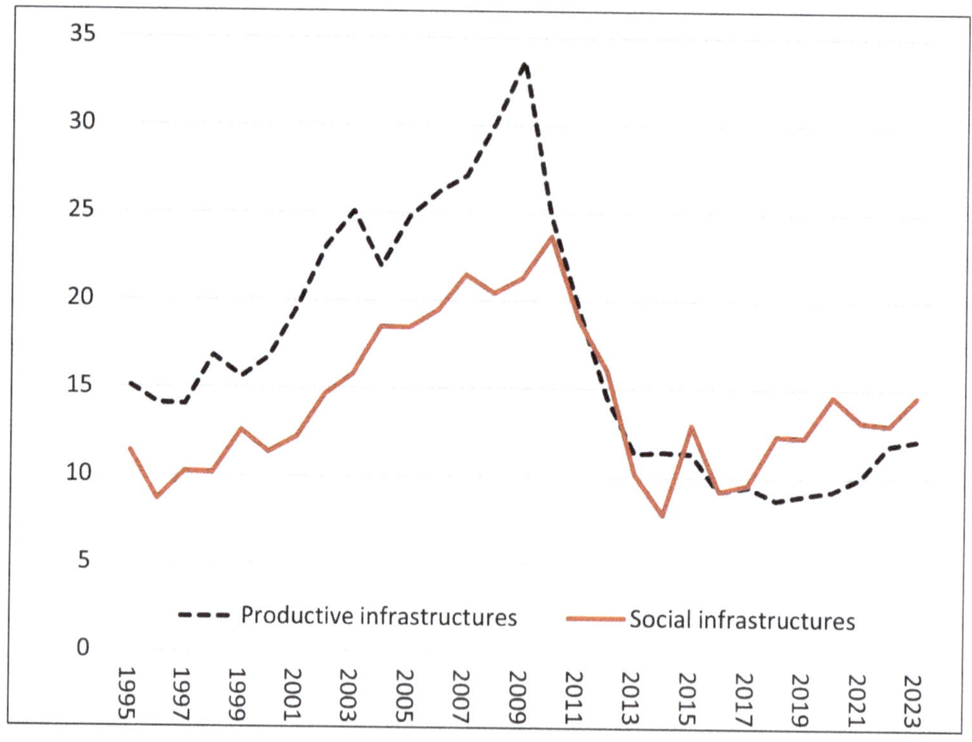

Fig. 5.3 Public infrastructure investment, Spain, 1995–2022 (billions of 2015 euros). *Source*: BBVA Foundation-IVIE and authors' calculations.

Moreover, starting in 2010, Spain entered a period in which the public sector's net fixed capital formation—that is, investment once capital consumption has been subtracted—was negative for a whole decade and did not even cover public capital's depreciation (Fig. 5.4).

The turning point in this anaemic evolution of Spanish public investment is not linked to the recovery of economic growth. In fact, the economy returned to solid growth between 2015 and 2019, and yet public investment remained stagnated as national authorities tried to rapidly reduce the public deficit by adjusting public investment downward.

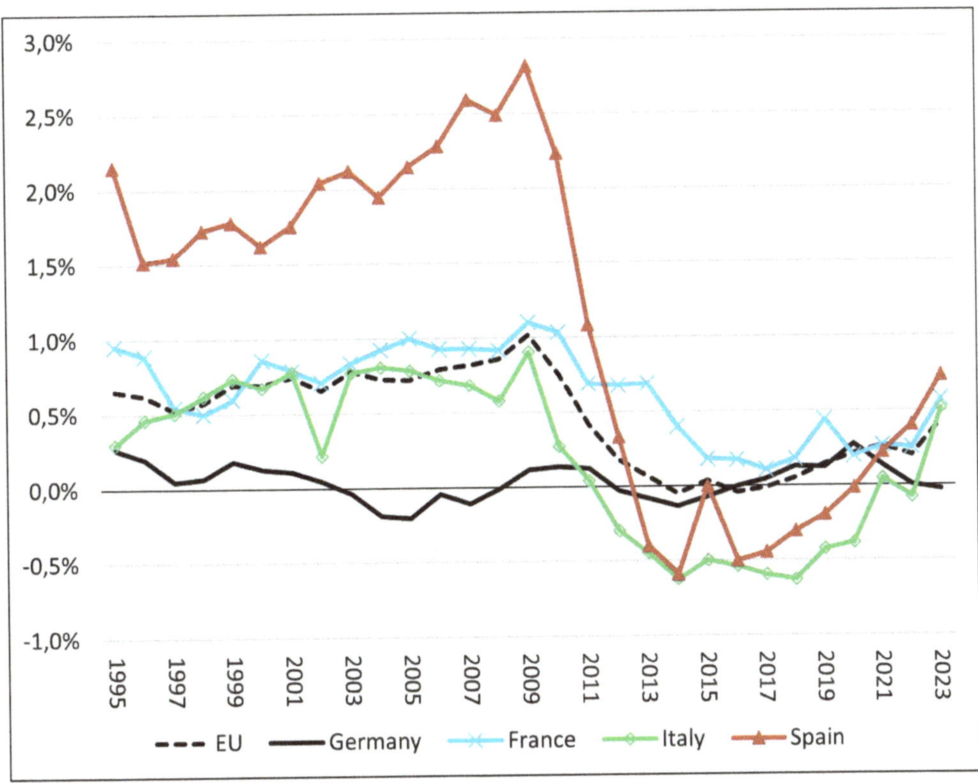

Fig. 5.4 Net public investment (as a percentage of GDP). *Source*: AMECO.

The change in the trend of public investment did not arrive until the COVID-19 pandemic, with a general turnaround in fiscal policies accompanying the disbursement of Next Generation EU funds. This has allowed both the investment effort as a percentage of GDP (Figs 5.1 and 5.4) and public investment levels (Fig. 5.2) to begin to rise. However, the critical question now is whether this change in trend will continue in the future, after the end of Next Generation funds and the reinstatement of fiscal rules.

5.3 From Investment to Capital Accumulation: The State of the Public Capital Stock in Spain

The evolution of the investment effort (flow) seen in the previous section is reflected in the public capital stock. During the 1990s and 2000s—and in parallel with the expansion of the economy itself—the stock of public capital grew rapidly in Spain, doubling in these years. This growth was maintained during the first years of the Great Recession (in 2008–2009), thanks to the so-called Plan E (a public investment program with which the government tried to tackle the recession at the time). However, the adoption of fiscal austerity policies in 2010 initiated a new phase, in which gross public investment could not even cover the depreciation of existing public capital and the stock began to progressively shrink (decreasing by 2% between 2010 and 2020, Figure 5).

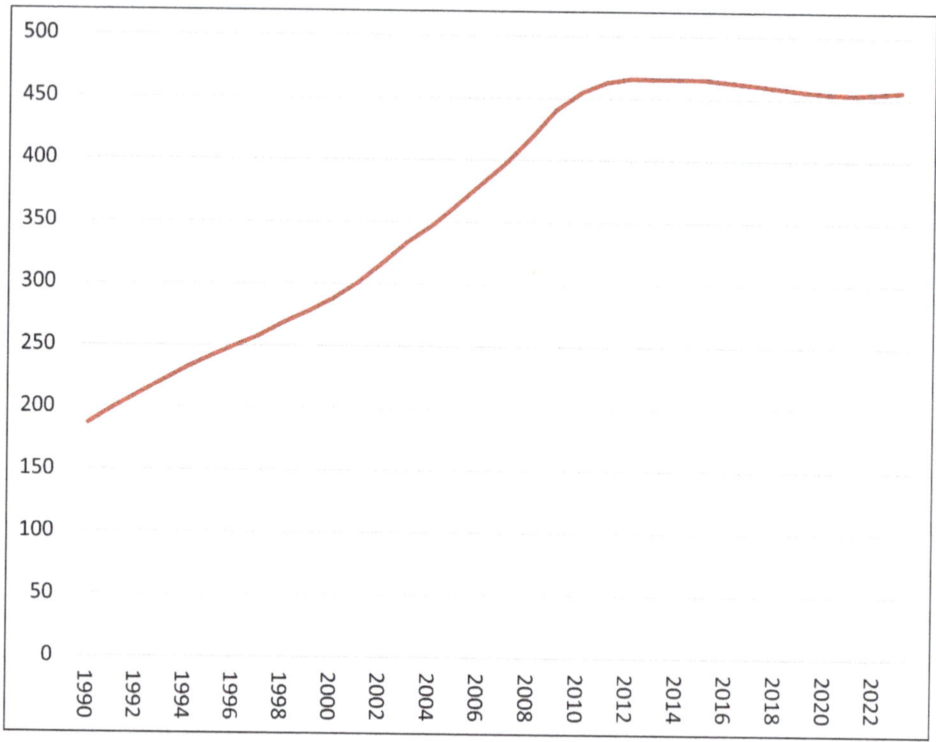

Fig. 5.5 Evolution of Net Public Capital Stock in Spain, 1990–2023 (billions of 2015 euros). *Source*: BBVA Foundation-IVIE.

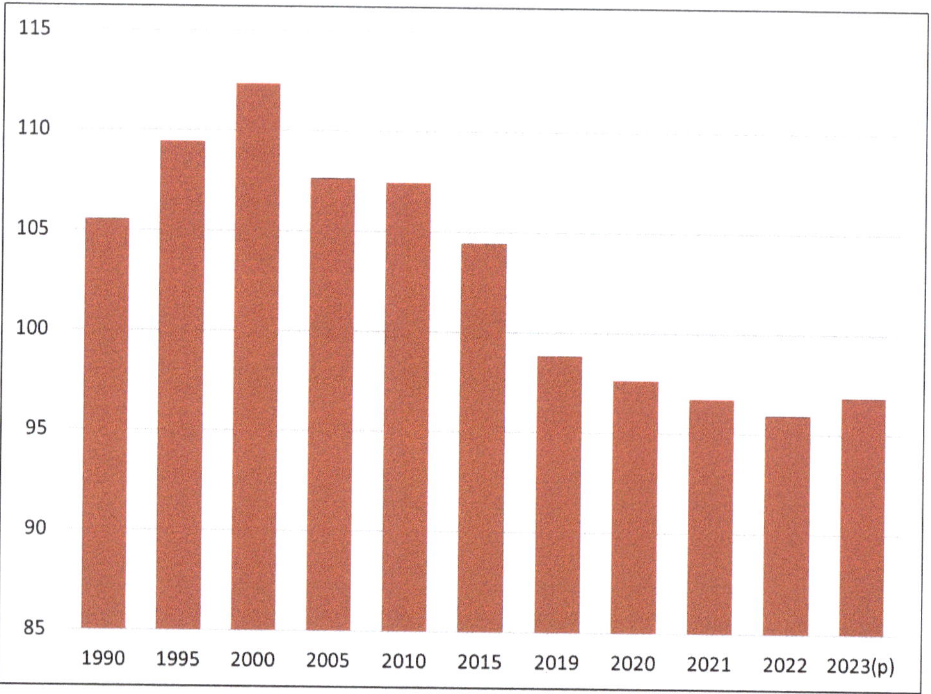

Fig. 5.6 Public capital stock per capita (Spain-Eurozone ratio, Eurozone=100). *Source*: Bank of Spain and authors' calculations.

This evolution of the public capital stock after the Great Recession has led to a "lost decade" in Spain in terms of new infrastructure development. As shown in Figure 5.6, Spain's public capital stock per capita moved away from the Eurozone average after the Great Recession due to the aforementioned short-circuit in public investment. In fact, between 2010 and 2019, the scarce investment flows have not been sufficient to maintain existing infrastructure in good condition, with the consequent loss of public capital and the aging of these infrastructures.

Looking at the evolution of public capital stock by asset types, we can observe a remarkable growth in all kinds of infrastructures up until the financial crisis (Fig. 5.7). Between 1995 and 2010, the share of transport infrastructure, particularly roads and railways, increased. Although on a smaller scale, the growth of airport infrastructure was also notable in Spain during these years. From 2010 onwards, however, hydraulic infrastructure and airports were particularly affected by the impossibility of covering the depreciation of their value.

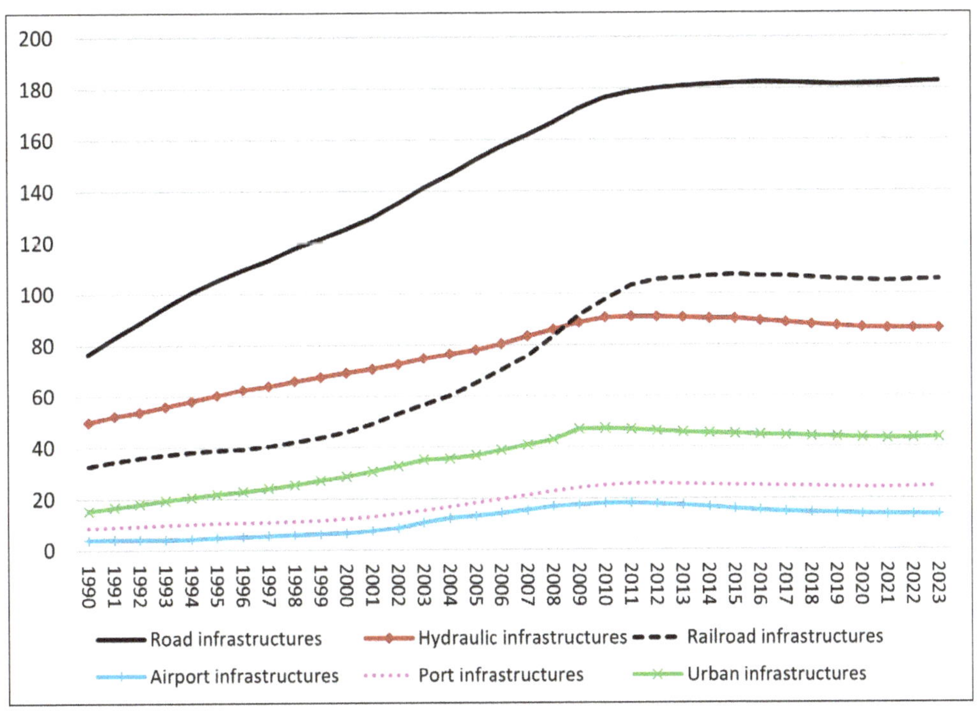

Fig. 5.7 Evolution of Net Public Capital Stock in Spain by type of asset, 1990–2023 (billions of 2015 euros). *Source*: BBVA Foundation-IVIE.

A consequence of the slow investment pace and depreciation of the public capital stock during 2010–2019 has been the progressive aging of assets. In 2007, the average age of Spanish infrastructure was very low compared to neighbouring countries. However, after a decade of not covering capital depreciation, this age increased sharply: assets older than twenty years represented 11% of total public infrastructure in 2007, having risen to 22.5% in 2016 (Fundación BBVA-IVIE 2019). If this slow pace of investment had been maintained, the percentage of infrastructure over twenty years old in 2030 would exceed 50% in the case of road (51%), rail (52.5%), and water (71%) infrastructure.

The inability of the Spanish economy to ensure the renewal of the capital stock during the decade following the financial crisis constitutes a very worrying dynamic, given that it could undermine the medium-term evolution of productivity and future growth. But at the same time, the Spanish experience should make us reconsider the need to thoroughly assess the costs and returns of certain inefficient infrastructure investments, such as some regional or local airports or certain road infrastructures. In the wake of this experience, there is a clear consensus on the need to prioritize those investments that are capable of driving the structural transformations that the country needs: for example, investments that lead the energy transition and allow Spain to change its competitiveness model from one based on low wages to another (more promising) one based on attracting industry thanks to clean, safe, and cheap energy.

5.4 Recovery, Transformation, and Resilience Plan: Impact in Spain

It is very unusual for the same generation to experience two major economic crises in a short period and thus be able to compare them. Nevertheless, this happened precisely with the Global Financial Crisis of 2008–2013 and the COVID-19 pandemic, when completely different economic policy measures were applied. Moreover, public investment is one of the areas where we can best see this change in economic policy strategy.

The response to the 2007 Global Financial Crisis was fiscal austerity, with significant cuts in public spending and investment. However, the response to the COVID-19 crisis was a stark contrast, in the form of an ambitious fiscal expansion program. This program, which includes more than €800 billion in loans and grants until 2026 to the different EU countries (€160 billion to Spain), has marked a shift in the use of public investment as an "adjustment variable" in the face of a crisis.

Figure 5.8 compares the pattern of public investment during the 2007 crisis and the COVID-19 pandemic. Between 2007 and 2011, public investment contracted by 21.3%, with public education (down 40%) and social services (cut by 32%) being the most affected components. The response to the COVID-19 crisis was very different. Not only did total investment not fall, but it grew by 19.2%, and so did its various components: education (41%), public health (29%) and social services (60%).

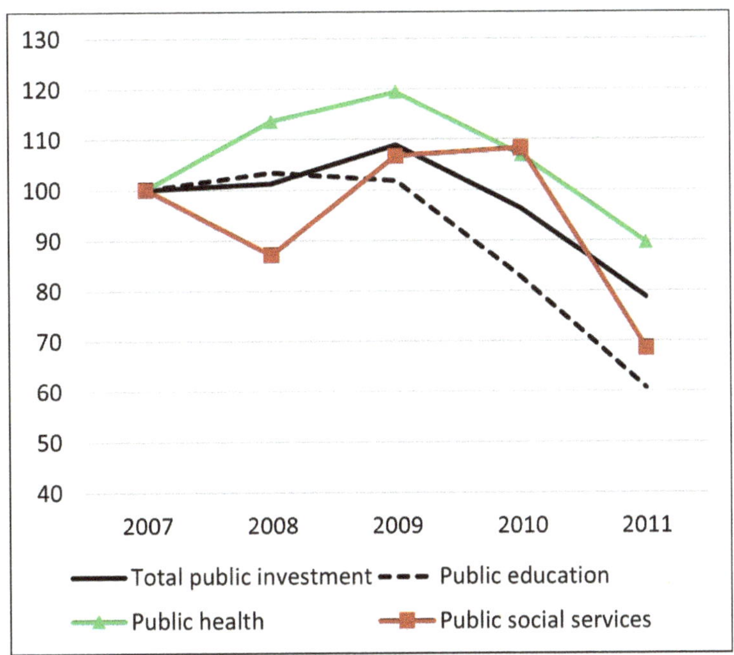

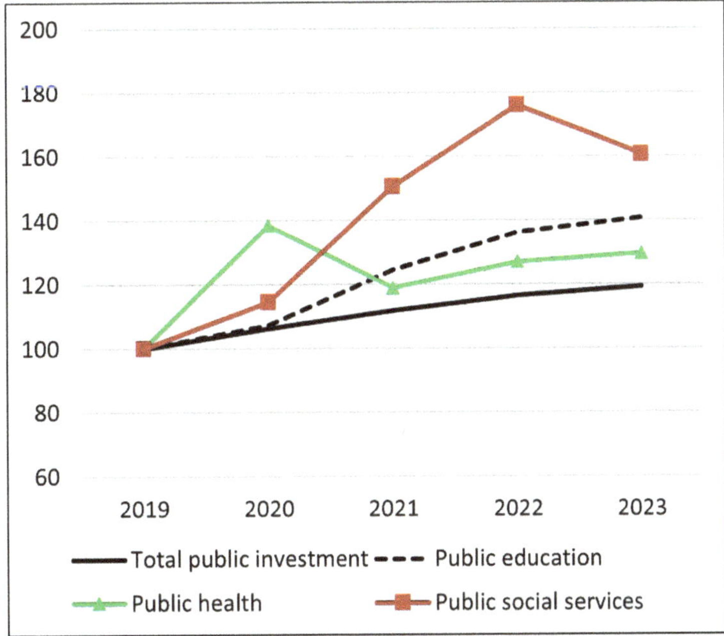

Fig. 5.8 Gross public investment. Great Recession compared to COVID-19 (Index 2007=100 and 2019=100). *Source*: BBVA Foundation-IVIE and authors' elaboration.

Spain is one of the countries with the largest allocation of Next Generation EU funds. Specifically, it has approximately €77 billion in transfers and up to €83 billion in loans, resources that have already been partially channelled into the economy during 2021–2023. This European funding has helped Spain to incorporate in its General State Budgets for 2021, 2022, and 2023 an average of around €30 billion per year in new public investment, making it one of the EU countries that is implementing the Recovery, Transformation, and Resilience Plan most rapidly. This implementation has been designed in two phases: a first one during the three-year period 2021–2023, focused on achieving a solid counter-cyclical impact, and a second one in 2023–2026, aimed at strengthening and completing the highest impact projects through the mobilization of loans.

This Recovery Plan has not only allowed a turning point in the dynamics of Spanish public investment, boosting aggregate demand and guaranteeing the growth of the country's public capital stock. It has also been accompanied by a new industrial policy—negotiated with the European Commission—selecting a series of priority sectors for this investment. Thus, twelve Strategic Projects for Economic Recovery and Transformation (PERTEs, in Spanish) have been launched, bringing together a total public investment of more than €40 billion and aiming to act as "missions" following Mariana Mazzucato's philosophy. These unique, large-scale projects aim to transform the country's productive structure to address major economic, social, and environmental challenges. To this end, these large projects coordinate efforts between public and private sectors, focusing fiscal stimulus on specific key sectors with high pulling power and strong multiplier effects. Table 5.1 shows the twelve PERTEs of this new industrial policy, as well as the amount of public investment allocated to each of them.

Table 5.1 Strategic Projects for Economic Recovery and Transformation (PERTEs), November 2023. Public investment in millions of euros. *Source*: Recovery, Transformation, and Resilience Plan, Government of Spain (2023).

Development of the electric vehicle	4.120 M€
Advanced healthcare	1.640 M€
Renewable energy, hydrogen and storage	10.797 M€
Agrifood supply chain	1.357 M€
New language economy	725 M€
Circular economy	792 M€
Shipbuilding industry	150 M€
Aerospace industry	931 M€
Digitization of the water cycle	3.485 M€
Microelectronics and semiconductors	12.250 M€
Social and care economy	1.766 M€
Industrial decarbonization	3.170 M€

This public investment plan, focused on some strategic projects, presents a second novelty: its link with an extensive and ambitious program of new structural reforms. These reforms are aimed at modernizing the Spanish productive structure and the Administration, renewing the regulatory framework to increase productivity and potential GDP, achieving more sustainable long-term growth, reducing job insecurity and strengthening the Welfare State and social cohesion. Table 5.2 shows the main advances in the structural reforms corresponding to Spain's Recovery Plan, which are directly linked to the above-mentioned public investments.

Table 5.2 Main advances in the Recovery Plan reforms (November 2023). *Source*: Recovery, Transformation, and Resilience Plan, Government of Spain (2023).

Business climate	Bankruptcy Reform
	"Create and Grow" Law
	Startups Law
	Securities Market Law Reform
	Reform of the Entrepreneur Support Law
	Improvement of the antitrust framework
Digitalization and innovation	5G Cybersecurity Law
	General Telecommunications Law
	Audiovisual Law
	National Security Scheme
	Spanish AI Supervisory Agency
	AI Sandbox
	Science Law
Green transition	Climate Change Law
	Waste and Contaminated Soil Law
	Energy efficiency in housing
	Spanish Circular Economy Strategy
	Reform of the Water Law
	Low Emission Zones

Employment and social protection	Labor market reform
	Rider Act
	Law for Reduction of Temporary Employment
	Employment Law
	Remote Work Law
	Regulation of hiring incentives
	Pension System Reform
	Minimum income scheme
Culture and education	Education Law
	Vocational Training Law
	Statute of the Artist
	Sports Law
	University System Law
	Spain Audiovisual Hub of Europe
	Intellectual Property Registry Regulation
Modernization of public administrations	National Public Procurement Strategy
	Civil Service Reform
	Digitalization of the Justice System
	Strengthening inter-regional cooperation
	Reform of Local Administrative Regimes

The economic impact of this investment program on Spanish economic growth is noteworthy. As is well known, an increase in public investment can positively affect economic growth for two reasons. First, it has a positive short-term impact on aggregate demand, increasing private investment, employment, and household consumption. Second, public investment also has a supply-side effect, boosting—as mentioned above—the economy's capital stock and, consequently, its efficiency and productive capacity in the medium and long term.

Empirical literature consistently highlights that the value of fiscal multipliers can significantly fluctuate depending on a variety of factors, such as the phase of the economic cycle, the level of public debt, the exchange rate regime and the degree of economic openness (Fatas and Mihov 2009; Gechert and Rannenberg 2014). However, there is a strong consensus that public investment's short- and medium-term multipliers, particularly in downturns, are notably high and almost always greater than 1 (IMF 2014; Auerbach and Gorodnichenko 2012).

This multiplier effect has been empirically tested in the case of the Spanish economy over the last three years. The Ministry of Economy estimates that over 2021–2023, the impact of the public investment program on GDP was 0.3% in 2021, 1.2% in 2022, and 1.4% in 2023, as we can see in Figure 5.9. These estimates are in line with the analysis of the Bank of Spain (Fernández Cerezo et al. 2023). In fact, economic authorities estimate that the economy recovered its pre-COVID-19 GDP level in 2022, two years ahead of schedule, thanks to the impact of the Recovery Plan. And they further expect the positive impact of public investment on GDP to remain high for the next three years, with an average annual impact of 1.2 % until 2026.

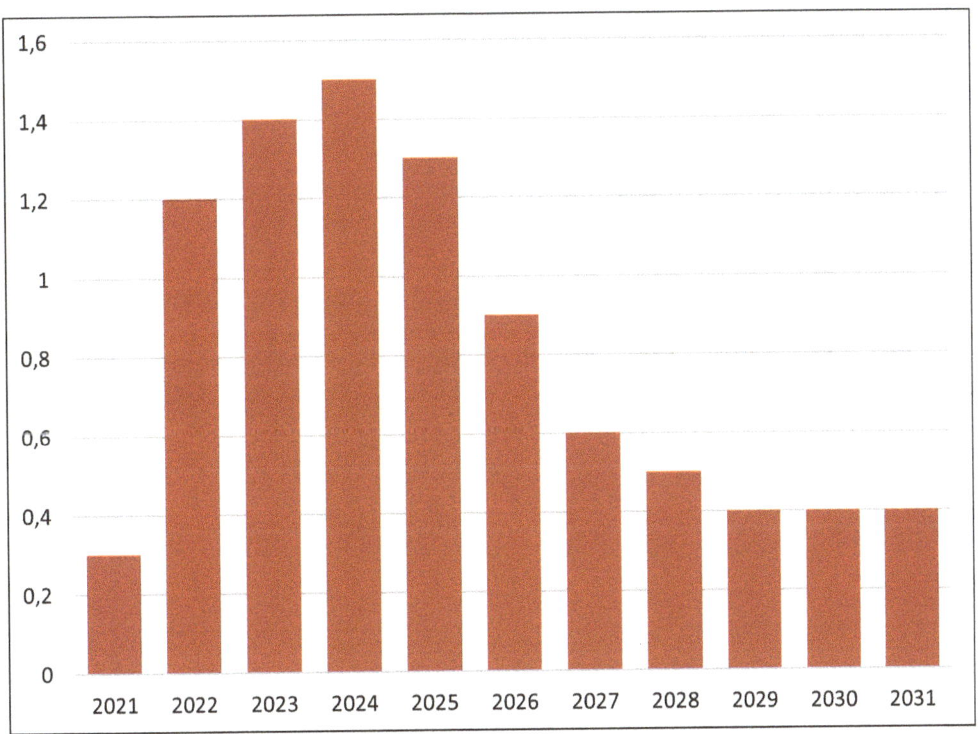

Fig. 5.9 Impact on GDP of public investments within the Recovery, Transformation, and Resilience Plan (percentage points of GDP over inertial path). *Source*: Ministry of Economy, Spain (2023).

The contribution of each type of investment to economic growth is certainly variable. As shown in Figure 5.10, sub-programs related to sustainable infrastructure, urban and rural development, and digitalization lead the impact of investment on GDP, concentrating 66% of this impact. Within these sub-programs, projects for the deployment of high-speed networks and other railway infrastructures, the MOVES plan (for electric mobility), and investment in broadband networks (digitalization) are particularly important.

These investments are followed by the science and health sub-program, which accounts for 11% of the total impact of the plan to date. Within this sub-program, investments related to health infrastructures, research projects in personalized precision medicine and the development of the Artificial Intelligence strategy stand out. In addition, the important process of modernization and digitization of public administrations contributes more than 7% of the total impact of investments on GDP.

Finally, investments directly related to the energy transition sub-program, as well as the launching of a new vocational training system, are of particular importance.

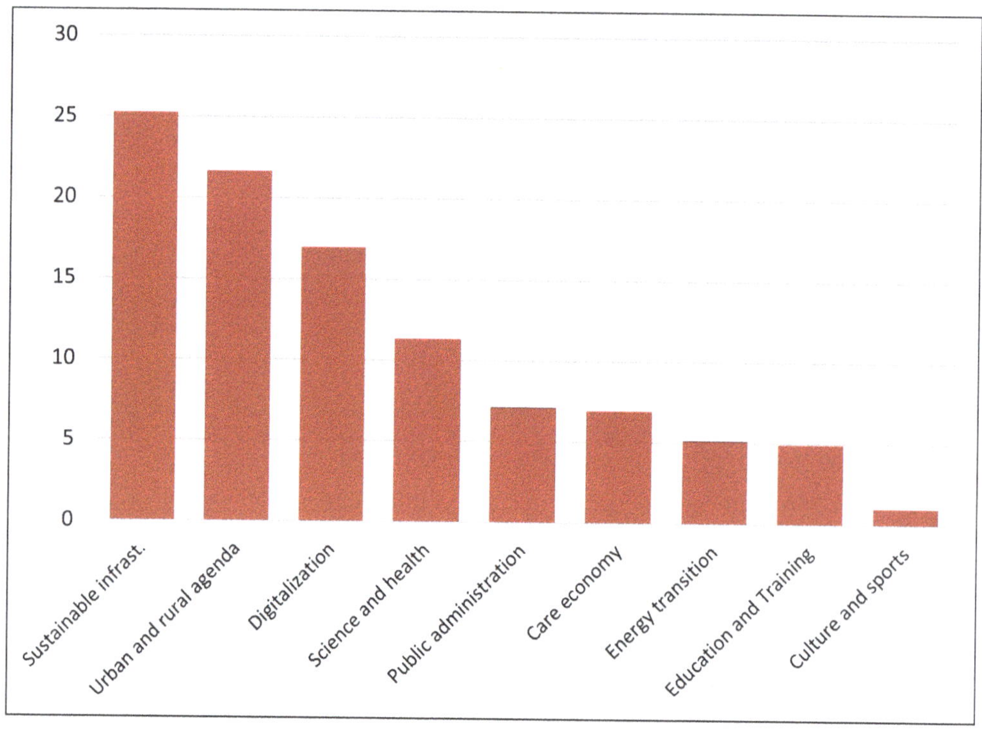

Fig. 5.10 Contribution of public investments to total investment impact on GDP (% of total investment impact, 2021–2023). *Source*: Ministry of Economy, Spain (2023).

5.5 Conclusions

The challenges ahead for the European Union are enormous, and member states need to take firm steps to ensure the green transition, the digitalization of the economy and the strengthening of industry while guaranteeing social cohesion. To meet the European Commission's own investment targets, the European Central Bank's Fiscal Policies Division recently estimated (Bouabdallah et al. 2024) that EU countries need to leverage additional public investment above what is already being implemented under the Next Generation EU funds. Specifically, they estimate the need to mobilize more than €900 billion for the whole of the EU during the period 2025–2031. Assuming that Spain takes up 10% of this investment (equivalent to the share of its GDP in the Eurozone), this would imply the need for an additional increase of almost €13 billion per year for the period 2025–2031, i.e. an increase of close to 1% of Spanish GDP in net public investment in the coming years (Fig. 5.11). The recent Draghi report on European competitiveness sets even more ambitious investment targets.

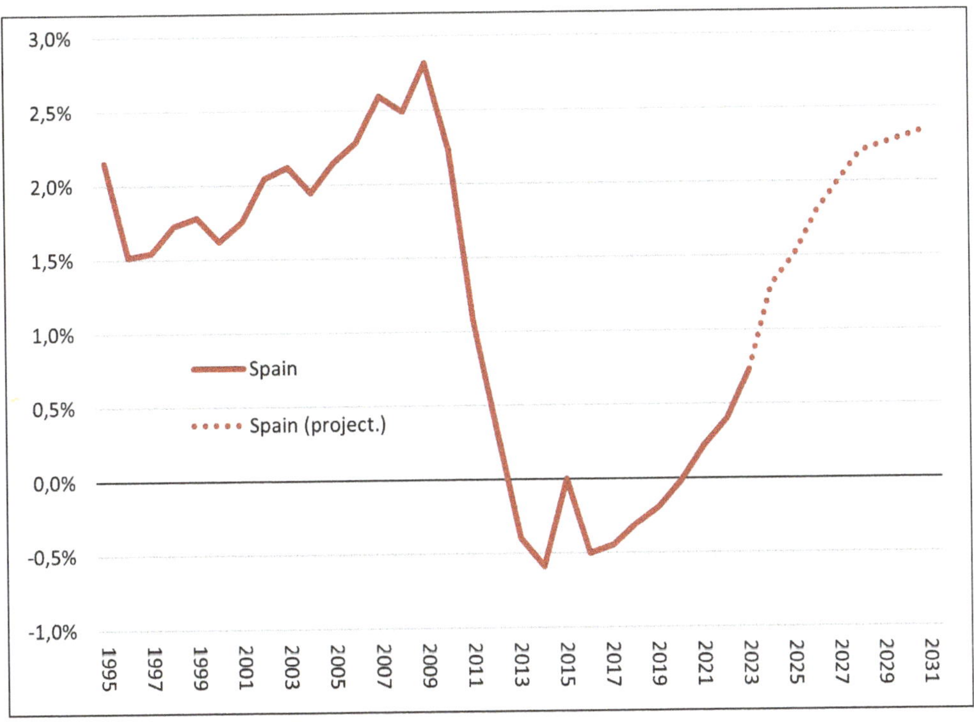

Fig. 5.11 Net public investment (as a percentage of GDP). *Source*: AMECO and authors' calculations. *Note*: Projection to meet the goals established by the European Commission, according to estimates developed by Bouabdallah et al. (2024).

Like the rest of its European partners, the critical debate facing the Spanish economy is evident: to what extent can these crucial investment needs be reconciled with the new fiscal rules?

Over the last few decades, numerous voices—from academia, governments and the business world—have questioned the Stability and Growth Pact due to its fiscal rigidity, its pro-cyclical nature and its inability to cope with recessions and economic crises, as well as its continuous contractionary effect on public investment. In March 2020, the European Commission activated its "general escape clause", which allowed the pandemic to be dealt with swiftly and flexibly. It also contributed to highlighting the need to reform the fiscal rules. This reform took place in the first half of 2024 and was approved by the European Parliament in April this year.

However, the new fiscal rules, despite being made more flexible in some aspects, still maintain a general orientation marked by the need to meet strict fiscal consolidation thresholds and have not incorporated any kind of Golden Rule to protect public investment. Therefore, there is a relevant threat of short-circuiting the recovery process of public investment in Spain and other countries, depending on how these new fiscal rules are implemented in the following year.

Last June, the European Commission opened the excessive deficit procedure for France, Italy, and five other EU countries. Spain has not been included in this procedure. However, the new fiscal rules establish that countries will be obliged to reduce their structural deficit by 0.4% per year, not only until the observed deficit reaches 3%, but also until the structural deficit reaches 1.5% to create a fiscal buffer for times of adversity. This implies that fiscal consolidation will have to continue over the coming years, also in Spain.

How should this fiscal consolidation be understood? The Directorate-General for Economic and Financial Affairs of the European Commission recently published "The Implications of Public Investment for Debt Sustainability" (Motyovszki et al. 2024: 1), which states that "without offsetting fiscal adjustments via the primary balance, a temporary increase in public investment implies a lasting increase in the debt-to-GDP ratio [...] In other words, debt stabilization would require subsequently higher primary surpluses, implying that public investments must eventually be paid for by fiscal adjustments".

In fact, according to Darvas et al. (2024), fiscal adjustments required under the new Stability and Growth Pact would be substantial for Spain: to achieve the intended structural primary balance objectives, the average annual fiscal adjustment would have to rise to 0.8% of GDP (in the case of a four-year adjustment period) and to 0.5% (in the case of a seven-year adjustment period).

The risk that this approach poses for public investment in countries like Spain is stark: the idea that a lasting increase in public investment is only feasible through continuous primary surpluses (probably sustained at the expense of public services) could undermine the current recovery of Spanish gross fixed capital formation, which has already been dragged down for a whole decade, as we have seen.

Moreover, this approach does not fit with recent empirical evidence from countries like Spain. We have already seen how fiscal consolidation in Spain was carried out during the Great Recession at the expense of public investment, which acted as an "adjustment variable" suffering massive cuttings. Paradoxically, this approach not only hindered effective fiscal policy but also damaged the very sustainability of public finances that it was intended to ensure, due to its contractionary effects on the economy (Labat-Moles and Summa 2023; Di Bucchianico 2019; Rosnick and Weibstrot 2015). However, over the last three years, Spain has adopted a very different approach to reducing deficit and debt over GDP ratios. Between 2020 and 2023, Spain has reduced them faster than was achieved in the 2010–2016 austerity period (Fig. 5.12). This has been possible through various tax reforms that have improved public revenues and, above all, due to economic growth, which has allowed the debt and deficit to be reabsorbed.

Obviously, the continuity of this growth is not independent of the fiscal policy pursued. As shown in Uxó et al. (2024), it is possible to design a fiscal policy strategy for Spain based on an expansion of public investment and an increase in public revenues (currently below the European average in the case of Spain).

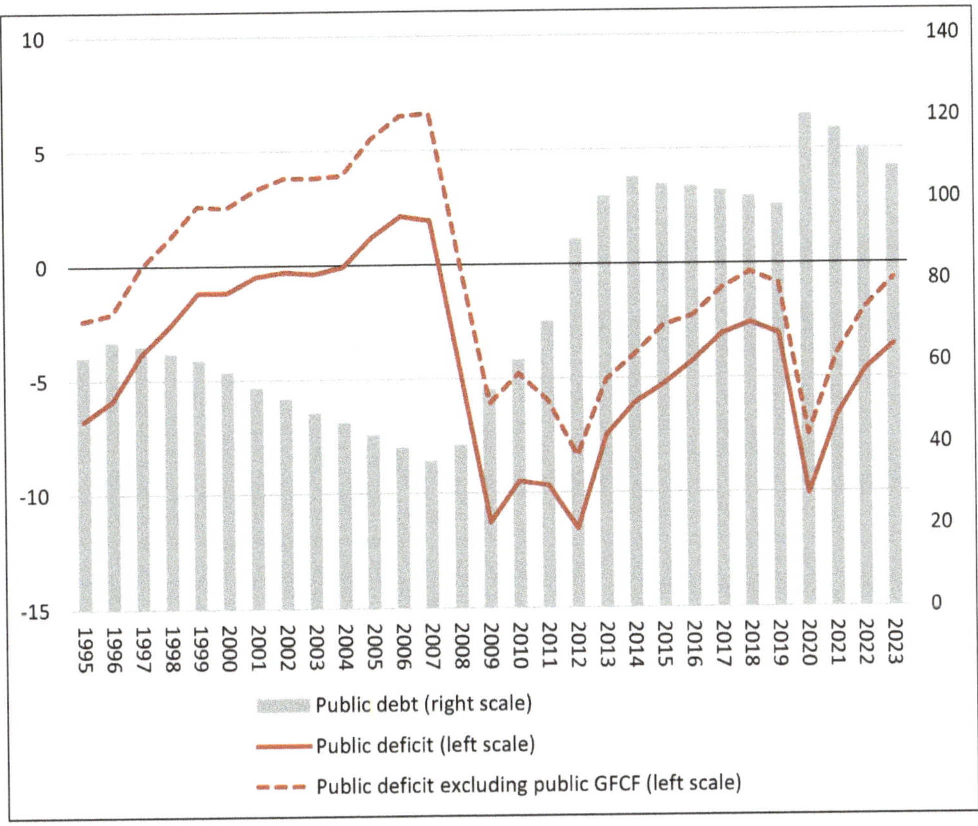

Fig. 5.12 Public debt and public deficit (Spain, % of GDP). *Source*: AMECO.

Online resources for Figs. 5.1–5.12 are available at https://hdl.handle.net/20.500.12434/a38b287c

This partially balanced budget expansion would allow the structural challenges of the Spanish economy to be faced, mobilizing more investment and reducing the unemployment rate while continuing to consolidate the public debt to GDP ratio. On the contrary, fiscal policies explicitly designed to reduce public deficit through freezing public expenditure will probably prove counterproductive.

Furthermore, and as we can see in Figure 5.12, the Spanish public deficit, excluding public gross fixed capital formation, is already nearly zero. Returning to the logic of public investment acting as the "adjustment variable" of fiscal consolidation and reducing this investment to ensure sustainable primary surpluses would be a policy mistake. It would reduce medium- and long-term economic growth potential, lower aggregate demand, and ultimately undermine fiscal sustainability itself.

References

Auerbach, A., and Y. Gorodnichenko (2012) "Fiscal Multipliers in Recession and Expansion", *NBER Working Paper* 17447, National Bureau of Economic Research, Cambridge, Massachusetts.

Bouabdallah, O. Dorrucci, E. Hoendervangers, L. and Nerlich, C. (2024) "Mind the Gap: Europe's Strategic Investment Needs and How to Support Them", *The ECB Blog*, 27 June, https://www.ecb.europa.eu/press/blog/date/2024/html/ecb.blog240627~2e939aa430.en.html

Consejo Económico y Social (2020) *La inversión pública en España: situación actual y prioridades estratégicas*, Colección Informes, Número 01/2020, Consejo Económico y Social.

Darvas, Z., L. Welslau, and J. Zettelmeyer (2024) "Incorporating the Impact of Social Investments and Reforms in the EU's New Fiscal Framework", *Bruegel Working Paper* 07/2024, https://www.bruegel.org/working-paper/incorporating-impact-social-investments-and-reforms-european-unions-new-fiscal

Di Bucchianico, S., (2019) "A Bit of Keynesian Debt-to-GDP Arithmetic for Deficit-capped Countries", *Bulletin of Political Economy* 13(1): 55–83.

Fatas, A., and Mihov, I. (2009) "Why Fiscal Stimulus Is Likely to Work", *International Finance* 12(1): 57–73

Fernández-Cerezo, A., E. Moral-Benito, and J. Quintana (2023) "The Recovery, Transformation and Resilience Plan and its Macroeconomic Impact from a Sectoral Standpoint", *Economic Bulletin*, Bank of Spain, 2023/Q1, https://repositorio.bde.es/bitstream/123456789/29539/1/be2301-art12e.pdf

Gechert, S., and A. Rannenberg (2018) "Which Fiscal Multipliers Are Regime-Dependent? A Meta-Regression Analysis", *Journal of Economic Surveys* 32(4): 1160–1182. https://doi.org/10.1111/joes.12241

Fundación BBVA-IVIE (2019) *El stock de capital en España y sus comunidades autónomas. Evolución de la edad media de las inversiones y envejecimiento del capital*, Fundación BBVA-IVIE.

Gobierno de España (2023) *Plan de Recuperación, Transformación y Resiliencia. IV Informe de Ejecución del Plan de Recuperación*, Gobierno de España, December.

International Monetary Fund (2014) "Is It Time for an Infrastructure Push? The Macroeconomic Effects of Public Investment", in *World Economic Outlook, October 2014: Legacies, Clouds, Uncertainties*. Washington, DC: International Monetary Fund, pp. 75–112.

Labat-Moles, H., and R. Summa (2023) "A Supermultiplier Demand-led Growth Accounting Analysis Applied to the Spanish Economy (1998–2019)", *European Journal of Economics and Economic Policies: Intervention* 21(1): 42–72, https://doi.org/10.4337/ejeep.2023.0115

Motyovszki, G., P. Pfeiffer, and J. Veld (2024) "The Implications of Public Investment for Debt Sustainability", *Discussion Paper* 204 (June), Directorate-General for Economic and Financial Affairs, European Commission, https://economy-finance.ec.europa.eu/system/files/2024-06/dp204_en.pdf

Pérez, F., and J. F. de Guevara (eds) (2024) *El stock de capital en España y sus Comunidades Autónomas 1995-2023. Cambios recientes en la composición de la inversión y en las respuestas a la crisis*, Documentos de Trabajo 1-2024, Fundación BBVA.

Rosnick, D., and M. Weibstrot (2015) "Has Austerity Worked in Spain?", *Center for Economic and Policy Research*, https://cepr.net/documents/Spain-2015-12.pdf

Uxó, J., E. Febrero, I. Ayala, and P. Villanueva (2024) "Debt Sustainability and Policy Targets: Full Employment or Structural Balance? A Simulation for the Spanish Economy", *Structural Change and Economic Dynamics*, 69: 475–487, https://doi.org/10.1016/j.strueco.2024.03.005

PART II—CHALLENGES

6. A New Industrial Policy as the Key to the Green Transition

Karl Aiginger[1]

The world is changing quickly. The former Soviet Union is gone and its successor, Russia, is seeking to reclaim parts of Soviet territory using military force. The United States (US) as a sole remaining superpower cannot take the lead, due to populism, failed democracy, and a lack of resilience. China is on the rise, but autocratic, longing for resources and facing a declining population. Europe is less dynamic and innovative, not yet seen as unified with common goals. New middle powers are gaining shares in production, but are themselves very different. The problems the world faces are changing: peace is no longer guaranteed, global warming is accelerating, poverty is on the decline but re-emerging in other ways, and migration policy is becoming more and more important. The green transition may be an engine of change and new dynamics, but there are also many backlashes. In this situation, a new industrial policy is needed—one very different from that of the past. We begin by describing the past policy as an isolated policy, along with the questions of whether such a policy is needed in a capitalistic economy and whether it should focus on "important sectors" (the sectoral or French approach) or "important activities" (the horizonal or German approach). We then turn to the increasing importance of international exports/ investments and the necessity for a green transition, but also new forms of protectionism and backlashes. This chapter builds on Aiginger and Rodrik (2020) with respect to "industrial policy for the 21st century", as well as on Aiginger and Ketels (2024) for its "reloading" after the most recent changes in the policy environment.

1 Vienna University of Economics; Policy Crossover Center Vienna.

 https://doi.org/10.11647/OBP.0434.07

6.1 The New World Order

The profile of the global economy is fundamentally changing, affecting policy priorities and the potential impact of policy actions.

The geographic footprint and responsibility for global GDP growth is changing. Today, developing countries produce half of the world's output, and they provide a rising share of trade and investment flows. The BRICS countries (Brazil, Russia, India, China, and South Africa) have invited six new members to join their ranks (BRICS Plus). Together they will account for roughly 30% of global GDP, challenging the dominance of the G7 countries (Canada, France, Germany, Italy, Japan, the UK, and the US). China, in particular, has enjoyed fast growth in the past. But it is now experiencing old and new problems, such as a decreasing population and macroeconomic imbalances with an ailing real estate market. There has been a decline in productivity dynamics, reducing its ability to drive global GDP growth in the future. Global trend growth is falling in China as well as in the advanced economies (Kose and Ohnsorge 2023).

Demographic trends are changing policy priorities. Many advanced economies, as well as that of China, are facing a rapid ageing of their populations. Japan has shown that this trend effects technical progress. Other regions, however, are facing a doubling of their population: Africa's population will rise from 1.4 billion to 2.5 billion people by the middle of the century, and then to 3 billion by the end of the century. India will continue to see its labour force grow for several decades, overtaking that of China. Ageing societies will experience demographics as a limiting factor for growth. While unemployment may become less of a challenge, skill shortages will increase. These countries would benefit from inward migration, but rising populism could prevent this from happening. Societies still experiencing population growth could give the global economy access to a growing labour force. But these are countries that have struggled to provide jobs for labour market entrants in the past; they face the threat of rising unemployment, poverty, and political tensions.

New technologies are changing the patterns of sector-specific opportunities for growth and job creation. Industry in the sense of manufacturing or infrastructure investment remains an important part of economic activities and global trade in particular. But production activities are made more valuable by services and new digital tools. And they provide less direct job creation opportunities than in the past, with productivity growth outpacing demand. New digital technologies like generative Artificial Intelligence (AI) will create further disruptions, providing opportunities for productivity growth but also threatening many existing jobs. Raw materials are still important, but growth is shifting to new materials like cobalt, copper, lithium, or nickel, which are important for the development of new technologies and decarbonization. Access to sources of renewable energy will become a critical asset; in the transition period, access to low-cost oil and gas resources will remain important, especially if conflicts threaten traditional sources, and policy fatigue could prevent innovations and change.

6.2 Past Industrial Policy

The starting point of the discussion was the question of whether an industrial policy is needed in a free-market economy dominated by the policy of the Washington Consensus. This approach is typical for US economists and the multinational institutions dominated by the US. In France, industrial policy is the successor of the "planification" model still reflected in the powerful state, in which sectors were selected as important to France and dominated by public support (sectoral industrial policy). Germany opposed this and focused on supporting activities important to all sectors, such as research and education (horizontal approach). The economic policy of the European Community initially focused on the horizontal approach, but soon incorporated some important sectors; this became known as the matrix approach in Aiginger and Sieber (2006). This led to a matrix, with industries as rows and policies as columns, and meant that, for example, the automotive industry required other policies than that of apparel.

6.2.1 The Green Transition and Its Backlashes

- The pandemic and its aftermath exposed both the fragility and the importance of global value chains. It drew attention to governments' abilities to provide medical products, basic health care, and other services to their populations. Resilience became a more important policy objective, and active government policy efforts a more important and accepted tool.
- Climate change is increasingly visible, with rising implications for prosperity, especially for those in poverty who suffer more from heatwaves and other weather extremes. The green transition is becoming a major policy objective across the world, with the need to manage that transition in ways that distribute the costs and opportunities of that transition across countries and parts of societies in balanced ways.
- Rising geopolitical tensions and active wars in Ukraine and Gaza are challenging the foundations of the global institutional structure that has sustained the last phase of globalization. They are also eroding the ability to mobilize global collective action to address climate change and other global challenges (Acemoglu 2023; Autor et al. 2021).

6.2.2 New Horizons

Recent changes have affected the debate and practices surrounding industrial policy. The following observations from the literature (drawn from Aiginger and Ketels 2024) stand out.

First, the focus of the industrial policy debate has increasingly shifted to "how to be successful in practice", and is no longer primarily about "whether to be justified in theory". Criscuolo (2012) and Juhász et al. (2023) outline new approaches for classifying and measuring industrial policy. This is seen as a critical step towards understanding what works and what doesn't, moving beyond the use of individual failures or successes to understanding broader patterns of impact. Industrial policy is much more successful in Asia than in other parts of the world. Export orientation appears to be a critical element of the "Asian miracle" (Birdsall et al. 1993) and thus a key characteristic of successful industrial policies.

Second, especially in advanced economies, there is a distinct shift in the objective function of industrial policy towards broader societal goals rather than a narrowing down to job creation or growth. This shift has also led to a significantly higher willingness to use policies that just a few years ago were considered distortive. Elisabeth Reynolds (2024) dissects the range of ambitious new policy initiatives launched by the Biden administration in the US. These policies combine the ambition to rebuild the industrial base in the US, especially in locations overwhelmed by rising Chinese imports over the past few decades (Autor et al. 2021), with a focus on creating high-quality jobs with social benefits, accelerating the green transition and strengthening the resilience and self-sufficiency of the US economy in key sectors. Reinhilde Veugelers, Simone Tagliapietra, and Cecilia Trasi (2024) contrast this approach with the efforts of the European Union to introduce a new green industrial policy. There are similarities with the US regarding broader ambitions related to the green transition and also the overall resources used. However, there are significant differences in the types of instruments used, and in Europe there are now clear concerns as to whether this difference in approach might also lead to a difference in impact.

Third, these changes in the policy posture of advanced economies have significant implications for emerging and developing economies. On the one hand, the change in the policy dialogue provides more justification for less advanced economies to set active policies that help accelerate their structural transformation (Lin and Monga 2017). On the other hand, these economies are facing increased rivalry from advanced economies with much deeper pockets, have weaker institutional structures to implement policies effectively, and are confronted with an economic context in which the export-driven growth of manufacturing is less feasible (Rodrik 2015). Deepak Nayyar and Gaurav Nayyar's (2024) article on India provides a concrete perspective on these challenges. India has moved beyond many of the ideological roadblocks that had held it back historically. But it is now facing the task of implementing ambitious policies to drive industrial development with institutional structures that are not fit for purpose. And it is facing a global market environment that is much less conducive to the types of export-oriented industrial policies that Fuad Hasanov and Reda Cherif documented as being historically more effective (Ketels et al. 2022).

6.3 Upcoming Trends

Industrial policy is here to stay. There is a rising demand for industrial policy, understood broadly as policies that aim to enhance the performance and profile of the economy using tools that move beyond sector-neutral and general 'rules of the game' policy actions. This demand is fuelled by new policy challenges and objectives, including achieving the green transition, driving shared prosperity growth, and enhancing resilience in a risky and fragmented geopolitical context. There is also a sense in the policy community that traditional policies to enhance overall framework conditions are insufficient on their own as a response. Thus, we observe less of a conceptual repudiation of the policies promoted since the 1990s than a reaction to changes in actual circumstances and needs.

The policy approach of the previous era, which focused on liberalization and improving framework conditions, was effective in many respects (see Irwin 2020 for the global perspective and Gil and Raiser 2012 for the European experience). However, the situation is different now, in part also as a direct consequence of the economic dynamics that the policy approach of the last few decades has created. This has shifted the balance of political opinion even in countries traditionally sceptical towards industrial policy, such as Germany and the US. And, as the memory of past industrial policy failures has faded somewhat, there is much less resistance to at least attempting new industrial policy measures. This could, however, change relatively quickly if the new industrial policies fail to deliver.

While still diffuse, elements of a new policy framework are emerging. New approaches, such as mission orientation, are considered promising, and may help identify critical dimensions of a new framework (Mazzucato 2021). Directionality in terms of aligning market signals with societal goals cannot be taken for granted, but needs to be embedded in policies, and policy action needs to mobilize a broader set of tools and actors to be effective. Yet, so far, actual initiatives in this vein have remained vague and have yet to show their potential in practice (Tõnurist 2023; Kelsey 2023). Old approaches towards industrial policy that worked, such as export orientation, may not be as effective in the new context (Rodrik 2015).

There is an emerging consensus that a policy approach that simply focuses on affecting the allocation of capital to new sectors is not enough. It also requires upgrading the fundamentals that drive productivity and innovation, along with their impact on resources. Boundaries with respect to innovation, trade, and infrastructure policies are becoming blurred—all of these are critical to the success of individual industries. Many of these fundamentals are, in fact, sector-specific, requiring policies to move beyond sector-neutral efforts. There is also an emerging consensus that success is driven by the alignment and coherence of policy actions, not simply by the features of any individual policy program. Such alignment and coherence require strategy, roadmaps, and collaboration—both between the public and private sectors, and within the public sector. Location-specific factors also play a role, as many actions and results are highly localized (Austin et al. 2018; Ketels and Duch 2022).

A new architecture will be needed to anchor national industrial policies in a stable global context. The past policy consensus was anchored in a set of global institutions and rules, and within Europe in the acquis governing the single market. It relied on collective action to sustain a cooperative equilibrium that was seen as benefitting everyone over time. But the willingness to behave cooperatively has eroded. Organization for Economic Cooperation and Development (OECD) economies feel that others, and China in particular, have not followed the spirit of the past consensus and have reduced their approach to "friend-shoring" (Yellen 2022) and "de-risking" their global economic relations (Ivanov 2023). Emerging economies, not only that of China, are at the same time concerned about steps taken by advanced economies that can erode the opportunities for catch-up via exports, which the past system promised. A combination of trade barriers, whether these are motivated by the green transition or geopolitical concerns, and more robust industrial policies by countries with deep resources is seen as disadvantaging emerging and developing countries (echoing an earlier argument made by Chang 2002).

Europe's role in the new world order is still to be designed. Draghi (2024) mentions three trends. First, Europe is no longer catching up with US productivity, and the gap in per capita productivity is widening, reflecting a growing innovation gap. Second, a joint plan for decarbonization and competitiveness is essential, as electricity and natural gas prices are significantly higher in Europe. Over the medium term, decarbonization will help to shift energy reliance towards more secure and low-cost sources. Third, increasing security and reducing dependencies on critical raw materials, as well as chips and digital technology, is crucial—a strategy we can refer to as "foreign economic policy" aimed at ensuring physical security. Investing in the future requires correcting for past nationalism and the overly timid use of international financing. The US has much higher debt yet pays lower interest rates. Finally, Europe must recognize its pivotal role in a new world order, where the countries from the Global South (see The Economist 2024) seek partners for equitable relationships. Europe can offer peace and innovation, and can spend on education and innovation.

Backlashes can already be seen. Although climate change has become ever more visible and well-documented by scientists and multinational organizations, social networks and fake news have continued to stoke the opinion that it does not exist. And if these tactics do not work, there is the argument that others have forced the problem on society or that environmental policy will only reduce competitiveness. The Green Deal elaborated by the EU has reduced the ability of parties in the centre to win elections and is not considered a powerful plan with which to increase well-being for all.

There is a clear danger that the more muscular use of industrial policies will lead to increasing tensions in the global international system. Competition could become more focused on capturing rents rather than creating value. This would have significant costs, even beyond those which a more limited erection of trade barriers would create (Javorcik et al. 2023; Aiyar et al. 2023). Yet, even if capturing rents is not the intention, a new balance will need to be found between market access, on the one hand, and the freedom to drive new industrial policies, on the other. In Europe, this became apparent when Germany launched large programs to support its companies during the pandemic and then during the energy crisis that followed Russia's invasion of Ukraine: other EU countries lacked the resources to match these programs and became concerned about their companies being at a competitive disadvantage on the EU single market as a consequence.

In 2024, industrial policy has not only been "reborn", but also "reloaded" (Aiginger and Ketels 2024). There is a large willingness of policy makers to engage in industrial policies, with unprecedented funding made available. We are experiencing industrial policy "at scale" (Rodrik and Stiglitz 2024): "In countries that are already rich, the state, after decades of free-market rhetoric, is back in a big way. Governments are spending hundreds of billions on handouts for industries they deem to be strategically important" (The Economist 2024).

New forms of protectionism occur. The US and, to a lesser extent, Europe is trying to reduce imports (such as electric cars) from China. China has reacted by preventing the exportation of rare earth minerals needed for many modern products in the US and Europe.

The shift is only partially a result of changes in conceptual thinking or the evidence surrounding industrial policy. Rather, it is primarily driven by changes in the political context, influenced by public demands on governments. This is particularly a concern, given the key elections scheduled this year (in the US, EU, and India), as well as the resulting pressures on an increasingly fragmented geopolitical system. It is also driven by new needs, in particular the green transition and rising concerns about shared prosperity. The past policy consensus is perceived as having been insufficient to provide policy makers with the necessary tools to address these challenges.

6.4 The Green Transition as an Engine of Change

Let us close with the following ten remarks:

1. The slogan that "no industrial policy is the best policy" is definitely wrong and is far from dominant even in the US today.
2. Industrial policy is no longer just about manufacturing; it also encompasses the boundaries of services and resources.
3. It is a matrix policy with different policy priorities for different sectors and columns.
4. Industrial policy can be different for advanced countries and emerging ones, for rich Asian countries, for poor provinces in the US, or for Europe.

5. It must follow new societal needs—it should be resilient, global, and social—and it should not be defined by GDP as a main goal, but rather by SDGs and healthy life expectancy.
6. It must take into account demographic trends, such as high ageing and a rapid decrease in the share of native populations in some countries, alongside the continued population growth in regions such as Africa.
7. Industrial policy will be different in regions, but all versions should be based on the need for better and more inclusive education, which provides the basis for the green transition.
8. While populism and "my country first" movements are on the rise, resorting to open or covert protectionism and imposing tariffs to limit imports from certain regions are misguided; instead, globalization must evolve.
9. A new industrial policy should not be national but rather international, and it should be driven by societal goals and the need for transition.
10. Backlashes will occur and must be countered by policy as well as civil society, using arguments and best practices.

References

Acemoglu D. (2023) "Letter from America: When Industry Means Hard Work", *Royal Economic Society*, https://res.org.uk/newsletter/letter-from-america-when-industry-means-hard-work/

Aiginger, K., and C. Ketels (2024) "Industrial Policy Reloaded", *Journal of Industry, Competition and Trade* 24(7), https://doi.org/10.1007/s10842-024-00415-8

Aiginger, K., and D. Rodrik (2020) "Rebirth of Industrial Policy and an Agenda for the Twenty-First Century", *J Ind Compet Trade* 20: 189–207, https://doi.org/10.1007/s10842-019-00322-3

Aiginger, K., and S. Sieber (2006) "The Matrix Approach to Industrial Policy", *International Review of Applied Economics* 20(5): 573–601, https://doi.org/10.1080/02692170601005507

Austin, B., E. Glaeser, and L. Summers (2018) "Saving the Heartland: Place-based Policies in 21st Century America. Brookings Papers of Economic Activity", *Brookings*, https://www.brookings.edu/articles/saving-the-heartland-place-based-policies-in-21st-century-america/

Autor, D., D. Dorn, and G. Hanson (2021) "On the Persistence of the China Shock", *Brookings Papers of Economic Activity* 2021(2): 381–476, https://doi.org/10.1353/eca.2022.0005

Aiyar, S., and A. Ilyna (2023) "Geoeconomic Fragmentation and the Future of Multilateralism", *IMF Staff Discussion Notes* 2023(001), https://www.imf.org/en/Publications/Staff-Discussion-Notes/Issues/2023/01/11/Geo-Economic-Fragmentation-and-the-Future-of-Multilateralism-527266

Birdsall, N. M., J. E. L. Campos, C. S. Kim, W. M. Corden, L. MacDonald, H. Pack, J. Page, R. Sabor, and J. E. Stiglitz (1993) *The East Asian Miracle: Economic Growth and Public Policy: Main Report (English). A World Bank Policy Research Report*. Washington, DC: World Bank Group, http://documents.worldbank.org/curated/en/975081468244550798/Main-report

Chang, H. J. (2002) *Kicking Away the Ladder: Development Strategy in Historical Perspective*. London: Anthem Press.

Criscuolo C., et al. (2012) "The Causal Effect of Industrial Policy", *NBER Working Paper* 17842, https://doi.org/10.3386/w17842

Draghi, M. (2024) *The Future of European Competitiveness*. Brussels: European Commission, https://commission.europa.eu/document/download/97e481fd-2dc3-412d-be4c-f152a8232961_en

Economist, The (2024) "Can India, Indonesia, and Saudi Arabia be the Next Great Economies", *The Economist*, 4 January, https://www.economist.com/leaders/2024/01/04/can-india-indonesia-and-saudi-arabia-be-the-next-great-economies

Gil, I. S., and M. Raiser (2012) *Golden Growth: Restoring the Lustre of the European Economic Model*. Washington, DC: World Bank Group.

Irwin, D. A. (2020) "The Washington Consensus Stands Test of Time Better than Populist Policies", 4 December, *Peterson Institute for International Economics*, https://www.piie.com/blogs/realtime-economics/washington-consensus-stands-test-time-better-populist-policies

Ivanov, I. (2023) "A Green Deal Industrial Plan for the Net Zero Age", *SHS Web Conf.* 176, https://doi.org/10.1051/shsconf/202317602009

Javorcik, B. S., L. Kitzmueller, H. Schweiger, and M. A. Yildirim (2023) "Economic Costs of Friend-shoring", *CID Faculty Working Paper* 422, https://growthlab.hks.harvard.edu/publications/economic-costs-friend-shoring

Juhász, R., et al. (2023) "The New Economics of Industrial Policy", *Annu. Rev. Econ* 16, https://doi.org/10.1146/annurev-economics-081023-024638

Kelsey, T. (2023) "When Missions Fail: Lessons in 'High Technology' from Post-War Britain", *Blavatnik School of Government Working Paper* 2023–056, https://www.bsg.ox.ac.uk/sites/default/files/2023-12/BSG-WP%E2%80%932023-056-When-Missions-Fail.pdf

Ketels, C., and E. Duch (2022) "Industrial Policy in a New Global Reality: Towards a More Location- and Sector-Driven Approach", *Private Sector Development Blog*, 11 July, https://blogs.worldbank.org/psd/industrial-policy-new-global-reality-towards-more-location-and-sector-driven-approach

Ketels. C., M. E. Porter, and A. Kapoor (2022) *Competitiveness Roadmap for India @ 100*. Delhi: Economic Advisory Council of the Prime Minister, https://www.hbs.edu/ris/Publication%20Files/Report_Competitiveness_Roadmap-25_August_2022_Web_Version_690d1fab-dce8-48a0-8cd5-6d6a63a6d5eb.pdf

Kose, M. A, and F. Ohnsorge (2023) *Falling Long Term Growth Prospects: Trends, Expectations, and Policies*. Washington, DC: World Bank, https://openknowledge.worldbank.org/handle/10986/39497

Lin, J. Y., and C. Monga (2017) *Beating the Odds: Jump-Starting Developing Countries*. Princeton, NJ: Princeton University Press, https://doi.org/10.2307/j.ctvc776tv

Mazzucato, M. (2021) *Mission Economy: A Moonshot Guide to Changing Capitalism*. London: Allen Lane.

Nayyar, D., and G. Nayyar (2024) "Made in India: Industrial Policy in a Changing World", *Journal of Industry, Competition and Trade* 24(1): 13.

Reynolds, E. B. (2024) "U.S. Industrial Transformation and the 'How' of 21st Century Industrial Strategy", *J Ind Compet Trade* 24: 8, https://doi.org/10.1007/s10842-024-00420-x

Rodrik, D. (2015) "Premature Deindustrialization", *NBER Working Paper* 20935, https://www.nber.org/system/files/working_papers/w20935/w20935.pdf

Rodrik, D., and J. Stiglitz (2024) "A New Growth Strategy for Developing Nations", *Harvard*, https://drodrik.scholar.harvard.edu/sites/scholar.harvard.edu/files/dani-rodrik/files/a_new_growth_strategy_for_developing_nations.pdf

Veugelers, R., S. Tagliapietra, and C. Trasi (2024) "Green Industrial Policy in Europe: Past, Present, and Prospects", *Journal of Industry, Competition and Trade* 24(1): 1–22, https://doi.org/10.1007/s10842-024-00418-5

Yellen, J. (2022) "Remarks at Microsoft in New Delhi", *US Department of the Treasury*, 11 November, https://home.treasury.gov/news/press-releases/jy1096

7. A “True” Industrial Policy for Europe Is a Technology and Innovation Policy[1]

Reda Cherif,[2] Fuad Hasanov,[3] and Xun Li[4]

Since the Global Financial Crisis of 2008, the “core” European countries have been losing their competitive edge in global markets for sophisticated products such as electronics and green transportation and power technologies, while also missing out on the earlier revolution in information and communication technology (ICT). Meanwhile, the “periphery” European countries have been slowing down and, in pre-crisis years, have mostly channelled their investment into non-tradable industries, concentrating their resources in relatively lower productivity and lower skill activities. The slowdown in growth and convergence highlights the need to reignite productivity and economic dynamism. Lessons from the Asian economic miracles and Europe’s own growth experience suggest the importance of developing sophisticated sectors. The development of these sectors is riddled with both government and market failures, requiring adequate policies to tackle them. We argue that a “true” industrial policy for Europe is a technology and innovation policy (TIP) that focuses on correcting market failures to spur innovation, scale up, and support production networks in sophisticated industries across Europe while reorienting the engines of growth of “periphery” economies toward sophisticated sectors and their complex value chains. TIP’s guiding principles are a focus on global markets, competition, and a strict accountability framework, where the “hard” tools such as tariffs and subsidies may not be necessary and may be potentially counterproductive.

1 The views expressed are those of the authors and do not necessarily represent the views of the International Monetary Fund (IMF), its Executive Board, or IMF management. We would like to thank the editors Floriana Cerniglia and Francesco Saraceno and IMF colleagues at the European Department, in particular, Helge Berger, Luis Brandao Marques, Stephan Danninger, Manuela Goretti, Gavin Gray, Andrew Hodge, Malhar Nabar, Roberto Piazza, and Hasan Toprak as well as Riccardo Ercoli and Annalisa Korinthios for helpful comments and suggestions. All errors are our own.

2 IMF, Bennett Institute for Public Policy (University of Cambridge), and Technology and Industrialization for Development Centre (University of Oxford).

3 IMF, Georgetown University, Bennett Institute for Public Policy (University of Cambridge), and Technology and Industrialization for Development Centre (University of Oxford).

4 IMF.

 https://doi.org/10.11647/OBP.0434.08

7.1 Introduction: The Challenge of Sustained, Sustainable, and Inclusive Growth

Europe is at the crossroads of economic challenges. Having intensified since the COVID-19 pandemic, these challenges are both old and new. Low productivity, declining dynamism, and the need for inclusive growth and well-paying jobs are seemingly being eclipsed by emerging challenges like intense competition from China, especially in renewables and electric vehicles (EVs), trade and geopolitical conflicts, and increased climate change uncertainties. In the aftermath of the pandemic, economic security, including resilience and supply chain diversification, has become an important policy issue. Moreover, increased global competition in sophisticated products, especially from China, have sent ripple waves across advanced countries such as the US and the European countries and have brought back the "spectre" of the 1980s, when Japan was rapidly gaining global market shares in sophisticated products like electronics and automobiles. The existing macroeconomic weaknesses, such as low productivity growth and stagnating real median incomes, are being amplified by the emerging challenges, worrying policy makers about growth prospects and economic security, amounting to the loss of advanced industries and well-paying jobs.

The fear of losing advanced industries, such as the automotive and clean technology (cleantech) sectors, along with well-paying jobs, encapsulates the key concerns facing policy makers. This fear is not unjustified, as large firms like Nokia in Finland and renewable industries like the solar manufacturing industry in Germany were lost previously. These sophisticated industries are key to innovation, productivity gains and growth, well-paying jobs, and inclusion (Cherif and Hasanov 2019a, 2019b; Cherif, Hasanov, and Aghion 2024). The lack of innovation and production in sophisticated sectors could inhibit the growth of well-paying jobs, reduce broad-based gains in market income ("predistribution"), and jeopardize the competitiveness of European firms in the global market. We argue that the old challenges of low productivity growth and declining dynamism and the new challenges of energy transition, climate change, and trade conflicts boil down to the key challenge of how to address market failures that hinder growth of sophisticated industries, including cleantech. Although, according to the IMF (2024b), a large share of the productivity gap is also due to the non-tech sector, productivity gains in sophisticated sectors have substantial spillover effects to other sectors, while technology diffusion from tech sectors could help narrow the productivity gap in non-tech sectors as well.

Sophisticated sectors generate productivity gains and sustained growth, as demonstrated by the experience of the so-called "Asian miracles", like Korea and Singapore. These sectors, mostly focused on tradable manufacturing goods, create spillovers to other tradable sectors such as supply chains, and non-tradable sectors such as services (Pisano and Shih 2012). These sectors, as measured by research and development (R&D) intensity, create opportunities in manufacturing-linked services while including professional/scientific and ICT services (Cherif and Hasanov 2019a). More importantly, they create well-paying jobs as high productivity growth and specialized skills are key elements of these sectors. Moreover, some sophisticated sectors such as EVs, renewables, and other clean technology sectors could generate sustainable growth while facilitating fast energy transition and reducing greenhouse gas emissions.

As the IMF (2024a, 2024b) argues, the standard growth approach that focuses on horizontal policies (applicable to all sectors), along with, in the context of Europe, tools to further European integration in support of the single market, would help alleviate the challenge of low productivity. In general, the standard growth approach primarily addresses government or policy failures. These failures include inadequate business environment, low spending on public goods, excessive regulations, and macroeconomic instability. Relative to other major economic blocs, Europe performs relatively well in tackling government failures in general, although policy improvements to improve the workings of the single market and reduce various barriers for business across Europe would be beneficial (IMF 2024a, 2024b; Letta 2024; Hodge et al. forthcoming). Promoting the single market, based on a level playing field, is important to create opportunities for firms and workers. Meanwhile, the level playing field should be complemented by more purpose-specific policies spurring firms to enter more decisively into sophisticated sectors.

The standard growth policy package may not be sufficient to provide incentives for firms to enter the sophisticated sectors because it does not address well what essentially all sophisticated sectors have in common—a myriad of market failures. Among these market failures are learning failure,[5] coordination and information failures, externalities, agglomeration effects, spillovers, unfavourable risk-return trade-offs, high uncertainty, and inadequate financing. The implication is that firms underinvest, produce less, or completely forgo entering these markets, potentially resulting even in "missing" markets.

A policy to tackle market failures riddling sophisticated sectors, aligning incentives for firms and workers, and coordinating across public and private stakeholders, is needed. We call it a "true" industrial policy (Cherif and Hasanov 2019a, 2019b). It is not a protectionist policy of the past industrial policies that mostly failed in the medium to long run, or a policy of blank check subsidies to firms ignoring market signal feedback, including the need to restructure failing enterprises. Rather, it is a technology and innovation policy, or TIP (Cherif and Hasanov 2019b).

A TIP for Europe is a coordinated European technology and innovation policy, complementing and reinforcing horizontal policies. It takes European regions as a unit of focus, emphasizing the importance of agglomeration and spillovers and combining pan-European and coordinated national policies. It promotes cross-border industrial

5 See Stiglitz and Greenwald (2014).

clusters and linkages, supporting integration and agglomeration forces. In addition, with a focus on coordination, provision of incentives, and direction for resource flows to tackle market failures, TIP would complement and reinforce horizontal policies for integration in the single market. As Letta (2024) states, the new single market framework to protect five freedoms—the free movement of people, goods, services, capital, and the newly added, research, innovation, and education—should also support "the objective of establishing a dynamic and effective European industrial policy", requiring speed, scale, and adequate financial resources. The European Commission (2024), in its note to the Eurogroup, argues that a European industrial policy can contribute to productivity growth and European competitiveness. Draghi (2024a, 2024b) further emphasizes the importance of advanced sectors and technology, including innovation and domestic manufacturing, with the need for a radical change in a European strategy with a clear focus on sophisticated sectors and large investments.

To succeed, TIP requires upholding three key principles. Overall, what needs to be done—fostering innovation and production in sophisticated sectors—is relatively clear, and it is a necessity for all European countries, which are relatively rich and largely at the technological frontier. Yet to achieve this goal, we argue that three key principles could facilitate the policy design and implementation: export orientation (a focus on global markets), competition, and multifaceted state support with accountability based on market signals—as the lessons from the successful growth of the Asian economic miracles illustrate—are a key part of TIP. Focus on global markets from the onset supports scale and scope of products. Competition not only internationally but also domestically increases the odds of the industry survival. "The state as a venture capitalist" approach, with a focus on industries or portfolios rather than particular firms, would further raise the chance of success. Various policy tools that provide the appropriate environment (e.g., specific infrastructure, regulation, financing, skill training) and incentives for firms to engage in innovation and production with clear accountability signals of progress and for workers to obtain needed skills, solve numerous market failures, improving the odds of developing competitive and innovative industries.

Lastly, the consistent implementation of TIP is crucial. Policy need not be written in stone and needs to be flexible. As with any policy (and not necessarily more fiscal spending), there are risks of rent-seeking and capture, requiring a careful design and implementation. A dedicated institution or a high-level council, endowed with "embedded autonomy", to coordinate across all the stakeholders, both public agencies and private firms, on country and European levels, thus resolving coordination and information failures, could drive the change. It is an institution that is in close contact with firms, has a deep knowledge of technologies and markets, and is shielded from external influence (e.g., political or rent-seeking). The focus and support to move toward new sophisticated industries, including the "industries of the future," would support productivity gains and dynamism and help generate sustained, sustainable, and inclusive growth.

7.2 A TIP for Europe

The following three case studies illustrate the main challenge facing Europe in critically important sophisticated sectors: disruption and international competition. They showcase examples where Europe held a strong initial advantage in an industry, which was subsequently disrupted or lost significant global market shares. These sectors are mobile phones, semiconductors, and EVs/batteries.

7.2.1 The Rise and Fall of Finland's Nokia

The rise and fall of Nokia highlight both the origins of Europe's strength in high-tech and the challenges and policy dilemmas it faces moving forwards. Out of a small and relatively poorer nation sprang a high-tech champion dominating the global mobile phone market for more than a decade. The success of Nokia, which started as a modest domestic conglomerate focused on wood pulp production, and later rubber boots and bicycle tires, depended largely on a multi-faceted state intervention helped by regional and EU policies to set up standards.

The rise of Nokia stemmed from a spirit of risk-taking combined with a wide spectrum of state interventions spanning procurement policies, active support for R&D through public research institutes and universities, and the existence of a powerful umbrella institution tackling coordination failures, including financing (Tekes). The company that became Nokia later pivoted to radio telecommunication because of a tender by the Ministry of Defence (which was later cancelled despite the incurred costs). Subsequently, the ministry of telecommunications set up a tender for firms to compete for a wireless communication system to be used along the roads in the northern part of the country where wire communication was costly to maintain due to the weather conditions.

The National Technology Agency (Tekes) funded and supported the technology sector in Finland for decades. Its support quickly concentrated on emerging technologies through sizable financial support to specifically develop Nokia's mobile and GSM (Global System for Mobile Communications) technologies in the 1970s and 1980s. More importantly, the strategic projects co-financed by Tekes were structured in a way that made it difficult for Nokia to withdraw. This proved useful during the early 1990s recession, when the temptation to cut back on "non-essential" projects was strong. Other tools, largely funded by the government, such as close links with universities and the public industrial research institute (VTT) were critical, as Nokia was given access to laboratories and scientists, and since education policy was geared toward engineering in the 1970s and 1980s.[6]

Subsequently, Nokia was disrupted by Apple as it missed out on the smartphone revolution in the 2010s. The disappearance of the mobile phone subsidiary accelerated

6 By doing so, the government addressed the market failure of inadequate financing for innovation.

with the takeover by Microsoft, shedding tens of thousands of highly qualified and experienced workers. Given the central role of Nokia in the Finnish economy as an anchor of a high-tech sector, the macroeconomic consequences persisted for at least a decade and may continue to do so. Finland's performance compared to its Nordic peers in terms of exports, growth, R&D, and productivity has been lagging since the closing down of the mobile phone subsidiary of Nokia (Ali-Yrkko et al. 2021).

How critical was European integration to the rise of Nokia? European integration played a critical role in terms of setting technology standards such as GSM that gave Nokia (and Swedish Ericsson) a valuable head start in the mobile phone market. European integration and cooperation also contributed indirectly by providing a conducive business environment. However, it is difficult to see other direct links of the European market integration with the early success of Nokia for the following reasons: the investment in strategic technologies took place in the 1980s and 1990s when the European market was less integrated than in the 2020s, and the stock price of Nokia peaked in 2000, around the time of the creation of the euro. Nokia was a global player, with the EU representing a significant portion of its market, but not the majority. Its production network was also globalized, with tens of thousands of workers employed outside Finland, mostly outside the EU. Nokia was listed on the New York Stock Exchange in 1994, but it was only listed on the Euronext Paris in 2015, after the decline of its mobile phone subsidiary.

7.2.2 Game of Chips: Semiconductor Rivalry Is Back

After decades of decline and stagnation, the European semiconductor industry became a minor player on the global stage when the COVID-19 pandemic pushed microchips to the fore as a critical product, perhaps only second to vaccines. Global shortages in a wide array of goods appeared in the wake of the pandemic, ranging from consumer electronics and appliances to cars. These shortages were attributed to a lack of semiconductors highlighting their ubiquitous applications. Global sales increased from $139 billion in 2001 to $527 billion in 2023 and are projected to reach about $650 billion in 2025 (SIA 2024). The European share in the global production declined from 44% in 1990 to 24% in 2000 and 8% in 2021 (Duchatel 2022; Huggins et al. 2023). The share of patents has been in decline as well while the remaining firms focused on niche markets (Huggins et al. 2023).

Losing advanced manufacturing to Asia and lagging behind the US and more recently China in fabless sales, or chip design, the European chip industry has maintained an important niche market in the semiconductor value chain. Out of twenty top semiconductor companies in the world by revenue in 2019, only four were European: ASML (equipment supplier), and three integrated device manufacturers (IDMs), STMicroelectronics, Infineon, and NXP Semiconductors (Huggins et al. 2023). In addition to ASML, suppliers such as ASM International in equipment, BASF in chemicals, and Siltronic in wafers are other players in the chip value chain. In the chip design space, the UK's ARM (owned by Softbank's Vision Fund and the object of a takeover attempt by the US's Nvidia) is a critical player while ASML is the sole supplier of cutting-edge lithography equipment to the foundries, or chip manufacturers, especially to TSMC. In addition, European IDMs have maintained relatively light production and relied on the Asian manufacturers, TSMS and Samsung, and Europe lacks foundries at the most advanced technological nodes. In terms of fabless sales, European firms have fallen behind China, which has been steadily gaining market share (Kleinhans and Baisakova 2020; SIA 2024).

With the disruptions in the global chip supplies during the COVID-19 pandemic as well as the increased technological rivalry between the US and China, especially in the cutting-edge semiconductor market, the future of Europe's chip industry has come to the forefront of the policy makers' agenda. The EU Chips Act that came into force in 2023 is designed to reinvigorate the European chip industry and increase its global market share of production capacity from 10% to 20% by 2030 (Huggins et al. 2023). The Act has allocated €43 billion to support new production facilities, create startups, and develop skills. It includes such initiatives as the supply chain mapping of the sector, the development of a virtual design platform to support firm entry, financing solutions through the Chips Fund, competence centres in all EU member states to provide access to the design platform, and the European Semiconductor Board to advise the European Commission (Kleinhans 2024). This array of policy tools is intended to tackle market failures that are particularly acute in the chips industry related to coordination among various stakeholders, economies of scale and learning, underinvestment in skills, and agglomeration externalities.

Concentrated in a few regions in Europe, the industry needs a focus on commercialization, collaboration across clusters, and increased investment to stage a comeback (Huggins et al. 2023). These semiconductor clusters are mainly located in Leuven (Belgium), Eindhoven (Netherlands), Dresden (Germany), Grenoble (France), Catania (Italy), and Cardiff (UK), the most recently created cluster. Huggins et al. (2023), having interviewed various actors in the industry, suggest that the European policy focuses mostly on research and much less on commercialization. There is a need for much higher scope for collaboration and knowledge sharing across clusters, which is being supported by Silicon Europe alliance. Manufacturing cutting-edge chips requires large investments, better integrated European supply chains, and local demand from end users of those chips.

The EU Chips Act calls for "digital sovereignty", but "indispensability" is another approach for the industry's revival. Self-sufficiency in semiconductors may be hard to achieve as the semiconductor industry is globally interdependent. Moreover, competition to attract incumbents could require giving large subsidies in the context of the US's Inflation Reduction Act (Cherif and Hasanov 2024). Although some question whether cutting-edge manufacturing is worthwhile to invest in before investing in chip design capabilities, a focus on key technologies and nodes in the value chain, emphasizing "indispensability" of the European firms (like Japan's model) could also be a feasible option (Kleinhans 2024; Duchatel 2022). Given the size of the European market, however, it is an open question whether to promote chip design first or target manufacturing and design simultaneously, and legislation would not necessarily solve it. Rather, policymakers and industry participants would have to decide which goals the European chips industry should pursue, redirecting policy tools and resources toward achieving those goals.

7.2.3 European Automotive Industry at the Crossroads

In the race to dominate the electric vehicle (EV) industry, a key cleantech technology, European firms started with clear advantages *a priori*. European firms were in the lead in the global markets of internal combustion engine (ICE) vehicles, including in China. They spanned all the segments of the market, from luxury to more accessible vehicles. The sector contributes to about 10% of manufacturing jobs in the EU, with production networks in several countries, accounting for a large share of the exports of Germany and several other European countries. The automotive industry also contributes massively to the total R&D expenditure and is one of the few high R&D intensity industries.

In the 2010s, the EV revolution was already gathering pace in the US and globally. While the cost of EVs was still high and the EV market share was below 1% of annual sales, evidence of a coming disruption was already clear by the mid-2010s (Cherif, Hasanov, and Pande 2017, 2021; Cherif, Hasanov, and Zhu 2021). Although major producers such as Volkswagen were already drafting ambitious plans to build EVs in 2017, they have been mostly playing catchup with Tesla in the luxury segment, and since the early 2020s with Chinese brands in all segments.

A few headwinds slowed the development of the European EV industry. European automotive firms were struggling to reach sufficient economies of scale in battery production, a critical input for EVs. However, beyond batteries, European firms have also been lagging behind US and Chinese counterparts in terms of software development, another key component of EVs. This is not surprising since leaders in the ICE market have not been well prepared for a radically different product structure, compared to new entrants building EVs from the bottom up.

An ambitious initiative, the European Battery Alliance (EBA), was put in place by the European Commission in 2017 to invest in battery technologies and production. The alliance gathers a wide array of actors such as EU national authorities, regions, and research institutes. Through an array of financial and regulatory tools (e.g., European Investment Bank), the EBA is designed to tackle market failures preventing the industry from reaching economies of scale and becoming competitive and innovative, by supporting all segments of the value chain, including by encouraging startups. By 2022, European investment in the battery ecosystem had already reached €180 billion.

7.3 A Few Stylized Facts: Relative Income, Investment, Exports, and Global Firms

A few stylized facts show that much of Europe has forged ahead while some countries have largely stagnated. Investment and manufacturing exports have slightly declined or barely have changed, but innovation has been low while large multinationals have fallen behind. Much of emerging Europe and the European periphery, including countries like Estonia and Ireland, have converged with advanced and core Europe, while some countries, like Greece and Italy, have fallen behind (Figs 7.1 and 7.2). The picture became much gloomier after the Global Financial Crisis (GFC) of 2008, resulting in slower growth in much of Europe, as in the US. Although investment and manufacturing exports have broadly held up on average, even before the 2008 crisis, innovation has been much lower than in the US while China has been fast in catching up. The share of European firms in *Fortune* Global 500 had been on a steady decline, and firms that have remained on the list are in traditional manufacturing sectors rather than high-technology sectors. The relatively good income performance was bound to come to an end once a large shock hit the economy, such as the 2008 Global Financial Crisis.

Fig. 7.1 The map of Europe. *Source*: Authors' classification.

The growth experience of the European countries for the 2000–2019 period (before the COVID-19 pandemic) suggests not only convergence for much of emerging Europe and some advanced European countries, but also stagnation or a decline for a few countries. In terms of relative income per capita compared to the US (measured in real GDP per capita in constant PPP dollars), most countries in Europe have improved their relative income rankings, especially in emerging Europe and core European countries, while the European periphery has stagnated or fallen behind (Fig. 7.2). All European countries (with Albania at the threshold) were either in the upper-middle-income category (above 20% of the relative US income) or high-income category (over 50% of the relative US income) in 2019.[7] Some of the lower-middle-income countries such as Bosnia and Herzegovina, Serbia, and Romania have crossed into upper-middle-income category while others in the upper-middle-income category, such as Estonia, Lithuania, and Poland, have reached high-income status by 2019. Several countries such as Hungary and Latvia have been converging slowly, remaining in the upper-middle-income category. Overall, they have done better than the rest of the emerging world (Fig. 7.2, green dots). Advanced Europe has broadly been closing the gap with the US, but many large countries, like France and the United Kingdom, have experienced growth similar to that of the US. Cyprus, Greece, and Italy have fallen behind, while Ireland, Norway, Luxembourg, and Switzerland have reached income per capita levels that exceed those of the US (literally, they are off the chart in Figure 7.2). Compared to other advanced countries (Fig. 7.2, yellow labels), the European core has been growing relatively well.

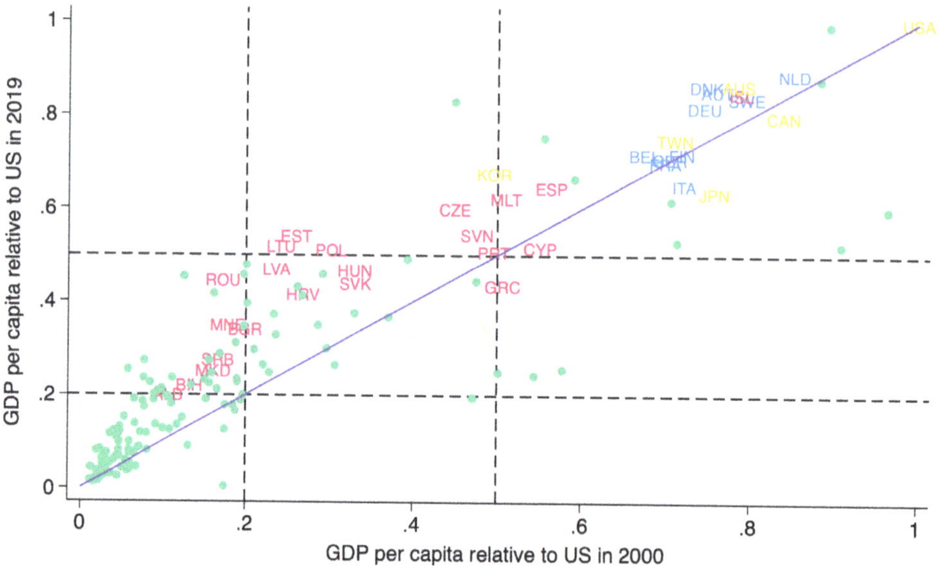

Fig. 7.2 The European growth experience, 2000–2019. *Source*: R. C. Feenstra, R. Inklaar, and M. P. Timmer (2015), "The Next Generation of the Penn World Table", *American Economic Review* 105(10): 3150–3182, https://doi.org/10.1257/aer.20130954

7 See Cherif and Hasanov (2019c) for a discussion of the middle-income trap and the income thresholds.

Yet this relatively optimistic picture of European growth becomes much less encouraging after the 2008 Global Financial Crisis. The European periphery in emerging Europe has been catching up but at a much slower rate, while Cyprus, Greece, and Spain have continued to fall behind. The European core countries have stagnated in relative income terms, growing as much as the US, with more countries such as Finland, Italy, and Netherlands falling behind (Figs 7.3 and 7.4). Relative incomes have not increased, including those in Germany and the UK (Fig. 7.3), and more worryingly, total factor productivity (TFP) has been on a declining or sideways trend in many European countries (Fig. 7.5). Germany seems to be an exception as its relative income has stayed the same, but its total factor productivity has grown since the GFC. For countries like Italy and Spain, it was mostly a declining trend with little growth in the late 2010s.

The growth picture becomes clearer in the recent decades when comparing TFP growth in the 2000s before the GFC and in the 2010s (Fig. 7.6). The TFP growth has slowed down almost everywhere and has turned to negative growth in some countries like Finland, Belgium, and Greece. In other countries like Portugal and Spain, TFP growth has become slightly positive, a better outcome compared to the numbers before the GFC, but still suggesting very low TFP growth. Even in Germany where TFP growth has stayed about the same, it is still relatively low, at about average 0.5% per year.[8]

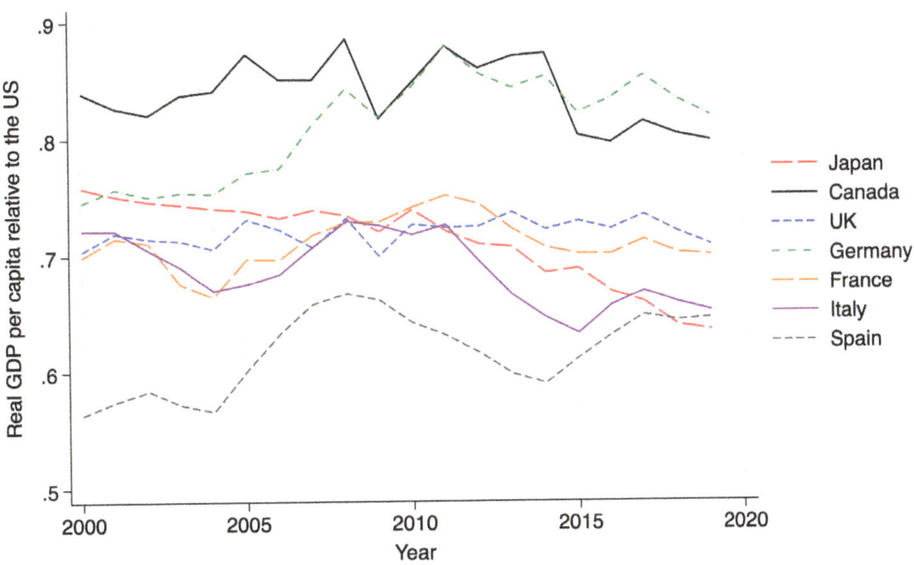

Fig. 7.3 Relative income for a few countries, 2000–2019. *Source*: R. C. Feenstra, R. Inklaar, and M. P. Timmer (2015), "The Next Generation of the Penn World Table", *American Economic Review* 105(10): 3150–3182, https://doi.org/10.1257/aer.20130954

8 The TFP data for the euro area and the UK through 2022 suggest that the gap with the US has not improved (Bergeaud 2024).

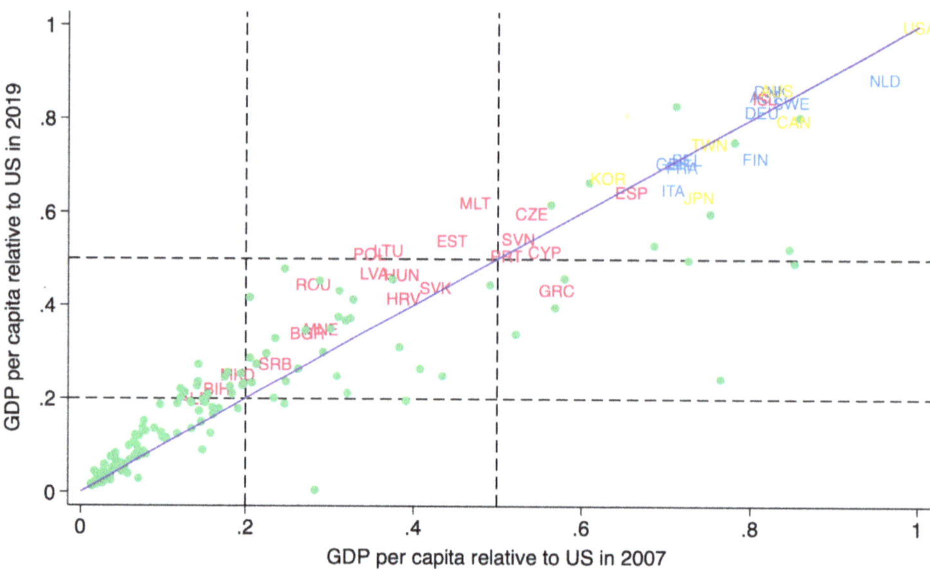

Fig. 7.4 Relative income, 2007–2019. *Source*: R. C. Feenstra, R. Inklaar, and M. P. Timmer (2015), "The Next Generation of the Penn World Table", *American Economic Review* 105(10): 3150–3182, https://doi.org/10.1257/aer.20130954

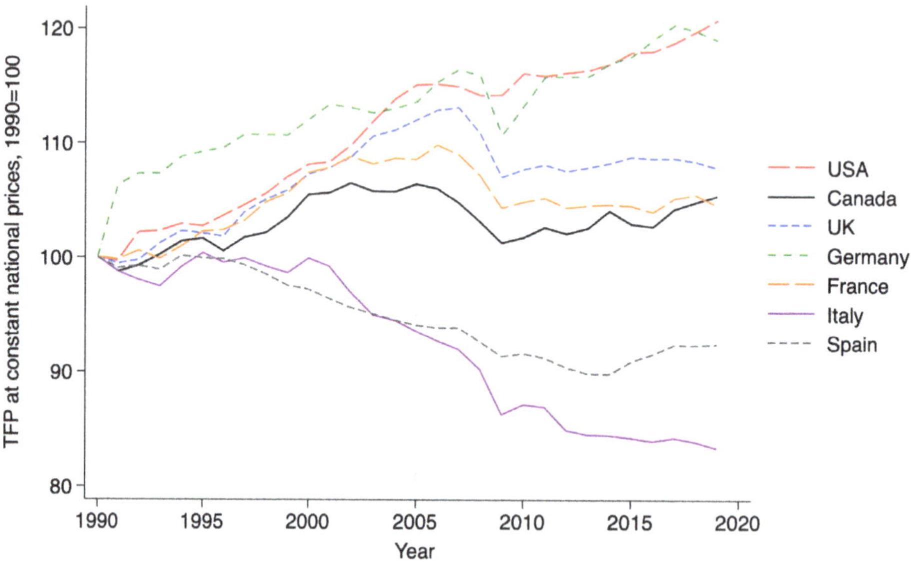

Fig. 7.5 Total factor productivity for a few countries, 1990–2019. *Source*: R. C. Feenstra, R. Inklaar, and M. P. Timmer (2015), "The Next Generation of the Penn World Table", *American Economic Review* 105(10): 3150–3182, https://doi.org/10.1257/aer.20130954

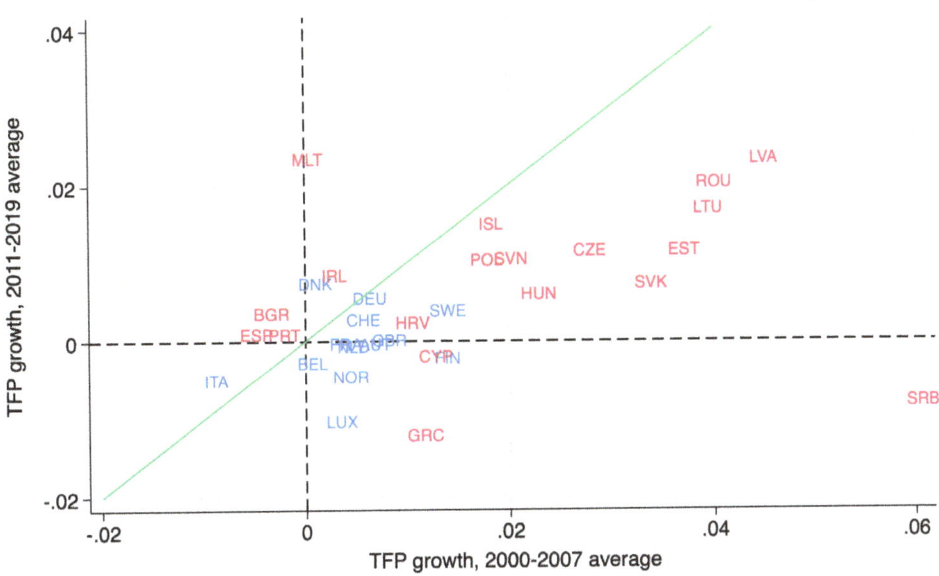

Fig. 7.6 Total factor productivity growth, 2000–2007 versus 2011–2019. *Source*: R. C. Feenstra, R. Inklaar, and M. P. Timmer (2015), "The Next Generation of the Penn World Table", *American Economic Review* 105(10): 3150–3182, https://doi.org/10.1257/aer.20130954

Although investment in machinery and transport has held up generally well, it has fallen since the 2008 GFC while manufacturing exports have not grown much. Both in the core and periphery Europe, investment fell to about 8% of GDP after 2008, as in other advanced countries like the US, although it was already on a declining trend in the European periphery (Fig. 7.7).[9] Real manufacturing exports per capita in the European core have been relatively high, about $15,000 per capita, and even the European periphery median investment of about $5000 per capita has been in line with that of other advanced countries. Yet in both European core and periphery, manufacturing exports' growth seems to have stalled. Total exports per capita exceed investment per capita in many countries, and richer countries have both high investment and exports per capita (Fig. 7.8). In addition, the global export market shares in sophisticated products like electronics, machinery, and vehicles of core European countries has been on a declining trend (Atlas of Economic Complexity 2024).

The striking pattern in the data is the relatively clear clustering of countries within three categories and the high level of dispersion among them. Periphery countries are clustered together and certain core countries are inching toward the periphery (e.g., Italy and Great Britain)—"main" core—while "advanced" core (e.g., Luxembourg and Switzerland) is clearly further away from the rest. On average, main and advanced core economies invest and export about two to three times, and five to seven times, respectively, more than the periphery economies. Meanwhile, some core European countries like Italy and the UK have relatively low investment and exports per capita, closer to those in the European periphery. Incidentally, these are the core economies that have been losing ground in terms of relative income and productivity.

9 Total investment is a bit above 20% of GDP on average in both European core and periphery.

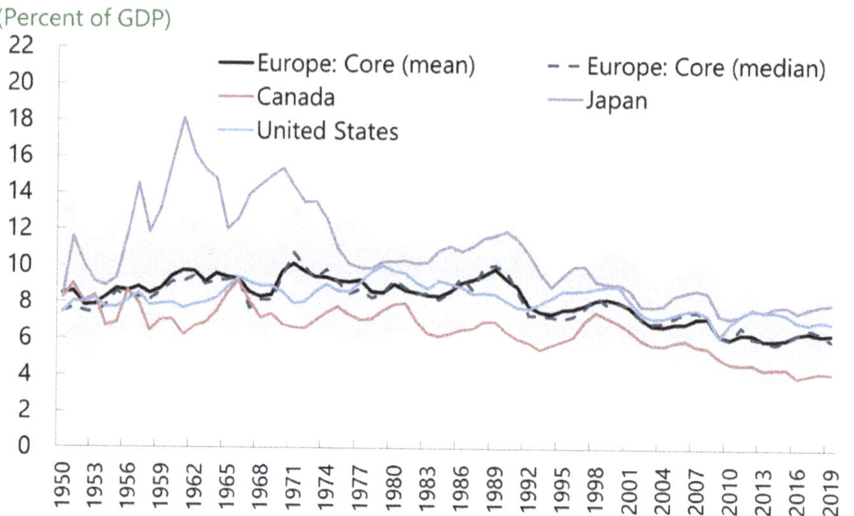

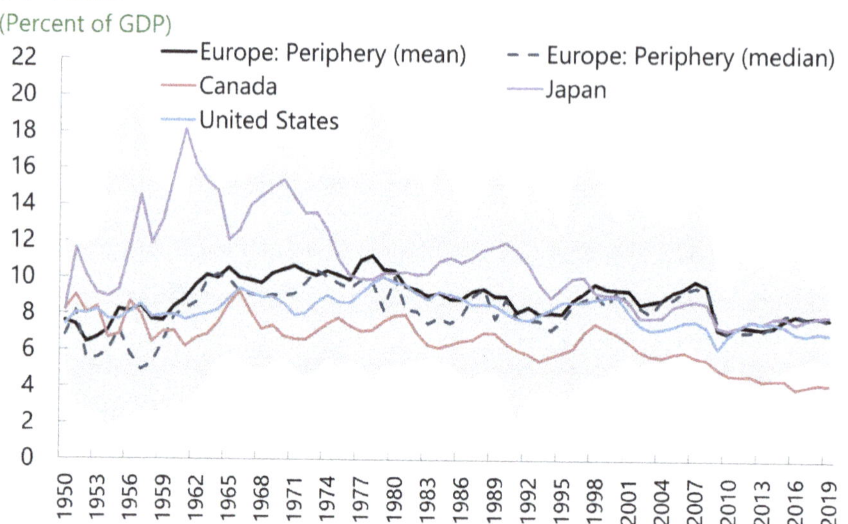

Fig. 7.7 Investment in machinery and transport equipment, 1950–2019, in (a) the core (above); (b) the periphery (below). *Source*: R. C. Feenstra, R. Inklaar, and M. P. Timmer (2015), "The Next Generation of the Penn World Table", *American Economic Review* 105(10): 3150–3182, https://doi.org/10.1257/aer.20130954. *Note*: shaded area indicates 5th to 95th percentiles of the core.

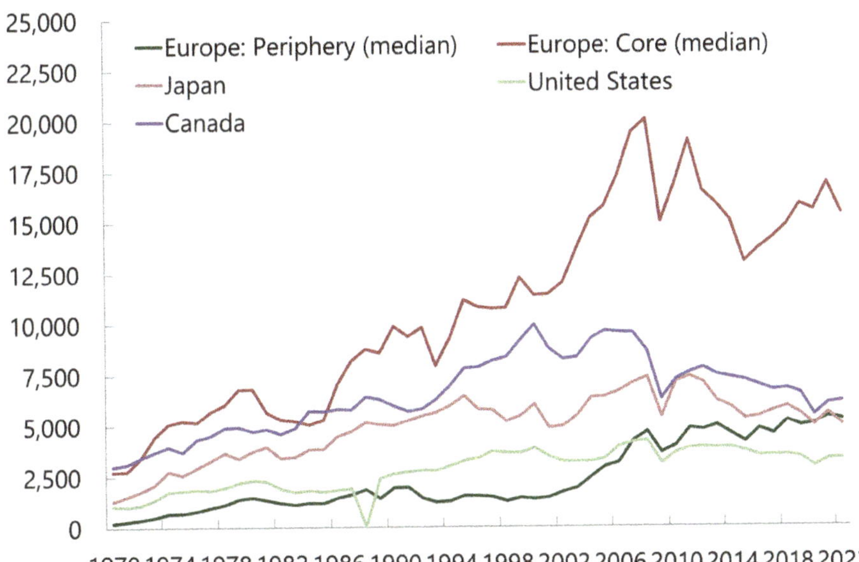

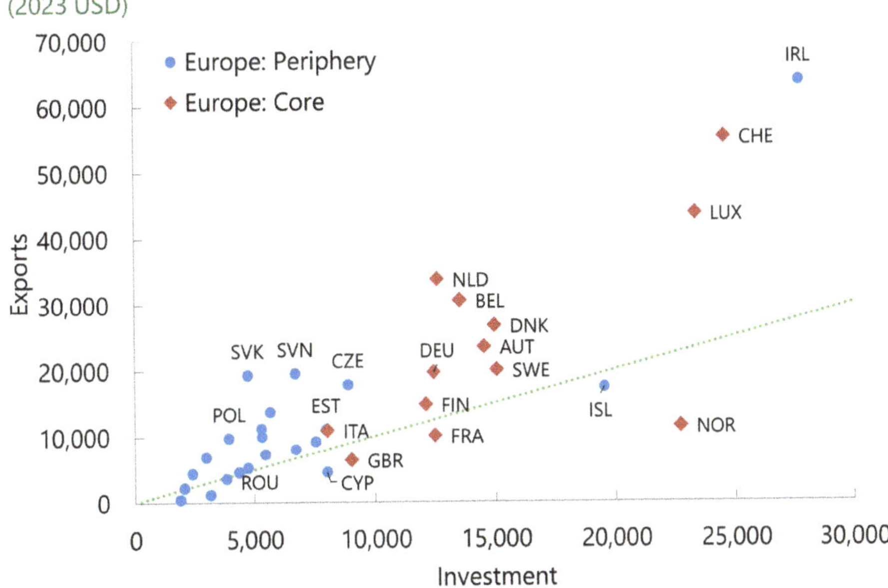

Fig. 7.8 Manufacturing exports and investment in (a) selected regions (constant 2022 USD) (above); (b) Europe (2023 USD) (below). *Source*: World Bank's World Development Indicators database and IMF's World Economic Outlook database. *Note*: the dotted line in (b) is a 45-degree line.

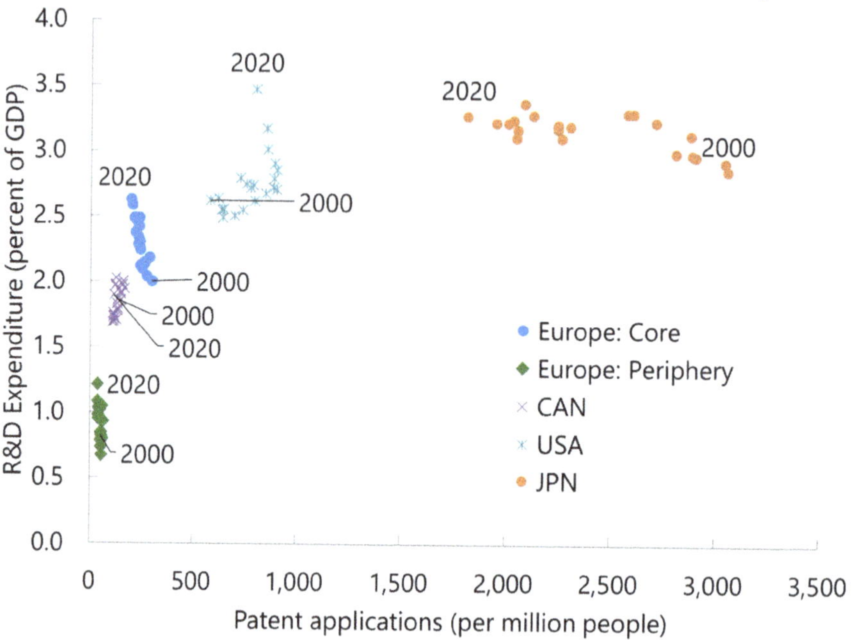

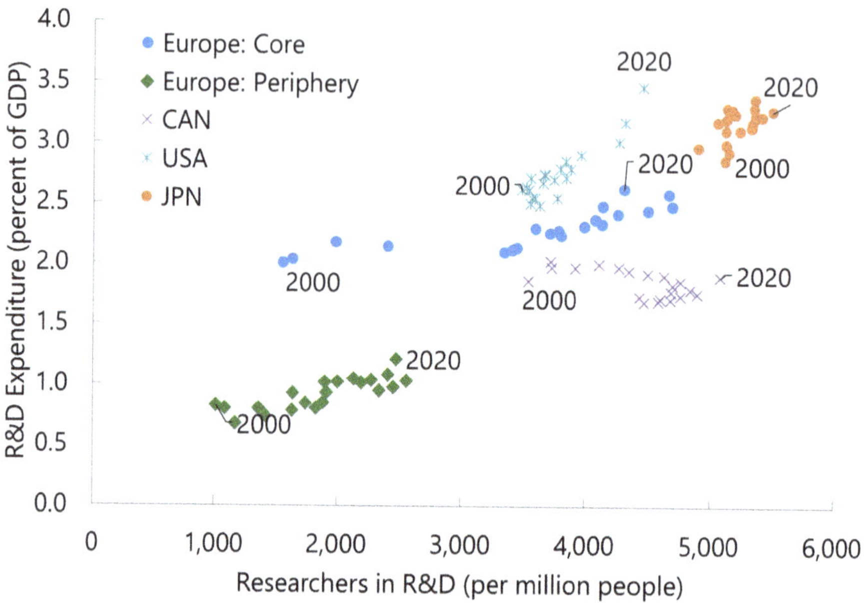

Fig. 7.9 Innovation in Europe: (a) patent application and R&D spending (above); (b) researchers in R&D and R&D spending (2000–2020) (below). *Source*: Our World in Data (2024) (data adapted from World Bank, United Nations) and World Bank's World Development Indicators database.

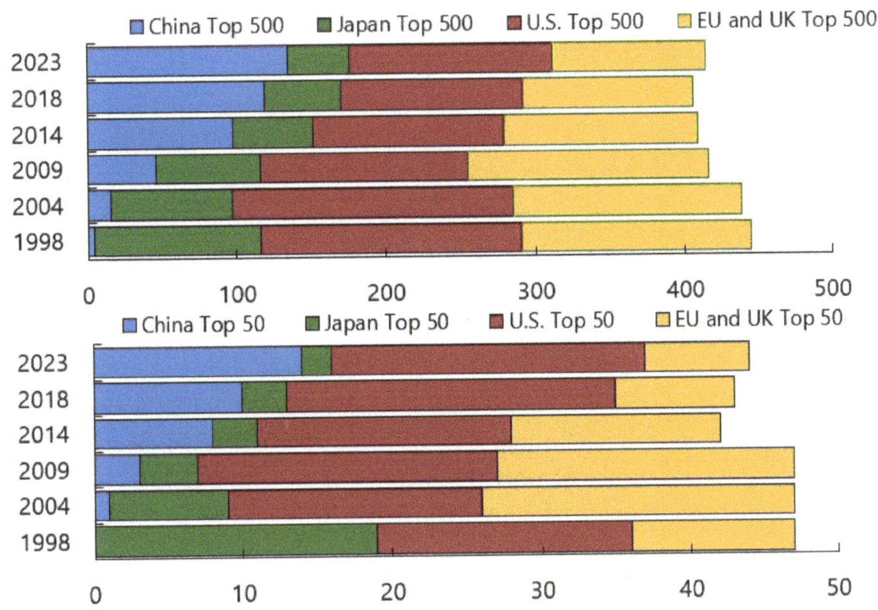

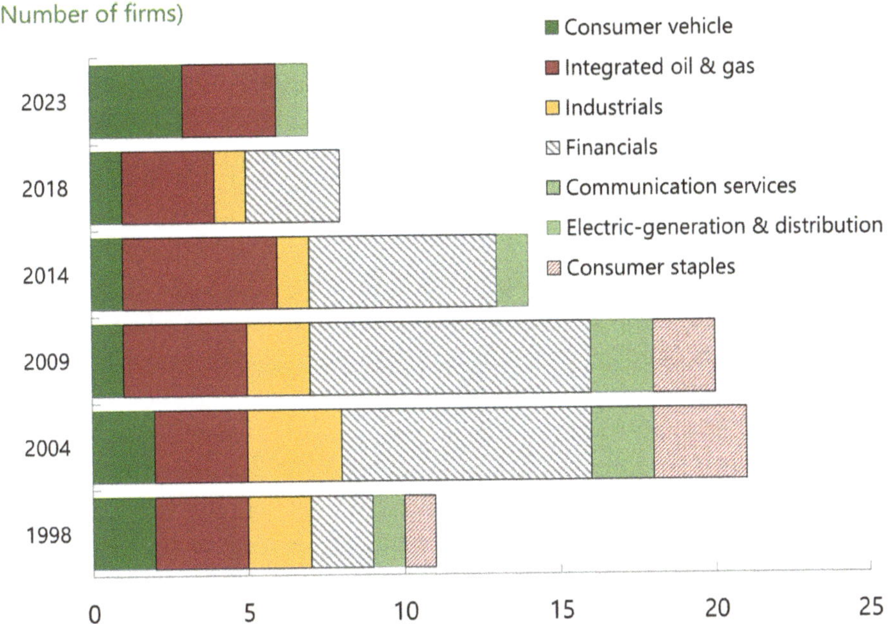

Fig. 7.10 *Fortune* Global 500. (a) Selected regions: *Fortune* Global 500 and 50 ownership (above); (b) EU and UK: *Fortune* Global 50 firm primary industry (below). *Source: Fortune* and S&P Capital IQ.

Lastly, more importantly, innovation indicators in Europe have largely been lagging behind those of the US and other top innovators, and large firms have been losing ground globally, which would have a negative effect on sophisticated sectors. The core Europe increased its R&D spending to about 2.5% of GDP by 2020 from 2% of GDP in 2000, still below the levels of the US and Japan, about 3.5% of GDP (Fig. 7.9). Bergeaud (2024) stresses the lower level of private R&D in Europe than in the US. This spending is mostly directed at mid-tech sectors such as automotive and chemicals, rather than high-tech sectors such as ICT and biotech, as in the US (Bergeaud 2024; Fuest et al. 2024). In addition, patent applications per capita, despite about the same number of researchers per capita as in the US and Canada, are much lower in Europe than in the US and are more comparable to that in Canada. The levels in the European periphery are much lower across various innovation indicators.

The sharp decline in the global standing of European firms is evident in their relative rankings in *Fortune* Global 500. In 1995, Europe had 153 firms on the list, but by 2023, that number had dropped to 103—a loss of 50 firms, less than Japan's decline (Fig. 7.10). The US lost only 18 firms, ending up with 136, while China gained ground substantially, increasing from just 3 firms to 135 by 2023. In addition, fewer than 10 European firms now rank among the global top 50, and most are in traditional manufacturing sectors rather than high-technology sectors (Fig. 7.10). This is consistent with the comparison of the US and European firms in terms of patents and R&D. In Europe, the top firms have broadly stayed the same since 2000 (mostly in chemicals, mobile communications, consumer electronics, and automotive) while in the US, they have changed substantially, moving from mid-tech to high-tech sectors such as software and advanced electronics (Bergeaud 2024; Fuest et al. 2024).

7.4 Technology and Innovation Policy—A TIP from the Asian Miracles and from Europe's Past

The sustained high growth of the Asian economic miracles, along with Europe's past successes, offer lessons for tackling growth and productivity challenges currently facing Europe. In particular, given declining export market shares in advanced products and the loss of global rankings of European firms, the creation and growth of sophisticated sectors should not be ignored. Indeed, Korea's experience, for example, is relevant for Europe's periphery where convergence has slowed down after 2008. The emergence of Korean and Taiwanese global players in high-tech sectors where they *a priori* had no prior experience (and even less "comparative advantage") is also instructive for European countries losing ground in the global top firm ranks. The experience of European economies, at the national level and through European-wide initiatives, as illustrated in the case studies, can help draw a path forward.

The key lessons from the Asian miracles can be summarized as follows: (i) a multifaceted state strategy that goes beyond traditional tools like tariffs/subsidies, to develop sophisticated, R&D-intensive industries; (ii) export, export, export: that is, an emphasis on export orientation and global markets; and (iii) the enforcement of accountability, even when the support received is indirect (e.g., collaboration programs with public research institutes or access to specialized infrastructure), along with fostering competition among firms (Cherif and Hasanov 2019a, 2019b). Spurring the creation and growth of firms in sophisticated industries is crucial. Export orientation should be key to increasing the scale and scope of industries and invigorating international competition. Providing support to these industries, rather than to particular firms, with clear conditions and progress monitoring in place, would increase the likelihood of success.

First, for the state to intervene in the economy, the focus on sophisticated sectors is key because this is where market failures are the most acute. These are high R&D-intensive sectors, which are largely advanced manufacturing and scientific and information technology services, most of which are linked to manufacturing (Cherif and Hasanov 2019a, 2019b). These sectors are riddled with market failures, and without state intervention, these sectors either do not exist or have low investment, R&D, and production. These sophisticated industries need to be selected. Various strategies such as quick wins and transformative strategies like leapfrogging and moonshots need to be pursued (Cherif, Hasanov, and Sarsenbayev 2024). Seizing opportunities in the existing industries such as automotive, aerospace, machinery, electronics, pharmaceuticals, and renewables could be quick wins with a focus on the short-term horizon, while the industries of the future like quantum computing, artificial intelligence (AI), and advanced cleantech and electronics would require leapfrogging and moonshot approaches, implying a longer horizon with substantial innovation and production support. This support does not imply protecting incumbent firms or outdated technologies like the internal combustion engine; rather, it is about providing support to build on new and emerging technologies like EVs.[10]

Second, export performance with a focus on global markets should be an important goal, and one at the heart of the accountability framework for firms receiving state support. This is a key insight from the Asian miracles, and the experience of European economies, and a defining difference between their successful industrial policies and the doomed import-substitution industrialization attempts of the 1970s and 1980s elsewhere (Cherif and Hasanov 2024). Competing with the best in the international markets requires improving cost competitiveness and efficiency and investing in product development and innovation from the onset. Competition in external markets provides the right incentives for firms to step up their game fast.[11] At the

---

10 See Cherif and Hasanov (2024) on the pitfalls of protectionism, who argue that protectionist policies may not help industries survive in the long run.

11 As economic pie is not fixed and trade is not necessarily a zero-sum game, a focus on exports without protectionism should not create a beggar-thy-neighbour environment and retaliation (Cherif and Hasanov 2024).

state level, export orientation would naturally entail exploring the European market, especially for periphery economies. It could be accomplished by supplying producers of sophisticated products or producing finished products. The European value chain network has supported the income convergence and could still be the key vehicle driving growth in the periphery. Yet one of the difficulties for the European periphery, especially in the eurozone, is the potential return of the "Dutch disease," as it is difficult to entice firms in the periphery to compete with firms in the core economies in sophisticated sectors when low-skilled service jobs are available (e.g., tourism), the dominant pattern before the 2008 GFC.

Third, the state support should only be provided with clear accountability signals. Export market performance serves as one of these market signals, as gaining global market shares allows the state to gauge performance and progress, as was the case in the Asian miracles. Domestic competition is another important element of the accountability framework. Supporting industries as a whole, rather than individual firms, is crucial because it is unclear which specific firm will succeed (Aghion 2016). Moreover, the industry support allows the state to redirect resources from laggards to frontier firms, thus ensuring the survival of the industry rather than propping up a failing firm. As firms fail, human and capital resources would not disappear, but rather would most likely move to other firms in the same industry, raising the chances of success (Ali-Yrkko et al. 2021). Supporting firm entry rather than only directing resources to incumbents is as important to the development of the industry in the global arena.

Europe already has in place most of the tools implemented in the Asian miracles, including business support and competition rules, skill training, financing, R&D support, and research and industry clusters, to be used for the creation and growth of sophisticated sectors. The single market provides technology standards, common rules, and favourable business environment as more work is underway to improve its workings (IMF 2024a, 2024b; Letta 2024; and Arnold, Claveres, and Frie 2024). Tackling market failures in sophisticated sectors, where firms may hesitate to enter or may underinvest, requires redirecting existing support tools toward these industries. Many countries already offer R&D grants and tax credits, while top research universities and public research institutes engage in a range of basic and applied research. Industry clusters further promote applied research and production. Commercialization of the technology is an important stage of TIP, and financing is key. Various investment and innovation schemes exist either via European institutions like the European Investment Bank (EIB) or the European Innovation Fund (EIF) or national development banks like Germany's KfW. There are ongoing discussions about creating breakthrough innovation initiatives similar to the US's Defense Advanced Research Projects Agency (DARPA).

Correcting market failures that prevent the development of sophisticated sectors must be at the top of government priorities:[12] this involves identifying or creating an

12 The lack or underdevelopment of sophisticated sectors stems from a myriad of market failures, requiring policy tools to address them.

adequate institutional apparatus where the highest levels of the government frequently monitor the progress and coordination of all stakeholders. This should be done through a high-level representation of all relevant stakeholders for the sophisticated sector(s) targeted (e.g., education, infrastructure, regulation, trade).[13] Following in the footsteps of the Asian miracles, it would also require acquiring (or often reacquiring) technical capabilities within government institutions to be able to collaborate, monitor, and receive feedback from the firms in a way that is impartial and independent from political interference—that is, "embedded autonomy" as outlined by Evans (1995). In addition, on the European level, an agency like the European Commission (EC) needs to coordinate policies and support across all countries, ensuring the flow of information, knowledge, and supporting tools. This approach, as exemplified by the EU Chips Act for the semiconductor industry, aims to tackle coordination and information failures.

All-in-all, at the European level, there are several ways to apply the principles of TIP. European policies and regulations could distinguish between the periphery and core, allowing for adjustments to competition and regulation policies that take into account the need for the periphery to catch up, especially in terms of exports of sophisticated products. Given the technological gap between core and periphery and the long time required to catch up, such a distinction is unlikely to alter or "distort" the single market and would eventually reinforce it. A particular emphasis could be placed on creating or extending value chains connecting the periphery to the core in sophisticated/complex industries. In parallel, as argued earlier, core Europe is facing the challenge of accelerated disruptions, including in industries where they have had a dominant position for decades, such as automotive and renewables. Far from trying to protect dying industries, policies applying existing business support tools could help incumbents pivot to more innovative products or industries while encouraging the creation and growth of new entrants. In other words, policies should also aim to create new firms in sophisticated industries—similar to the emergence of Tesla, challenging established auto firms back in the 2010s.

In practice, the following broad economic issues could be considered for a TIP in Europe:

First, a redeployment of European support tools toward the development of sophisticated industries,[14] not only for innovation but also for production and diffusion to reach economies of scale and support knowledge spillovers, is in order. This implies spending differently and potentially spending more. For example, since its inception and until 2023, agricultural subsidies represented the largest share of the European budget (about a third on average), and it is more unequally distributed to favour large firms over small farmers (Aghion, Cherif, and Hasanov 2022). Meanwhile, agriculture represents a small fraction of employment, on average

13 For example, biotech would require coordinating with the Ministry of Health.

14 See footnote 13.

about 1%, and contributes marginally to R&D expenditure and productivity gains, which potentially redirected financing could support, promoting innovation and technology deployment and diffusion, solving market failures of inadequate access to finance and technological uncertainties. While increased spending may lead to a rising deficit and public debt in the short run—a potential challenge when these are already relatively high—the potential for higher productivity growth in the medium to long run, driven by sophisticated sectors and their spillover effects on other industries, could make this a worthwhile trade-off. Growth is one of the most significant drivers of public debt dynamics (Cherif and Hasanov 2018). In addition, the accountability framework and governance structure of the state support to industries and firms are key to the successful implementation of the policy and need to be designed correctly with the emphasis on a few critical elements: "embedded autonomy" of the institution, clear market signals from firms receiving support (e.g., exports, innovation, and global market shares), strong domestic competition, and the withdrawal of support if market signal criteria are not met.

The redeployment of resources could not only involve fiscal policy but also use various public investment vehicles to catalyze private finance. EIB, EIF, national development banks, and other institutions are key to derisking private investment and innovation spending (Mazzucato 2013). Funds of funds are needed to provide more directed funding to venture capitalists (VCs), enabling them to invest in these sophisticated sectors to create and grow startups. Next, commercial banks, pension funds, insurance companies, and other financial intermediaries could be given incentives to provide necessary funding for scaleups (Arnold, Claveres, and Frie 2024). In brief, the whole innovation chain needs to be provided with adequate financing to succeed.

What is important for productivity gains and growth is not only innovation but also manufacturing with a focus on the portfolio approach, which we call "the state as a venture capitalist". This approach implies that the state programs have to take a portfolio view in providing support to industries and firms just like VCs take a portfolio view in their investments. For instance, a financing program acting as a catalyst alongside traditional private investors for scaleups would be evaluated at a program or portfolio level. This evaluation would compare the benefits obtained from loans to successful companies like Tesla with losses of failed ventures like Solyndra. In addition, as innovation produces designs and prototypes and employs highly skilled workers, it may not be sufficient for a broad-based inclusive growth, reaching out to many regions and different types of workers. Manufacturing of these newly developed advanced goods and products is important for spillovers and feedback loops in and across industries. This approach is part of a broader competition policy needed to create a flow of new entrants into the markets that innovate and produce, a key feature of the Schumpeterian growth paradigm. Whether for innovation or manufacturing, as support is given to firms, flexible rather than rigid accountability frameworks focused on principles rather than prescribed rules for all possibilities would allow adaptation and pivoting as circumstances change. It is "the state as a venture capitalist" approach to supporting industries that allows flexibility with a focus on an industry or a set of industries with various policy tools, including financing programs, skill training, regulatory and legal overhaul, and the provision of purpose-specific infrastructure. While it is impossible to identify ex ante which specific firms will succeed, it is feasible to select winning sophisticated industries as a portfolio (Adler 2021). This can be achieved by implementing the right set of policy tools and accountability frameworks.

Second, a better coordination of policy tools and stakeholders, including financing vehicles, universities, and public research institutes, across countries would facilitate the formulation of a coherent strategy. Drawing from the experience of Nokia in the 1980s and 1990s, a coordination of European policies would help identify technologies of the future, create European technology standards (such as GSM), ensure close collaboration with the private sector when setting up standards, and finally leverage procurement to spur innovation. This approach could be spearheaded by the EC at the European level while national agencies or ministries could be focused on the country's progress.

Third, while the European market is one of the largest in the world, and the benefit of geographic proximity gives a natural advantage to intra-European trade, the experience of the last decade (e.g., chips, Nokia, and EVs) has shown that for sophisticated industries, the markets are global. In other words, policies should aim at achieving international competitiveness rather than protecting incumbents in their domestic or regional markets. Tariffs, for example, do not necessarily provide an incentive to attain cost competitiveness and may only delay the inevitable demise of the industry (Cherif and Hasanov 2024). Rather, the focus on exports and global markets to compete with the best, continuously innovating on a product level and manufacturing processes, is the path to success.

7.5 Concluding Remarks

The European integration showed broadly impressive results up to the 2008 GFC, with the periphery catching up rapidly with the core, while the core was catching up with the US. However, the initial growth models, with relatively low levels of exports of sophisticated products in the periphery and low R&D investment in most of Europe, showed their limits in the post-GFC era. The rate of convergence of the periphery slowed down dramatically, while some large core economies stagnated. Moreover, in the core economies, the spectre of disruption from international competitors looms large. The cases of Nokia, the semiconductor industry in Europe, or the EV industry in the 2020s illustrate this challenge well. This is confirmed by the secular decline in the number of European firms appearing in the top rankings of global firms, especially in sophisticated and high-tech industries.

One can distil lessons from the growth experience of the Asian miracles and the European growth experience to explore growth strategies in Europe. It comprises following three simple principles: steering resources toward correcting market failures to support the development of sophisticated industries; emphasizing exports and global markets; and enforcing competition and accountability. In practice, it means a reappraisal of the approach toward sophisticated sectors to help spur more technology creation in the periphery and the core, produce newly developed goods and services, and connect supply chains in sophisticated industries. Far from the caricatural "hard" industrial policy tools of the past (e.g., tariffs and unconditional subsidies), this effort requires policy tailored to correcting market failures, as part of a holistic approach (e.g., purpose-specific investment and regulation), a continuous market feedback, flexibility, and a tolerance for risk-taking. This approach should lead to an increase in R&D expenditure, which ultimately produces more innovation and advanced manufacturing, resulting in higher productivity and income growth.

At this critical juncture, Europe would benefit from a strong coordination among states and a reorientation of policy tools to spur dynamism and competition in sophisticated industries to keep creating new champions, capable of competing internationally and reaching the list of top global firms.

References

Adler, D. (2021) "Inside Operation Warp Speed: A New Model for Industrial Policy", *American Affairs* V(2): 3–32, https://americanaffairsjournal.org/2021/05/inside-operation-warp-speed-a-new-model-for-industrial-policy/

Aghion, P. (2016) "Growth Policy Design for Middle-Income Countries", in R. Cherif, F. Hasanov, and M. Zhu (eds), *Breaking the Oil Spell: The Gulf Falcons' Path to Diversification*. Washington, DC: International Monetary Fund, pp. 117–130.

Aghion, P., R. Cherif, and F. Hasanov (2022) "Competition and Innovation", in V. Cerra, B. Eichengreen, A. El-Ganainy, and M. Schindler (eds), *How To Achieve Inclusive Growth*. Oxford: Oxford University Press, pp. 212–237.

Arnold, N., G. Claveres, and J. Frie (2024) "Stepping Up Venture Capital to Finance Innovation in Europe", *IMF Working Paper* 24/146.

Atlas of Economic Complexity, The (2024) Harvard University, Growth Lab, https://atlas.cid.harvard.edu.

Bergeaud, A. (2024) "The Past, Present, and Future of European Productivity", Working Paper, ECB Forum on Central Banking, July 1–3, https://www.ecb.europa.eu/pub/pdf/sintra/ecb.forumcentbankpub2024_Bergeaud_paper.en.pdf

Ali-Yrkkö, J., R. Cherif, F. Hasanov, N. Kuosmanen, and M. Pajarinen (2021) "Knowledge Spillovers from Superstar Tech-Firms: The Case of Nokia", *IMF Working Paper* 2021/258, https://www.imf.org/en/Publications/WP/Issues/2021/10/29/Knowledge-Spillovers-From-Superstar-Tech-Firms-The-Case-of-Nokia-501347

Cherif, R., and F. Hasanov (2018) "Public Debt Dynamics: The Effects of Austerity, Inflation, and Growth Shocks", *Empirical Economics* 54(3): 1087–1105.

Cherif, R., and F. Hasanov (2019a) "Return of the Policy That Shall Not Be Named: Principles of Industrial Policy", *IMF Working Paper* 2019/74, https://www.imf.org/en/Publications/WP/Issues/2019/03/26/The-Return-of-the-Policy-That-Shall-Not-Be-Named-Principles-of-Industrial-Policy-46710

Cherif, R., and F. Hasanov (2019b) "Principles of True Industrial Policy", *Journal of Globalization and Development* 10(1): 1–22.

Cherif, R., and F. Hasanov (2019c) "The Leap of the Tiger: Escaping the Middle-income Trap to the Technological Frontier", *Global Policy* 10(4): 497–511.

Cherif, R., and F. Hasanov (2024) "The Pitfalls of Protectionism: Import Substitution vs. Export-Oriented Industrial Policy", *Journal of Industry, Competition and Trade* 24(1): 1–34.

Cherif, R., F. Hasanov, and A. Pande (2017) "Riding the Energy Transition: Oil Beyond 2040", *IMF Working Paper* 2017/120, https://www.imf.org/en/Publications/WP/Issues/2017/05/22/Riding-the-Energy-Transition-Oil-Beyond-2040-44932

Cherif, R., F. Hasanov, and A. Pande (2021) "Riding the Energy Transition: Oil beyond 2040", *Asian Economic Policy Review* 16(1): 117–137.

Cherif, R., F. Hasanov, and M. Sarsenbayev (2024) "Call of Duty: Industrial Policy for Post-Oil Era", *IMF Working Paper* 2024/74. https://www.imf.org/en/Publications/WP/Issues/2024/03/29/Call-of-Duty-Industrial-Policy-for-the-Post-Oil-Era-546941

Cherif, R., F. Hasanov, and P. Aghion (2023) "Fair and Inclusive Markets: Why Dynamism Matters", *IMF Working Paper* 2021/29, https://www.imf.org/en/Publications/WP/Issues/2021/02/06/Fair-and-Inclusive-Markets-Why-Dynamism-Matters-50052

Cherif, R., F. Hasanov, and M. Zhu (2021) "The Electric Vehicle Revolution Goes Global", August 30, *Project Syndicate*, https://www.project-syndicate.org/commentary/electirc-vehicles-in-developing-and-emerging-economies-by-reda-cherif-et-al-2021-08

Draghi, M. (2024a) "Radical Change—Is What Is Needed", Speech at the High-level Conference on the European Pillar of Social Rights, Brussels, April 16, https://geopolitique.eu/en/2024/04/16/radical-change-is-what-is-needed/

Draghi, M. (2024b) *The Future of European Competitiveness*. Brussels: European Commission, https://commission.europa.eu/document/download/97e481fd-2dc3-412d-be4c-f152a8232961_en

Duchatel, M. (2022) "Semiconductors in Europe: The Return of Industrial Policy" *Institut Montaigne*, Policy Paper, https://www.institutmontaigne.org/ressources/pdfs/publications/europe-new-geopolitics-technology-1.pdf

European Commission (2024) "Euro Area Competitiveness: Opportunities and Value Added of a European Industrial Policy. A Note to the Eurogroup for June 20, 2024 Meeting", https://www.consilium.europa.eu/media/dfcjg0yd/com-note-ea-competitiveness-industrial-policy.pdf

Evans, P. (1995) *Embedded Autonomy: States and Industrial Transformation*. Princeton, NJ: Princeton University Press.

Fortune (1998) "The World's Largest Corporations", 138(3): F1–F10.

Fortune (2010) "Global 500", 162(2): 153–F7.

Fortune (2015) "Global 500", 172(2): F1–F6.

Fuest, C., D. Gros, P. Mengel, G. Presidente, and J. Tirole (2024) "How to Escape the Middle Technology Trap", *EconPol Policy Report*, April, https://www.econpol.eu/publications/policy_report/eu-innovation-policy-how-to-escape-the-middle-technology-trap

Heimer, M. (2019) "The List", *Fortune* 180(2): 122–118.

Heimer, M. (2023) "The List", *Fortune* 188(1): F1–F6.

Hjelt, P. (2004) "The Fortune Global 500", *Fortune* 150(2): 159–186.

Hodge, A., R. Piazza, F. Hasanov, X. Li, M. Vaziri, A. Weller, and Y. C. Wong (forthcoming) "Industrial Policy in Europe: A Single Market Perspective", *IMF Working Paper*.

Huggins, R., A. Johnston, M. Munday, and C. Xu (2023) "Competition, Open Innovation, and Growth Challenges in the Semiconductor Industry: The Case of Europe's Clusters", *Science and Public Policy* 50: 531–547.

IMF (2024a) "Euro Area Policies—2024 Annual Consultation", *IMF Country Report* 24/248, https://www.imf.org/en/Publications/CR/Issues/2024/07/29/Euro-Area-Policies-2024-Annual-Consultation-Press-Release-Staff-Report-and-Statement-by-the-552578

IMF (2024b) "Soft Landing in Crosswinds for a Lasting Recovery", *IMF Regional Economic Outlook*, April, https://www.imf.org/en/Publications/REO/EU/Issues/2024/04/05/regional-economic-outlook-europe-april-2024

Kleinhans, J.-P. (2024) "The Missing Strategy in Europe's Chip Ambitions", July, *interface*, https://www.interface-eu.org/publications/europe-semiconductor-strategy

Kleinhans, J.-P., and N. Baisakova (2020) "The Global Semiconductor Value Chain: A Technology Primer for Policymakers", October, *Stiftung Neue Verantwortung Policy Paper*.

Letta, E. (2024) *Much More Than a Market*, https://www.consilium.europa.eu/media/ny3j24sm/much-more-than-a-market-report-by-enrico-letta.pdf

Mazzucato, M. (2013) *The Entrepreneurial State: Debunking Public vs. Private Sector Myths*. New York: Public Affairs.

Pisano, G., and W. Shih (2012) *Producing Prosperity: Why America Needs a Manufacturing Renaissance*. Cambridge, MA: Harvard Business Review Press.

SIA (2024) "Semiconductor Industry Association Factbook", *SIA*, https://www.semiconductors.org/resources/factbook/

Stiglitz, J. E., and B. C. Greenwald (2014) *Creating a Learning Society: A New Approach to Growth, Development, and Social Progress*. New York: Columbia University Press. https://doi.org/10.7312/stig15214

8. Industrial Policy and Security. The European Union and the Double Challenge: Strengthening Competitiveness and Enhancing Economic Security

Paolo Guerrieri[1] *and Pier Carlo Padoan*[2]

This chapter argues that the European Union's (EU) dual challenge—enhancing both competitiveness and economic security—must form the core of its open strategic autonomy framework, which integrates national security considerations with economic policy. The chapter explores the vulnerabilities and strengths of the EU's industrial and technological strategies, emphasizing the need for deeper European integration and more robust governance to meet these challenges. Central to this effort is the provision of European public goods (EPGs), such as climate policy, energy security, and technological development, which require stronger EU-level governance and financial resources. To ensure long-term resilience and relevance in a fragmented world, Europe must undertake a profound restructuring of its economic governance and enhance its strategic autonomy.

8.1 Introduction

The European Commission released its latest package of economic security measures at the end of January 2024 (European Commission 2024). It includes a broad range of initiatives: enhancing screening for inbound and outbound investments, controlling

1 Luiss Institute for European Analysis and Policy (LEAP) and Paris School of International Affairs (PSIA), Sciences-Po.

2 Luiss Institute for European Analysis and Policy (LEAP).

 https://doi.org/10.11647/OBP.0434.09

sensitive exports, and increasing research funding for dual-use technology. The package implements and further develops the European Economic Security Strategy launched in June 2023 (European Commission 2023b). The objective is to foster growth, defend the European Union against unfair trade practices, and collaborate with allies, aligning it with the principles of "promoting, protecting, and partnering".

The European Commission's release of measures underscores the increasing importance of economic security in the EU's agenda, particularly in light of political tensions and global economic shifts like the Russian invasion of Ukraine. In addition, the new global context poses significant challenges to the EU's long-term economic competitiveness. Europe has been one of the largest beneficiaries of the intense globalization in recent decades, relying on a growth model based on cheap imported energy, medium- and low-tech industries, and net exports to the rest of the world, especially China. The ongoing reconfiguration of the global economy, driven by rising energy prices, fragmentation of the global trade regime, and the emergence of new technological digital clusters, has rendered this traditional growth model unsustainable. To regain competitiveness, Europe's productive supply needs radical restructuring and reconversion (Guerrieri and Padoan 2024).

Europe therefore faces a twofold challenge in this turbulent world: strengthening competitiveness while enhancing economic security. A greener and more competitive Union can indeed provide an effective response to make the EU more resilient and secure. But it is a complex task that requires a series of highly complex initiatives and policies, both domestically and internationally, with a lot of trade-offs between promoting growth and reducing risk. As will be argued in this chapter, this dual challenge must form the basis of Europe's so-called open strategic autonomy (OSA), a concept that has long been debated in Europe and has played a central role in defining the strategies of the von der Leyen Commission in recent years (Steinberg and Wolff 2023). The concept emphasizes the need for Europe to become a stronger player in the geopolitical arena while maintaining an open and competitive market economy. OSA integrates "national" security considerations into EU economic policy, akin to approaches taken in the United States and Japan. The fact is that you can't separate the agenda of economic security from that of European competitiveness, as done in the past. The EU has taken some steps in this direction. But much more needs to be done.

This chapter delves into the multifaceted dimensions of OSA (section 2), analyzing vulnerabilities and strengths of the EU in competitiveness and economic security, and proposing policy solutions. It explores the challenges to Europe in industrial strategies and policy (sections 3 and 4), economic security measures (section 5). These challenges characterize the current global scenario and have relevant spillover effects on the EU economy. The last part of the chapter (section 6) points out that the twin goals of enhancing economic security and competitiveness require deepening European integration, providing EU governance with more effective policy tools and increasing financial resources at the European level.

8.2 The Concept of Strategic Autonomy

The term "strategic autonomy" first emerged over a decade ago in the context of European security and defence issues (Tocci 2021). However, its usage later shifted towards European economic matters, such as ensuring the security of supply chains and fostering technological sovereignty. This shift was prompted by a series of events and crises that characterized the international scene over the past decade, including the rise of China under Xi Jinping, Donald Trump's protectionist policies, the COVID-19 pandemic, and more recently, energy shocks and the invasion of Ukraine.

And it is with reference to its economic aspects that this chapter analyzes EU strategic autonomy. It will highlight how in Europe the concept has often been defined as "open strategic autonomy" (OSA) stressing the need for a delicate balance between safeguarding European strategic assets and the imperative of maintaining the EU's economic openness and integration with international markets (European Commission 2021).

The precise definition and scope of strategic autonomy have been subjects of many debates and different interpretation across Europe (Tamma 2020; Meunier and Nicolaidis 2019; Schmitz and Seidl 2023; Lavery 2023; Wigger 2023). In June 2023, the Commission published its "Economic Security Strategy and Strategic Autonomy" document, focusing on promoting competitiveness, protecting citizens, forging partnerships, and providing general guidelines to inform member countries' choices and policies (European Commission 2023b). More recently, by the end of January, the Commission—as already noted—published its second package of economic security measures (European Commission 2024)

The heightened attention to the concept of strategic autonomy is a response to the new phase of geopolitical rivalry shaping international economic relations. In this context, the balance of power between countries, particularly the clash between the US and China, takes precedence over multilateral rules and institutions (Lake 2021). Uncertainty and risk increasingly influence economic life, with interdependence becoming a source of both opportunity and vulnerability, often referred to as "weaponized interdependence" (Farrell and Newman 2019). Consequently, the traditional concept of national security is evolving to include economic security.

This new world has created difficult challenges for the EU, whose institutions were designed to operate in a rules-based world. Unlike the US and China, foreign and security policy within the EU largely remains the prerogative of Member States (Zuleeg 2023). Economic security and geopolitics were thus far removed from the "four freedoms" (free movement of goods, services, people, and capital) that have characterized how the European economy has functioned for decades. However, this detachment is no longer sustainable. The EU must now navigate a global context marked by major power competition while ensuring its own security through economic means, necessitating the integration of economic and geopolitical decision-making processes (Guerrieri and Padoan 2024).

Awareness of this challenge is growing in Europe, yet the EU remains relatively unprepared for a world of geopolitics and great power competition. This vulnerability is compounded by the loss of competitiveness suffered by Europe vis-à-vis the US, China, and other advanced countries. In the following sections, we will analyze these vulnerabilities, beginning with Europe's greatest challenge: the ecological transition and the Green Deal.

8.3 The Key Role of Industry and Industrial Policy

The energy crisis, coupled with escalating geopolitical conflicts, has posed significant challenges to the growth model of continental European economies (Baccaro and Hadziabdic 2023), as previously discussed, and has consequently affected their productive structures. The current hardships faced by Germany and its manufacturing industry confirm this reality. Given Germany's status as Europe's economic powerhouse, the ripple effects of Germany's economic issues are felt throughout Europe.

A fundamental transformation of European manufacturing is imperative. It involves shifting away from energy-intensive production towards less energy-intensive industrial segments and embracing digital technologies to enhance competitiveness. This presents a formidable challenge for Europe amidst international industrial and technological competition, particularly between the United States and China, both of which are implementing expansive industrial policies and mobilizing substantial public resources.

However, achieving these goals is complicated. The objectives of a green industrial strategy extend beyond enhancing productivity and fostering innovation to encompass securing Europe's technological and industrial position. Closing the gap with the US and China in technological prowess, particularly in the digital realm, is crucial for economic security and the attainment of genuine strategic autonomy of Europe. In a geo-economic world, enhanced technological capacity serves as a deterrent and containment measure against the advancement of rival technological industries.

This is more the case as Europe's competitive lag has significant implications for key sectors central to the current digital revolution, such as microprocessors, big data, and Artificial Intelligence (AI). Addressing this lag necessitates substantial adjustments and restructuring processes, which is primarily the responsibility of individual European countries. That this will not be enough and that no European country will be able to do it alone is a widespread and well-documented conviction.

Strengthening and restoring the industrial and technological competitiveness of the EU goes beyond national policies. It requires a concerted effort at the European level, avoiding protectionist tendencies and benefitting on a European scale. This is the key to success in many areas, such as AI, where Europe is particularly lagging behind. While the EU and the United States have roughly the same number of startups, the Americans have access to ten times more funding than their European counterparts, which allows them to scale up their industries more quickly.

In the digital world, we think and act on a planetary scale. To compete with non-EU big tech, Europe needs to join forces so that "European champions" can emerge from national industrial ecosystems on a global scale. To strengthen its techno-industrial position, the EU needs to create centralized resources. This will enable the Commission to co-finance early-stage, capital-intensive critical technology projects. This applies not only to high tech, but also to defence and national security.

The first initiatives promoting economic resilience and industrial capacity, particularly in green and technology sectors, have already been made (e.g., European Chips Act, Green Deal Industrial Plan, the Net-Zero Industry Act) (Tagliapietra and Veugelers 2023). Nonetheless, the European Union is still very far from having developed an effective and adequate industrial policy strategy. For example, measures to achieve the goals in these plans of securing significant market shares for EU production concerning several green and digital technologies are lacking. Reliance solely on incentives and subsidies to alter long-term comparative advantages is relatively naïve (Aghion 2023). On the contrary, they can easily become unaffordable.

Instead, strengthening the digital single market, increasing investment in knowledge and human capital, and enhancing venture capital funding for startups is essential. However, Europe cannot win the technology race with public money alone. It needs to unlock private capital and work hard on its overall competitiveness. Collaboration on a European scale is crucial to foster "European champions" capable of competing globally. A focus on innovation and competitiveness is paramount, rather than striving for complete autonomy over entire production chains (Guerrieri and Padoan 2020).

Moreover, strategic investments in critical technologies must be made, ensuring production is based in the EU and draws from a diversified supply chain. Like in quantum computing and sensing technologies. A security-driven investment plan that helps Europe's leading industrial innovators to upgrade in a collaborative way is needed for the EU's economic security posture. Important Projects of Common European Interest (IPCEIs) will be relaunched and strengthened in this respect. In the same vein, the Commission has made an interesting proposal for the creation of a "European Sovereignty Fund". Its role would be to launch EU-wide actions in cleantech frontiers where the European scale is needed. This is the case in many areas of R&D spending, where Europe has lost a lot of ground to other major competitors. Yet, disagreement among Member States has hindered progress. In its place, a much less ambitious program has been approved, the so-called STEP (Strategic Technology for European Platform), initially with a budget of just €10 billion for the scaling-up of critical technologies, particularly in the field of digital and clean energy, but more recently with a budget of only €1.5 billion and directed entirely at defence-related projects. Such a decision is an indication of the fragile political support behind the industrial and technological agenda. Equally clear, Europe's economic security will deteriorate without a more serious promotion agenda.

Furthermore, the Commission's calculations clearly underestimate the considerable common financial resources needed to finance these industrial policies, as in the case of energy and environment. Due to the strong divisions between Member States, it will be very difficult to acquire these funds. On the one hand, there are countries like France which want to see a more assertive industrial policy. They argue that the EU needs to change course radically and adapt to the new competition among major powers. On the other hand, countries like the liberal, export-oriented open economies of northern Europe argue for substantial non-intervention under the banner of traditional free market principles. Precisely because of the divisions between Member States, the interesting proposal of the European Strategic Fund has quickly been shelved, at least for the time being.

However, with the EU lacking new common instruments and funding, its current reliance on gradual relaxation of European state aid rules in response to the US Inflation and Reduction Act (IRA) extended after COVID-19 in March 2023 is even more worrying. The risk is distorting the single market and eroding cohesion among Member States. Indeed, the strongest countries, first of all Germany, will take advantage of this, as it happened during the recent energy crisis, triggering a subsidy race and creating new deep divergences between member countries. Though difficult, a common policy agenda is necessary to enhance Europe's industrial and technological capability and safeguard its economic security (Guerrieri and Padoan 2024).

8.4 Deepening the Single Market and Reconfiguring GVCs

One of the most significant risks confronting Europe today is the potential further relaxation of European state aid rules, which could compromise the integrity of the EU's internal market. The single market not only stands as a cornerstone of European competitiveness but is poised to become the focal point for the EU's sustainable growth with the Green Deal, once the current over-reliance on exports is diminished. However, its effectiveness needs to be reinforced and complemented with policies and measures aimed at safeguarding its vital interests, thus becoming a cornerstone for building the EU's strategic autonomy in terms of heightened competitiveness and security.

Firstly, a new and effective EU green industrial policy should aim at enhancing the overall attractiveness of the EU's internal market as a green investment destination. This entails completing the internal market (IM) by encompassing service sectors that have remained outside its purview, notably in energy, telecommunications, and digital diffusion. Services account for a significant share of GDP in all advanced economies and are poised to shape the future global economy. Even the growth gap between the European Union and the United States counts among its main causes Europe's lower productivity growth in those service sectors in which the integration process is most deficient (Guerrieri and Padoan 2020).

Manufacturing services—the so-called advanced tertiary sector—have become a fundamental and complementary input for the industry. They include digital services, and in particular knowledge-intensive business services (KIBS), where the EU's competitiveness has declined significantly in recent years. These are all fast-growing sectors that are driving structural changes and productivity gains essential for countries' long-term economic growth in the ecological and digital transition.

The deeper integration of the services market could thus be pivotal for Europe's future competitiveness. Further liberalization and integration within the internal services market could provide strong incentives for the restructuring of European economies and enterprises at a continental scale, fostering positive changes in production and innovation systems, leveraging economies of scale, and facilitating appropriate facility relocations within the EU. A recent International Monetary Fund (IMF) study suggests that deeper integration within the EU could potentially boost Europe's GDP by 7% (IMF 2023).

Moreover, the internal market could serve as a robust foundation for the reorganization or establishment of European value chains in the face of new strategic and security conditions. It is important to recall that the EU is highly integrated in global value chains (GVCs) in both manufacturing and services, with considerable heterogeneity across EU Member States in terms of the degree of dependence on GVCs. Deep and resilient value chains are therefore crucial for Europe's economic competitiveness in the long term (Bontadini et al. 2023).

GVC disruptions caused by the Covid pandemic and the war in Ukraine have led not to re-shoring, as many had expected, but to greater diversification (and nearshoring), along with a shift from global to regional supply networks. To address these challenges, the EU should leverage new international partnerships and trade relations, accompanied by financial support, to promote the diversification of critical value chains, thereby strengthening them and mitigating risks of economic dependency, including potential export restrictions on critical commodities.

Despite certain weaknesses that make Europe particularly exposed to the changes taking place globally, the EU's diverse composition of advanced and emerging economies positions it favourably to restructure its production offer in terms of value chains (Guerrieri and Padoan 2024). Its mix of innovation and manufacturing strength presents a unique ecosystem compared to the US, which is relatively more specialized in innovation, and China, which is more focused on manufacturing, enabling it to respond more effectively to the pressures of economic fragmentation. Ultimately, the EU has the potential to reorient global production towards low-cost, low-adjustment production sites in Eastern Europe, thereby enhancing its economic resilience and security.

8.5 Protecting European Strategic Interests and the Over-dependence on China

The green transition is highly mineral-intensive and will significantly increase the EU's demand for specific critical materials essential for the environmental and digital transformation. Currently, most of these materials are sourced from outside the EU, primarily from China. In fact, the EU imports 93% of its annual consumption of strategic materials from China, rendering it vulnerable to external shocks and potential trade weaponization. To mitigate this risk, the EU must ensure secure and reliable access to critical materials.

To address this challenge, alongside the industrial policies mentioned earlier, the EU initiated the European Raw Materials Alliance (ERMA) program in 2020 (European Commission 2020). The ERMA aims to enhance the EU's autonomy in critical material supply for the energy and digital transition. Additionally, in March 2023, the Commission introduced the Critical Raw Materials Act, a comprehensive set of measures to achieve a "secure, diversified, and sustainable" supply of strategic raw materials. These measures include diversifying supply chains, increasing domestic production, and promoting recycling and recovery of critical materials, thereby strengthening the circular economy (European Commission 2023c).

However, safeguarding against asymmetric interdependencies that may jeopardize EU security extends beyond addressing over-reliance on strategic materials. In line with the European Economic Security Strategy launched in June 2023, as mentioned at the beginning of this paper, the European Commission recently proposed various measures. Among the many proposals and initiatives, those in favour of a revision of the European law on the control of foreign direct investment are worth mentioning (European Commission 2024). Under these measures, all Member States would be obligated to introduce FDI monitoring and impose bans on investments that pose threats to European security. This contrasts with the current scenario, where not every country has FDI laws, and the criteria for their application vary widely. Furthermore, the scope of control would extend to investments from within the EU if the investors are controlled by foreign companies. However, the potential damage stemming from the implementation of restrictive measures must be carefully considered when calculating security risks, and discretion in using such instruments should be carefully monitored to prevent protectionist abuse by Member States.

Regarding outbound investment control, an even more controversial issue, the Commission has published a White Paper, which intends to launch a debate and discussion among Member States with a view to drawing some policy conclusions. The White Paper is also devoted to the issue of more effective EU controls on the export of dual-use goods (civilian and military), which may pose security problems within the EU. Calls for a coordinated EU-wide approach in such cases have intensified following pressures last year from the US on the Netherlands to impose restrictions on the Dutch chip equipment supplier ASML.

While the Commission advocates for "Europeanization" of EU security rules to ensure consistency among Member States' measures, the latest proposals are not in the direction of interventions at the EU level. Primarily they urge Member States to take further action and engage in consultations for additional policy initiatives. It should also be considered that the evolving global landscape necessitates adaptive responses to shocks, including the use of "offensive" instruments like sanctions alongside defensive ones. But this is a difficult area for Europe to enter. The EU's treaties, designed to uphold openness to international investment and finance, prohibit restrictions on capital and payment movements between the EU and third countries. Consequently, strengthening the EU's ability to act effectively on the international stage is essential.

All these instruments were initially crafted with an implicit focus on China (Beaucillon 2023), although they were designed to be applicable in a broader context concerning dealings with third countries. Indeed, particularly in strategic sectors like clean energy, where items such as batteries for electric vehicles, photovoltaic panels, wind turbines, and critical materials are vital, Europe's primary concern is mitigating its over-reliance on Chinese companies and global supply chains. This is accentuated by China's reputation as an unfair competitor, characterized by massive subsidies to its companies and a disregard for workers' rights. Establishing reciprocity and a level playing field in economic relations with Beijing is thus imperative.

Relations between Brussels and Beijing have further soured as China emerges as an assertive systemic rival on the international stage. More recently, China's stance of "active neutrality" regarding Ukraine, often perceived as veiled support for Moscow, and its unequivocal statements regarding reunification with Taiwan, exemplify the escalating tensions.

More recently, the EU has proposed a strategy of "de-risking" to address vulnerabilities stemming from economic interdependence while preserving an open global economy. In the case of China, this strategy aims to prioritize national and European security interests in economic and political dealings with Beijing (Guerrieri and Padoan 2024). Unlike the American proposal of "decoupling" from China, which is deemed unfeasible due to huge and intricate production and trade ties between the two superpowers, Europe favours a strategy focused on managing risks rather than abrupt disengagement.

It is worth noting that the United States has also recently embraced the idea of "de-risking", although specific details regarding the strategy's implementation remain elusive (Sullivan 2023). However, close collaboration with the US administration empowers Europe to exert greater influence over Beijing.

Nevertheless, the EU's internal disunity remains a significant obstacle in its relationship with China. Individual Member States' interests often take precedence, hindering the implementation of a unified and effective strategy of confrontation and competition with Beijing. While some Member States have taken steps to enhance economic security by adopting measures against China, different views on China persist within the EU. This lack of cohesion allows China to exploit divisions within Europe, undermining its ability to negotiate independently on the international stage (Bergsten 2022). Achieving consistency and unitary European strategy should thus be a paramount objective of a unified European economic security strategy.

8.6 European Public Goods and EU Governance

The European Union is facing a monumental task: establishing an autonomous capacity to assert and safeguard its economic-strategic interests, encapsulated in the concept of open strategic autonomy. It is a matter of strengthening Europe's competitiveness while enhancing its economic security.

However, charting this path forward is no easy feat. It requires addressing a myriad of complex domestic and international trade-offs and challenges. And it will not be easy, as we have seen, to identify the problems that need to be addressed, together with the policies and the instruments of intervention that need to be used.

Mere reinstatement of past policies won't suffice to deal with the major challenges, from the ecological transition to industrial and technological competition, to revitalizing relations with the Global South countries. Europe must adapt and innovate to meet these new tests head-on. Some steps have already been taken, and they are in the right direction, but a great deal remains to be done.

Central to Europe's agenda for greater competitiveness and strategic autonomy is the provision of so-called European Public Goods (EPGs) (Buti et al. 2023), spanning climate policy, energy security, and industrial and technological endeavours. In all of them, the Union represents an essential means for individual European countries to recover their sovereignty and capacity for action in areas and fields where individual efforts fall short (Draghi 2019).

Nevertheless, realizing these EPGs necessitates additional political instruments and financial resources at the European level. Only through a profound restructuring and renewal of its economic governance architecture can Europe equip itself (Guerrieri and Padoan 2023).

The current decision-making mechanisms are labyrinthine and cumbersome, ill-suited for agile crisis management. Overcoming the unanimity rule in favour of qualified majority voting in pertinent fields is imperative to facilitate swifter, more effective decision-making aligned with Europe's growth and security objectives.

Furthermore, there is an urgent need for augmented common financial resources. The ecological and digital transition requires a monumental investment, spanning both public and private sectors. However, individual Member States, already burdened by public debt consolidation, cannot shoulder the full financial load. Moreover, the new Stability and Growth Pact, enacted in 2024, leaves limited fiscal space for Member States to address the additional financial demands associated with the green transition.

It requires the creation of an investment and financing capacity at European level.

For instance, joint financing and investment programs to initiate energy transition policies and develop an autonomous European technological capability. They should be financed by the issuance of EU sovereign debt and should be centrally managed. However, unlike the NGEU, joint investments should be neither limited nor temporary; they should be made permanent.

Increasing the allocation of "own resources" to European institutions and granting them new fiscal powers could serve as another important solution to address the challenges ahead. This step would mark the beginning of a common fiscal capacity at the European level, crucial for financing the substantial public expenditure required for Europe's environmental transformation. A centrally managed fiscal capacity of significant size would also ensure that resources be allocated based on where they can generate the greatest benefits, rather than being dependent on individual countries' capacity and willingness to provide state aid.

Furthermore, budget reforms are essential to finance the ambitious policies the Union will pursue in the coming years. The success of programs like Next Generation EU (NGEU) by 2026 would be crucial to demonstrate the advantages of common financing and centrally managed fiscal capabilities for all Member States.

Addressing the scarcity of resources for private investment across Europe is another critical aspect. Currently, this scarcity persists partly due to the underdeveloped state of the Unification of the European capital markets, hindered by the incomplete European banking union and the absence of a European safe asset. Completing both the Banking Union and the Capital Markets Union is thus imperative. Without fundamental steps in this direction, achieving the dual green and digital transition in Europe would remain elusive.

Regrettably, little to no progress has been made in these areas in the recent period. If anything, there have been a few steps backwards in the last two years. And the results of the recent European elections have given mixed signals, strengthening the previous majority at the helm of Europe (EPP, SD, and Liberals), but at the same time strengthening right-wing parties and movements, even the most radical ones, which oppose further steps forward in the integration process. However, In the five years of the new legislature Europe must initiate and reinforce a profound restructuring and revitalization of its economic governance architecture to equip itself for the challenges ahead. This entails surmounting bureaucratic hurdles, enhancing decision-making agility, and securing the required financial resources. Maintaining the status quo risks rendering European countries irrelevant and marginalized in a fragmented and conflict-ridden world. What is urgently needed is a significant strengthening of the Union's sovereignty and resilience to advance open strategic autonomy while safeguarding economic security and competitiveness. The key challenge for the future global growth of the Union lies in taking decisive steps in this direction by setting up a policy response that suits the new geopolitical environment (Guerrieri and Padoan 2024).

References

Aghion, P. (2023) "An Innovation-Driven Industrial Policy for Europe" in S. Tagliapietra and R. Veugelers (eds), *Sparking Europe's New Industrial Revolution: A Policy for Net Zero, Growth and Resilience*. Brussels: Bruegel, pp. 29–41, https://www.bruegel.org/sites/default/files/private/2023-08/Bruegel%20Blueprint%2033_chapter%202.pdf

Baccaro, L., and S. Hadziabdic (2023) "Operationalizing Growth Models", *Quality and Quantity* 58: 1325–1360, https://doi.org/10.1007/s11135-023-01685-w

Beaucillon, C., and S. Poli (2023) "Special Focus on EU Strategic Autonomy and Technological Sovereignty: An Introduction", *European Papers* 8(2): 411–416, https://www.europeanpapers.eu/en/europeanforum/special-focus-eu-strategic-autonomy-and-technological-sovereignty-introduction

Bergsten, C. F. (2022) *The United States vs China: The Quest for Global Economic Leadership*. New York: Polity Books.

Bontadini, F., V. Meliciani, M. Savona, and A. Wikierman (2023) "Nearshoring, Global Value Chains' Structure and Volatility", *LEAP Working Papers* 8/23, https://leap.luiss.it/wp-content/uploads/2023/09/WP8.23-Nearshoring-global-value-chains-structure-and-volatility2.pdf

Buti, M., A. Coloccia, and M. Messori (2023) "European Public Goods", June 9, *CEPR*, https://cepr.org/voxeu/columns/european-public-goods

Dadush, U. (2022) "Is the Post-War Trading System Ending?", *Policy Contribution* 04/2022: 1–12, https://www.bruegel.org/sites/default/files/wp-content/uploads/2022/02/PC-04.pdf

European Commission (2020) "European Raw Materials Alliance (ERMA)", *European Commission*, https://single-market-economy.ec.europa.eu/industry/industrial-alliances/european-raw-materials-alliance_en

European Commission (2021) "Trade Policy Review: An Open, Sustainable and Assertive Trade Policy", COM(2021) 66, February 18, https://eur-lex.europa.eu/legal-content/EN/ALL/?uri=CELEX%3A52021DC0066

European Commission (2023a) "A Green Deal Industrial Plan for the Net-Zero Age", COM(2023) 62, February 1, https:// eur-lex.europa.eu/legal-content/EN/ TXT/HTML/?uri=CELEX:52023DC0062

European Commission (2023b) "Joint Communication to the European Parliament, the European Council and the Council on 'European Economic Security Strategy', JOIN(2023) 20, June 20, https://eur-lex.europa.eu/legal-content/EN/TXT/?uri=CELEX:52023JC0020

European Commission (2023c) "Joint Communication to the European Parliament and the European Council on 'A Secure and Sustainable Supply of Critical Raw Materials in Support of the Twin Transition", COM(2023) 165, March 16, https://eur-lex.europa.eu/legal-content/EN/TXT/?uri=COM%3A2023%3A165%3AFIN

European Commission (2024) "Communication from the Commission to the European Parliament and the European Council on Advancing European Economic Security: An Introduction to Five New Initiatives", COM(2024) 22, January 24, https://commission.europa.eu/system/files/2024-01/Communication%20on%20European%20economic%20security.pdf

Farrell, H., and A. L. Newman (2019) "Weaponized Interdependence: How Global Economic Networks Shape State Coercion", *International Security* 44(1): 42–79, https://doi.org/10.1162/isec_a_00351

Georgieva, K., G. Gopinath, and C. Pazarbasioglu (2022) "Why We Must Resist Geoeconomic Fragmentation and How", *IMF Blog*, May 22, https://www.imf.org/en/Blogs/Articles/2022/05/22/blog-why-we-must-resist-geoeconomic-fragmentation

Guerrieri, P., and P. C. Padoan (2020) *L'economia europea. Tra crisi e rilancio*. Bologna: il Mulino.

Guerrieri, P., and P. C. Padoan (2024) *Sovereign Europe. An Agenda for Europe in a Fragmented Global Economy*. Brookfield, VT: Edward Elgar.

Hoekman, B. M., and L. Puccio (2019) "EU Trade Policy: Challenges and Opportunities", *RSC Policy Papers* 6, https://hdl.handle.net/1814/61589

IMF (2022) "Geo-Economic Puzzle: Policy Making in a More Fragmented World", *Finance and Development* 59(2).

IMF (2023) "Geoeconomic Fragmentation: What's at Stake for the EU", *IMF Working Papers* 245, https://www.imf.org/en/Publications/WP/Issues/2023/11/29/Geoeconomic-Fragmentation-Whats-at-Stake-for-the-EU-541864

Lake, D. A., et al. (2021) "Challenges to the Liberal Order: Reflections on International Organization", *International Organization* 75(2): 225–257, https://doi.org/10.1017/S0020818320000636

Lavery, S. (2023) "Rebuilding the Fortress? Europe in a Changing World Economy", *Review of International Political Economy* 31(1): 330–353, https://doi.org/10.1080/09692290.2023.2211281

Meunier, S., and K. Nicolaidis (2019) "The Geo-politicization of European Trade and Investment Policy", *Journal of Common Market Studies* 57(S1): 103–113, https://doi.org/10.1111/jcms.12932

Schmitz, L., and T. Seidl (2023) "As Open as Possible, as Autonomous as Necessary", *Journal of Common Market Studies* 61: 834–852, https://doi.org/10.1111/jcms.13428

Steinberg, F., and G. Wolff (2023) "Dealing with Europe's Economic (In-)security", *Global Policy* 15(1): 183–192, https://doi.org/10.1111/1758-5899.13303

Sullivan, J. (2023) "Renewing American Economic Leadership", Speech Given at Brookings Institution, Washington DC, April 27.

Tagliapietra, S., and R. Veugelers (eds) (2023) *Sparking Europe's New Industrial Revolution: A Policy for Net Zero, Growth and Resilience*. Brussels: Bruegel.

Tamma, P. (2020) "Europe Wants 'Strategic Autonomy'. It Just Has to Decide What That Means", October 15, *POLITICO*, https://www.politico.eu/article/europe-trade-wants-strategic-autonomy-decide-what-means/

Tocci, N. (2021) "European Strategic Autonomy: What It Is, Why We Need It, How to Achieve It", *Istituto Affari Internazionali*, https://www.iai.it/sites/default/files/9788893681780.pdf

Wigger, A. (2023) "The New EU Industrial Policy and Deepening Structural Asymmetries, *Journal of Common Market Studies* 61(1): 20–37, https://doi.org/10.1111/jcms.13366

Zuleeg, F. (2023) "Economic Security: A New EU Paradigm?", Discussion Paper, European Policy Centre, June 8, https://www.epc.eu/en/publications/Economic-security-A-new-EU-paradigm~516bc0

9. Trends in Defence Spending in the European Union[1]

Alessandra Cepparulo[2] and Paolo Pasimeni[3]

After more than sixty years of peace, in 2022 Europe has faced a watershed moment in its security, which is leading to higher and more integrated defence spending in the European Union (EU). This article uses new sources of data to illustrate the evolution of defence spending in the EU and its composition. It also looks at the articulation of responsibilities for defence spending in a multi-level governance system, such as the EU. The institutional evolution of defence policy in the EU tries to build on a progressive convergence of foreign policy objectives and points towards some concentration of defence spending at the supra-national level. The key question for the future is to what extent this convergence will hold and to what extent it will be reflected in new provisions for defence in the common budget.

9.1 Introduction

Much of the economic literature relegates defence spending to the realm of strategic choices connected to security, threats, or arms races; in the post-Cold War years, the evolution of military spending has been shaped also by internal groups of interest. Additionally, defence spending, especially when considered in its various components, has implications for employment, investment, and the economic growth of a country. The empirical literature on the defence–growth nexus is not unanimous;[4] little consensus exists on the relationship, as well as on its direction of causality and nature. Alptekin and Levine (2012) and Churchill and Yew (2018), in their meta-analysis of empirical studies found that positive economic impacts are more frequently reported in wealthy countries than in less developed ones.

1 The views expressed in the text are the private views of the authors and may not, under any circumstances, be interpreted as stating an official position of the European Commission.

2 European Commission.

3 Brussels School of Governance (BSoG) at the Vrije Universiteit Brussel (VUB).

4 For a theoretical discussion on the defence-growth nexus see also Pivetti (1989; 1992) and Smith and Dunne (1994). For a recent survey of the empirical literature on the direction and nature of the defence-growth nexus in advanced economies see Cepparulo and Pasimeni (2024).

 https://doi.org/10.11647/OBP.0434.10

On a larger sample including developing countries, Yesilyurt and Yesilyurt (2019) find no significant effect, considering not only as dependent variable the share of military expenditure in GDP but also other functions of it (logarithms, differences, etc.). According to Santamaría et al. (2022), only about one in four articles, published between 1995 and 2019, support the existence of a positive relationship between military spending and growth, 16% support a negative relationship while nearly 38% are either heterogeneous or inconclusive. The findings are dependent on the time horizon and the methodology used. In particular, Dunne and Tian (2016), reviewing 168 studies, find that the horizon considered influences the results favouring a negative effect when using post-Cold War data.

According to the literature, favourable trends in investments and its components, such as equipment and R&T (research and technology) spending, can be deemed growth-enhancing. These economic implications deserve consideration in the current historical phase, when European countries are reassessing and increasing their defence spending, its quantity and composition, following years of steady decline.

Several advanced countries have seen a significant decrease in defence spending over the past seventy years. In the United States (US), after the peaks connected to the Cold War period and the 'war on terror' in Iraq and Afghanistan, the share on military spending has decreased to about 4.5% GDP. In the European Union (EU) countries, as well as in New Zealand, and Japan, this decline has been less pronounced, also because the initial levels were considerably lower (Fig. 9.1). As a result of the Global Financial Crisis, a new downturn in military spending has taken place in the main advanced economies and, in particular, in certain EU countries (Bulgaria, Lithuania, Latvia, Greece, Slovakia, Slovenia, and Malta) where cuts have exceeded 20%.

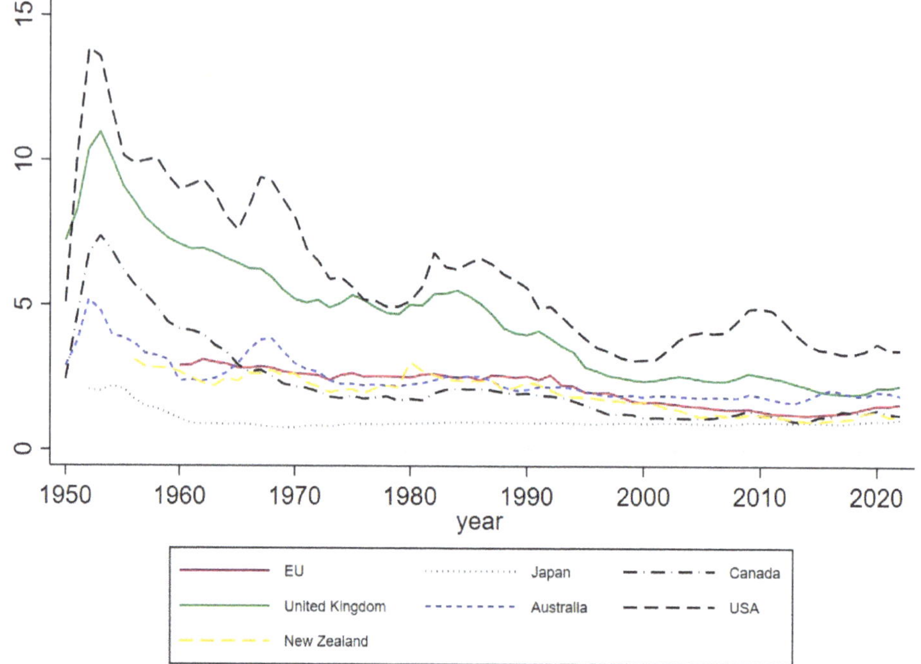

Fig. 9.1 Defence spending (% of GDP): EU countries vs advanced economies. *Source*: SIPRI.

The invasion of Crimea by Russia and the NATO Readiness Action Plan, signed in 2014 to respond to instability and deteriorating security on the global front (NATO 2014), have reverted the trend. At that time, the US accounted for more than half of all transatlantic defence spending and NATO members agreed to reach a minimum spending of 2% of GDP in a decade. A further push in this direction, for the EU countries, came in 2017 when, as part of the Permanent Structured Cooperation (PESCO),[5] they agreed to increase their defence budgets in real terms on a regular basis as one of their twenty common commitments. Finally, the invasion of Ukraine in 2022 has prompted a reappraisal of NATO and European countries' defence spending with the view of bolstering their military strength.

The recent resurgence in defence spending raises multiple strategic, political and economic questions. The structure of the chapter is as follows. Section 2 discusses the economic, political, and institutional arguments about the attribution of defence spending responsibilities at different levels of government. Section 3 presents the institutional evolution of EU defence policy. Section 4 looks at the evolution and the composition of defence spending. The chapter ends with a conclusion.

9.2 Defence Spending in a Multi-Level Governance System

Given the nature of defence as a public good, a relevant question refers to the level of government best suited to finance it. The theory of fiscal federalism (Oates 1999, 2005) can inform this reflection. The traditional distinction of the key responsibilities of public finances highlights three main functions: allocation, redistribution, and macroeconomic stabilization (Musgrave, 1939). While the second and the third are usually performed more efficiently by the higher level of government (a federal or common budget), the function of allocation is often considered as one that is more effectively performed by lower levels of government, closer to citizens' preferences.

There are, nevertheless, exceptions to this idea, notably related to the provision of public goods, a category to which defence belongs. Indeed, defence spending enjoys the non-rivalry and non-excludability features that characterize public goods. Hence, the only way to provide a sufficient level of defence is to entrust it to the highest level of government—be it central or federal—and fund it accordingly through its budget. However, an increasing number of activities related to defence policy—including policies related to common procurement, shared infrastructures, common arms export policies, and joint defence initiatives (Fuest and Pisani-Ferry 2019)—present non-rivalry and non-excludability features at the EU level, as they can ensure consistent and uniform security standards and equal protection and territorial integrity to all regions/states of the Union. Accordingly, to the extent that the Member States decide

5 PESCO in the area of security and defence was firstly introduced by article 42(6) of the Lisbon Treaty on European Union (TEU).

to transfer certain competences in the defence field to the EU level, this could be accompanied by and reflected in new provisions in the common budget.

A fundamental argument in favour of central EU spending on defence is to achieve economies of scale. Defence spending often requires significant upfront costs for acquiring and maintaining equipment, infrastructure, and technology. The recent report on the future of European competitiveness (Draghi 2024b: 166) argues that "complex next-generation defence systems in all strategic domains (air, land, space, maritime and cyber) will require massive research investment that exceeds the capacity of any Member State alone". Considering the pace of technological innovation, EU Member States are unable individually to "finance, develop, produce and sustain the necessary defence capabilities and enabling infrastructure". This may likely lead to inefficient and insufficient investment in defence, compared to other countries, thereby favouring technological dependence.

The central budget can pool resources, negotiate better contracts, and streamline procurement processes, leading to cost savings and efficiency gains. This approach is especially beneficial for smaller states that may not have the necessary resources to independently build and maintain robust defence capabilities. Fragmentation and duplication in spending are a source of inefficiency, dampening the positive effects of synergies and scale: in the EU, just 18% of all defence investments are undertaken collaboratively, according to the "Coordinated Annual Review on Defence" report (EDA 2022). In the case of R&T spending the percentage of collaboration is reduced by half. According to the European Commission (2022b), EU Member States frequently act in isolation rather than coordinating their military efforts, with the cost of this lack of collaboration ranging from €25 billion to €100 billion per year.

A further argument refers to defence externalities and spill-over effects. By centralizing defence spending, the EU could better account for interdependencies and externalities, ensuring a coordinated response. Moreover, investment in defence infrastructure, research and development (R&D), and defence-related industries can have spill-over effects on the economy, in the form of technology advancement and innovation. Mowery (2010) and Mazzucato (2013), based on the US experience, show how military R&D has been a crucial driver of technological innovation, with substantial spillover effects on the rest of the economy. However, Mowery (2010) notices how the extent and efficiency of these spillovers depend on factors such as openness, collaboration, and sustained investment. These benefits may extend beyond regional or national boundaries. These arguments are relevant from an economic point of view, in particular, because efficiency considerations seem to matter greatly when analysing the nexus with economic growth (Angelopoulos et al. 2008).

Finally, common defence spending can also be, in principle, a tool to better promote common strategic and foreign policy objectives. Centralizing defence expenditure would enable the EU to allocate resources strategically, respond to emerging threats, and project national power effectively on the international stage. These theoretical arguments support the assignment of some tasks of defence policy at the EU supranational layer. The current geopolitical situation would also suggest some form of pooled sovereignty, or at least enhanced European cooperation (Fuest and Pisani-Ferry 2019).

The EU, however, is not a federation, like other complete federal states; it is instead a union of sovereign countries in which political and budgetary responsibilities are delegated (with many limitations) by the national to the supranational level. The EU has evolved into "an environment of increased interconnectedness, but also heightened vulnerability, with rampant externalities and spillovers" (Buti and Papaconstantinou 2022: 1); for this reason, it is entrusted with some shared responsibilities across different policy areas and provides some public goods whose benefits are enjoyed at the EU level and that are also known as European Public Goods (EPG).

Due to the extent of the common military funding needs, the EU budget allocation alone is insufficient; both public and private resources are required. Public procurement can play an important role in reducing the defence market's fragmentation, which is estimated to cost over €100 billion a year (Letta 2024). There have been discussions about the possible emission of defence Eurobonds or specialized credit lines for national defence spending, utilizing the European Stability Mechanism (ESM). The European Council (March 2024) agreed that the European Investment Bank could support the defence industry, while "core defence activities" remain excluded from the support. Such exclusion, as observed by the Draghi report (2024b) is also applied by other public and private banks limiting the possibility of the defence sector to fully benefit from EU financial instruments and private financing.

For the moment, in general, collaboration in defence spending is promoted only when it aligns with national goals or benefits the national industry, and this points to another fundamental criterion that has to be assessed when thinking of shifting decision and budgetary powers to the supranational level. Defence has typically been at the core of national interest because it has the ultimate task to provide security, it is an expression of sovereignty, and contributes to shaping a country's role in the international community. To the extent that these objectives are shared among countries, these functions can be centralized, but the process is likely to be slow and delicate.

9.3 Institutional Developments in the EU Defence Policy

According to the current legal framework, defence policy is an intergovernmental competence, since the establishment of the EU Common Security and Defence Policy (CSDP) in 1999. The CSDP aims to provide the EU with the capability to effectively respond to international crises, contribute to international peace, and strengthen global security; it integrates both civilian and military tools.

In line with the Treaty limitations (TEU, Art. 41(2)), the EU budget can only cover the operating expenditure for civilian CSDP missions that contribute to maintaining regional and global security and stability, whereas the *operations that have military or defence implications* or the purchase of military equipment for third countries cannot be borne by the EU budget. The big legal question today refers to the nature of these "operations" that cannot be financed by the EU budget, and in particular whether Article 41(2) refers only to own operations of the Union or also to operations conducted by other entities (such as, for instance, Ukraine).

Since 2014, a growing perception of a threat following Russia's annexation of Crimea and the war in eastern Ukraine has prompted European defence cooperation. The EU global strategy addressed five priorities: (1) the EU's own security; (2) enhancing the resilience of the neighbourhood; (3) the use of an integrated approach when dealing with war and crisis; (4) support for stable regional orders around the world; and (5) effective global governance. This implied further developments for the Common Security and Defence Policy-CSDP, which is now distinguished by a coherent mechanism to enhance collaborative defence capability planning, development, procurement, and operation.

The EU Council established a specific mechanism called Athena (EU 2014), to finance common costs[6] associated with some operations as well as the national contingents' costs (such as lodging or fuel), back in 2004. In 2021, the Athena Mechanism and the African Peace Facility (which financially supported peace operations led by African states and regional bodies) were merged into the European Peace Facility (EPF), an off-budget account, funded by allocations from the Member States based on their gross national income. Since its creation, the EPF has been mobilized to support military assistance activities in a number of third countries, and it has played a key role in supporting Ukraine, as it allowed the reimbursement of EU member states for their donations of military equipment. The financial ceiling of the EPF was set at €5.7 billion (in current prices) for the years 2021–2027 when it was first established. It has, then, been increased to €8 billion in December 2022 and then to €12 billion in June 2023, to ensure that additional financial needs can be covered.

In December 2017, the European Council established a "framework and a structured process to gradually deepen defence cooperation" and create "a more coherent European capability landscape", in order to enhance the collaboration between participating EU Member States. It also endorsed the modalities for establishing the Coordinated Annual Review on Defence (CARD) which provides Member States with a comprehensive overview of the European defence landscape (capability, research, and industrial aspects) in order to better identify opportunities for new

6 These costs include: HQ implementation and running costs, including travel, IT systems, administration, public information, locally hired staff, Force Headquarters (FHQ) deployment and lodging for forces as a whole, infrastructure, medical services (in theatre), medical evacuation, identification, acquisition of information (satellite images), and reimbursements to/from NATO or other organizations (e.g. the UN).

collaborative initiatives. Finally, to reduce the European dependence on non-European actors in developing new and defence technologies, the Commission introduced in the Multiannual Financial Framework of the Union 2021–2027, the European Defence Fund (EDF).

The 2021–2027 EU Multiannual Financial Framework (MFF) has introduced, for the first time, a heading (number 5)[7] dedicated to Security and Defence (European Commission 2021). Heading 5 is the smallest of all headings, accounting for 1.2% of the overall budget. In particular, the defence programmes cover 65% of the amount dedicated to this heading, the bulk of it going to the EDF (€7.29 billion in current prices) and military mobility (€1.75 billion in current prices).

The EDF co-finances Member States' defence capability development costs (1/3 of the total) and provides funding for cooperative defence research initiatives at all levels of R&D (2/3). This fund combines two pre-existing programs funded by the 2014–2020 MFF as trial or preparation actions, namely the Preparatory Action on Defence Research (PADR) and the European Defence Industrial Development Programme (EDIDP),[8] funded through the "Smart and Inclusive Growth" (heading 1).

Military mobility, instead, finances projects for dual-use transport infrastructure under the Connecting Europe Facility (CEF), mostly on the railway and roads infrastructures across Europe, in order to make the movement of the European armed forces faster and on a sufficient scale to respond to crises erupting at and beyond the EU's external borders.

The Strategic Compass approved, in 2022, outlines the strategic direction and priorities for the EU on common defence policy until 2030, to enhance the EU's capacity for autonomous action, and crisis management. The Compass overtly identifies Russia and China as threats or rivals and recognizes the geopolitical changes due to Russia's invasion of Ukraine (Fiott 2023).

To address the EU's most urgent and critical defence capability gaps, in 2023 the European Commission put forward a proposal for a regulation establishing the European Defence Industry Reinforcement through the common Procurement Act (EDIRPA), which would create a short-term joint defence procurement instrument and incentivize the EU Member States to procure defence products jointly, and the Act in Support of Ammunition Production (ASAP), a temporary instrument ensuring that the EU can ramp-up its production capacity. Both ASAP and EDIRPA are financed via the EU Budget, with an envelope respectively of €500 million and €300 million.

Finally, in March 2024, the European Commission (2024) has tabled a proposal for a new defence industrial strategy (EDIS), with the objective of stepping up its defence readiness. Based on an analysis of investment and capability gaps, it calls for more investment in defence, a more secure supply, and deepened partnership. This strategy

7 For a detailed description of the negotiations of this heading see Mazur (2021).

8 EDIDP is dominated by four big European businesses (Airbus, Leonardo, Thales, and Indra Sistemas) that are partially owned by their respective governments and by US investment funds.

sets three clear targets to be achieved by 2030: intra-EU defence trade to represent at least 35% of the value of the total EU defence market; at least 40% of defence equipment should be procured in a collaborative manner; and at least half (and 60% by 2035) of defence procurement should be sourced internally in the EU.

The rapid unfolding of new initiatives testifies of this new trend, started after Russia's occupation of Crimea, and accelerated after its invasion of Ukraine. These events have prompted the European Commission to increase its ambition and expand its role to advance the integration process. However, the final outcome will be influenced by both supranational entrepreneurship and the collective political will of member states (Fiott 2023; Håkansson 2023).

9.4 Defence Spending in the EU Countries

9.4.1 Methodological Aspects

This section presents an examination of the evolution and composition of defence spending in the EU countries, drawing on multiple data sources: (i) the Stockholm International Peace Research Institute (SIPRI) Military Expenditure Database,[9] which provides continuous time series data for 155 states from 1949 to 2022; (ii) the European Defence Agency,[10] which provides data on defence spending and its composition since 2005 for EU Member States;[11] (iii) NATO defence database that provides the decomposition of defence expenditure by main categories for 24 EU countries;[12] (iv) EU countries Stability and Convergence Programs, that provide medium-term projections of defence spending, and, finally; and (v) the EU budget. Given that military spending accounts for around 90% of EU defence budgets (Fig. 9.2) referring to military spending or defence data guarantees consistency.

9 See https://www.sipri.org/databases/milex
10 See https://eda.europa.eu/home
11 The data collection started gathering data from twenty-two countries extending to all others over time. Denmark joined only on 23 March 2023.
12 Ireland and Austria are not members of the NATO alliance while Sweden became NATO's newest member on 7 March 2024.

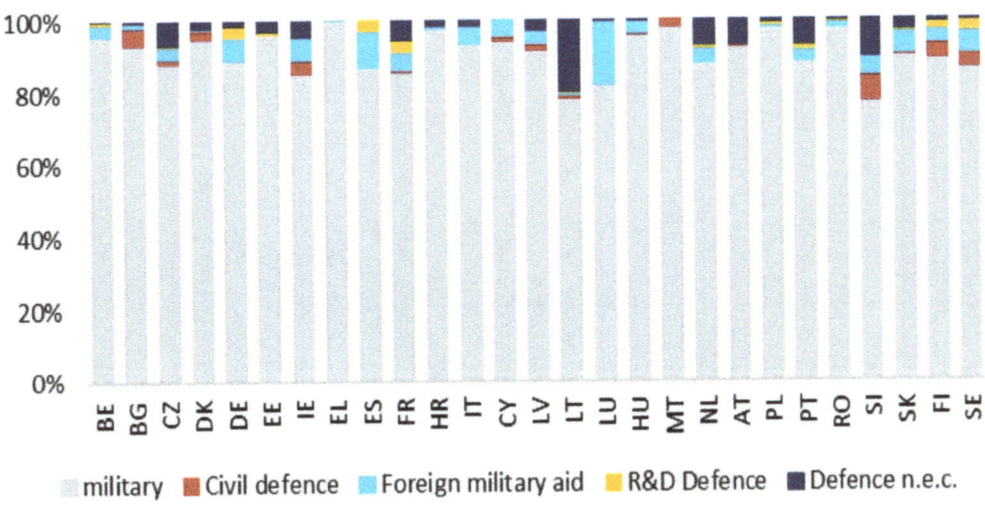

Fig. 9.2 Defence expenditure by function: average (2012–2022). *Source*: Eurostat.

9.4.2. Recent Trends

In 2022, defence spending in the EU hit a record of €240 billion, a 6% rise over 2021 in constant terms (EDA 2023), keeping a trend of consecutive increases for the eighth year, following the invasion of Crimea. Almost all EU countries have increased military spending in the past decade. Four categories of countries can be distinguished based on the most recent data (Fig. 9.3a). The first group comprises countries that are not NATO members (such as Ireland, Austria, and Malta) or are small countries (Luxembourg): they spend less than 1.1% of their GDP.

Instead, the bulk of European countries fall into the second category, with expenditures ranging from 1.1 to 2% of GDP, with Finland (1.94%) and France (1.88%) spending the most in this cluster. The third and fourth groupings include the Baltic Republics, Poland, and Greece, who spend more than 2% in accordance with NATO commitments and more than the EU average of 1.5%. Greece is the only country with a level of expenditure higher that 3%, up to roughly 4% of GDP, something probably due to the long-standing tensions at its borders with Turkey. According to NATO forecasts, the number of countries spending more than 2% of GDP should have doubled in 2023. Poland is predicted to have the greatest increases, with a growth of more than 60%, followed by Finland and Romania, where spending is expected to rise by more than 40%.

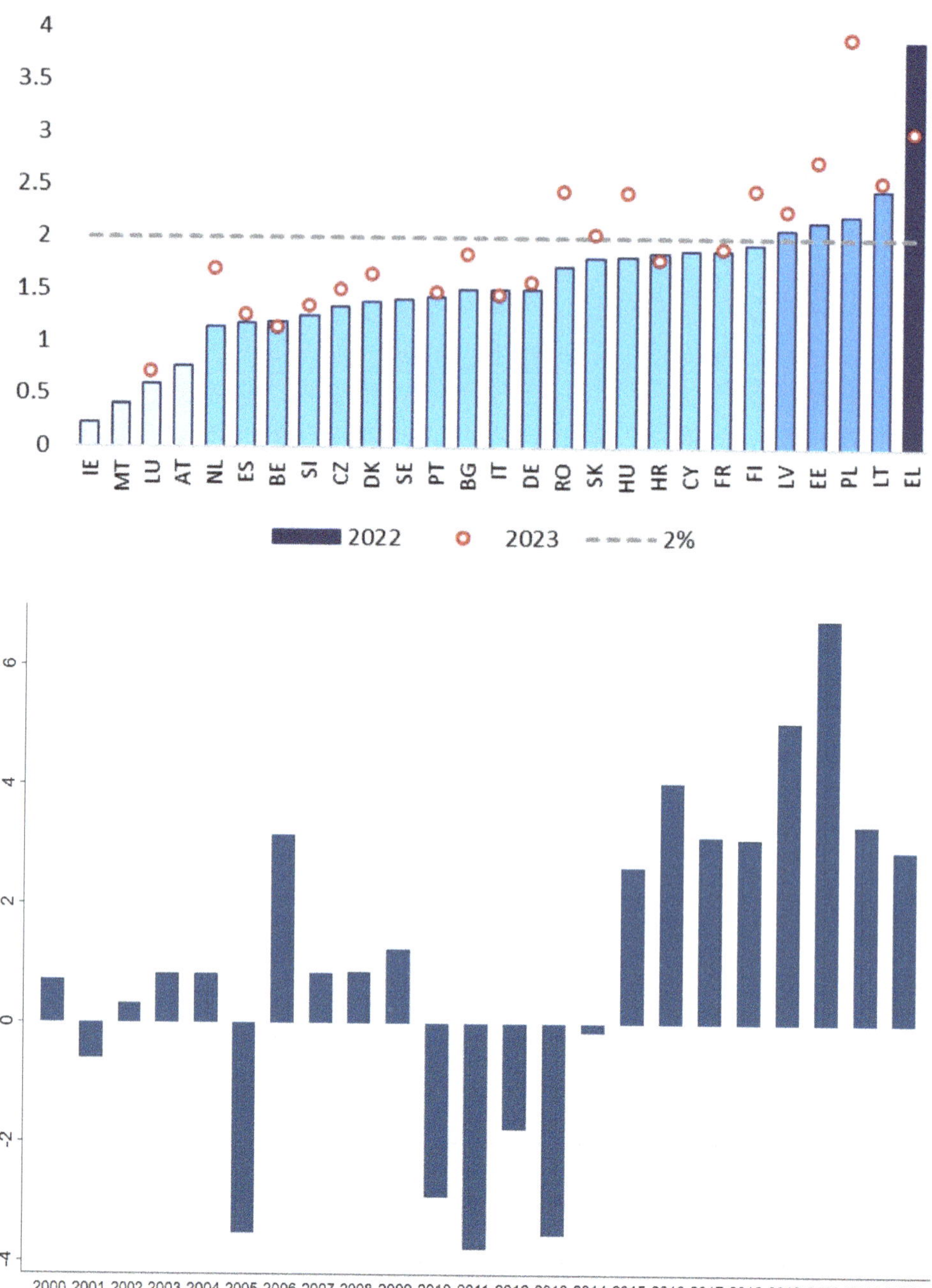

Fig. 9.3 Defence spending. (a) EU countries (% GDP) (above); (b) EU growth: 2000–2022 (below). *Source*: EDA Defence data 2022, NATO and SIPRI database. *Note*: EU countries are represented by their two-letter country codes. EU figures correspond to the average among EU countries. NATO database doesn't include the data for Ireland, Malta, Austria, Cyprus, and Sweden.

EU Member States are not only guided by the NATO commitments but, as part of PESCO, they agreed in 2017 to increase defence budgets in real terms on a regular basis as one of their twenty common commitments. Half of the countries met their commitment with a consistent increase across the past four years. Only one country (Croatia) has shown positive growth in two years. Malta[13] is not among the PESCO participating members and did not commit to any specific target.

The Russian invasion of Ukraine, in February 2022, has drastically shaken the geopolitical equilibria; as a consequence, further increases in defence spending are expected. According to the 2023 Stability and Convergence Programmes,[14] at least nine European countries plan to increase defence spending by 2026 (Fig. 9.4). Czechia (by 1% of GDP) and Finland[15] (by 0.7% GDP) are on top of this list. The Netherlands, Estonia, and Spain intend to increase defence spending by 0.5, 0.4, and 0.3 percentage points of GDP, respectively. Four other countries (Slovakia, Latvia, Luxembourg, and Bulgaria) expect an increase of less than 0.2% of GDP by 2026. The national programmes of eight other countries[16] mention the future budgetary impact of defence spending although no quantitative information is provided. Only the programmes of the remaining eight countries have no mention of defence spending.[17]

More generally, the Council of the EU confirmed future higher spending commitments in the Strategic Compass (Council of the EU, 7371/22), in which Member States committed to increasing defence expenditures to close critical military and civilian capability gaps and strengthen the European Defence Technological and Industrial Base strategy, inaugurated in 2007 to better coordinate defence policies and the related industrial activities.

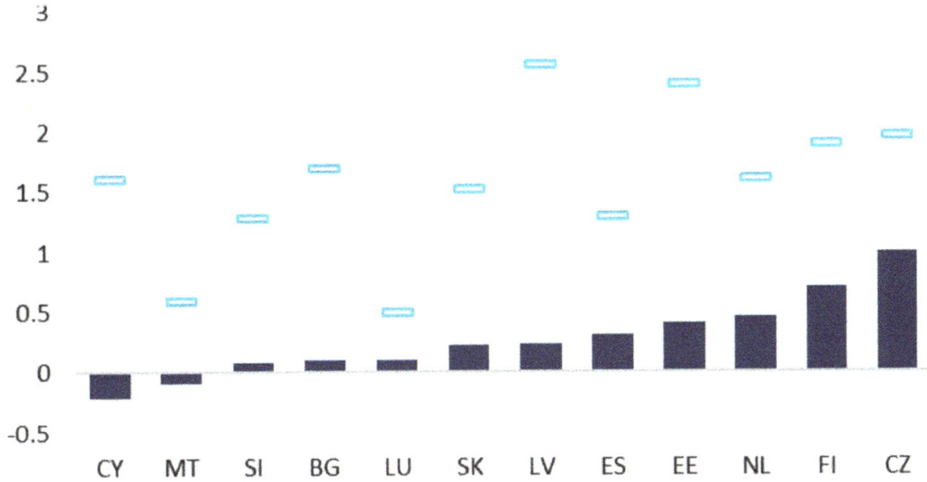

Fig. 9.4 Defence expenditure planned in selected EU countries for 2026 (% of GDP). *Source*: 2023 Stability and Convergence Programmes.

13 Denmark joined formally PESCO on May 2023.

14 Every April, EU Member States are required to lay out their fiscal plans for the next three years.

15 In the case of Finland, the expected increase of spending is also related to the NATO membership.

16 Austria, Croatia, Italy, Sweden, Denmark, Germany, Lithuania, and Poland.

17 Belgium, Greece, France, Ireland, Hungary, Romania, Portugal, and Slovenia.

9.4.3 The Composition of Defence Spending

The composition of defence spending has some relevance, not only in terms of effectiveness of the defence capabilities of a country, but also in terms of economic effects. Some studies argue that spending on non-equipment can be associated with a potential crowding-out effect of the private sector, while the equipment budget, linked to procurement and R&D, can generate a crowding-in effect.

From a functional perspective, there are four components of defence spending: equipment,[18] personnel,[19] infrastructure,[20] and other operating spending.[21] Using data from NATO and the EU, we observe that personnel spending absorbs the majority of resources dedicated to the defence function, in all advanced countries (Fig. 9.5a). While it accounts for roughly one-third of total spending in the UK and the US, it represents slightly less of half of total spending for the EU countries and Canada.

Historically, the EU has spent the most in personnel spending. This category accounts for around 46% of defence expenditure in 2023, which is 64% more than the amount spent by the country that spends the least (US). On average over the period 2010–2022 this item accounted for 56.5% of GDP. Although the share of personnel spending has been declining since 2014 (Fig. 9.5b), the EU countries will still have the highest level, with Cyprus (74% of total expenditure) and Ireland (81% of total expenditure) topping the list (Fig. 9.5c).

These figures seem to confirm the theory of burden shifting inside the NATO alliance (Becker 2017; 2021). In case of peer pressure or fiscal pressure, reallocation of resources within the defence budget are a somehow hidden way of burden-shifting. In order not to lose the benefits of being part of an alliance, countries can favour, within the defence budget, those expenditure categories with more direct domestic benefits. As a result, personnel would be the most appealing short-term choice, given the immediate gains in terms of employment stimulus. This situation is all the more probable in times of peace, when there is no specific threat that pushes towards a strategic direction. Becker (2021) finds evidence that countries facing unemployment tend to reduce defence spending and divert resources from acquiring capability-enhancing equipment. Instead, they prioritize personnel spending as a stabilizing measure.

---

18 Equipment expenditure includes major equipment expenditure and R&D devoted to major equipment according to the NATO definition.

19 Personnel expenditure includes military and civilian expenditure and pensions according to the NATO definition.

20 Infrastructure expenditure includes NATO common infrastructure and national military construction, according to the NATO definition.

21 Other expenditure includes operations and maintenance expenditure, other R&D expenditure and expenditure not allocated among above-mentioned categories.

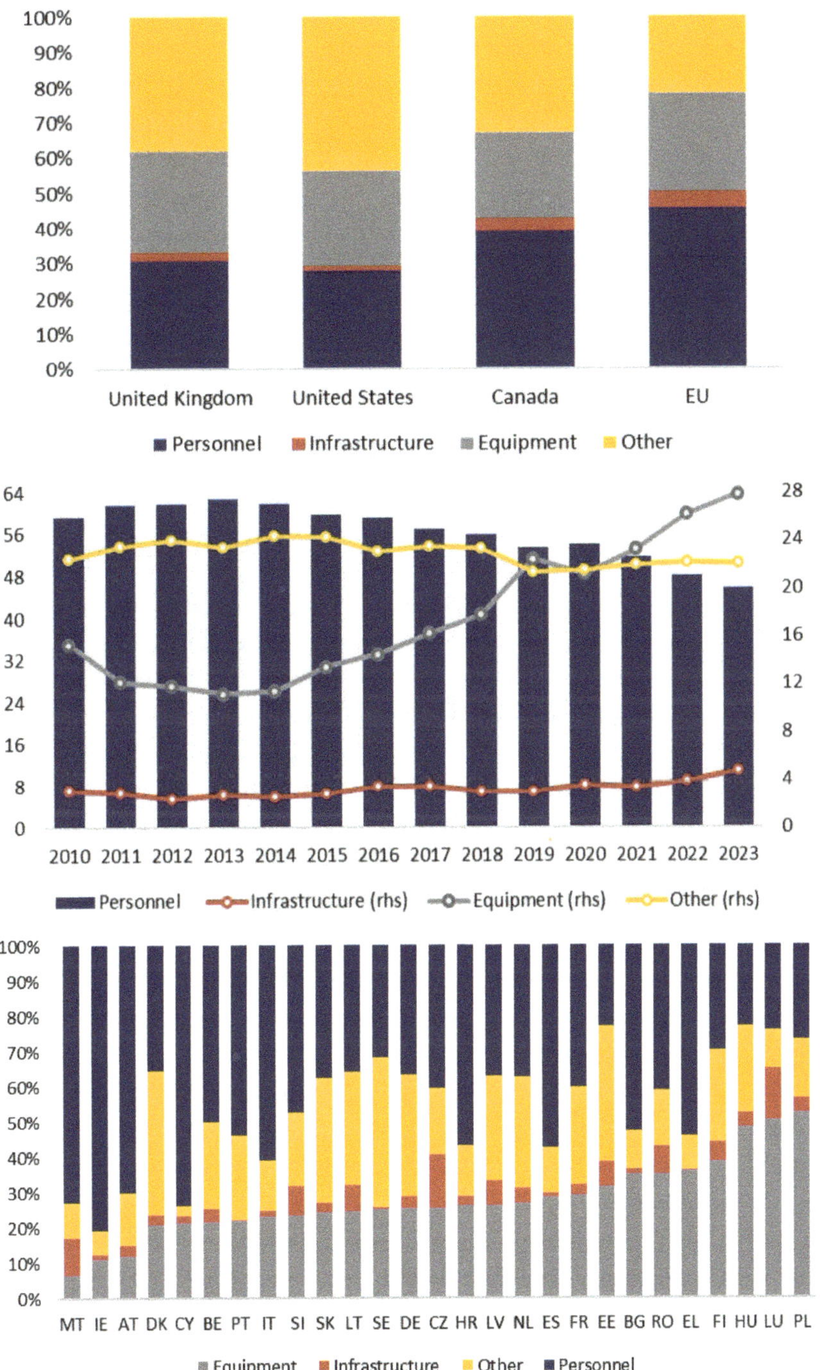

Fig. 9.5 Decomposing the defence spending (% of total defence expenditure). (a) Advanced economies in 2023 (above); (b) EU: 2010–2023 (middle); (c) EU countries in 2023 (below). *Source*: NATO and EDA defence data 2022. *Note*: EU figures correspond to the average among EU countries.

In contrast to other advanced economies, EU members spent the most on infrastructure in 2022 (about 4%) (Figs 9.5a and 5b). On average, this category in the EU accounts for around twice as much as in the US. All advanced economies have boosted expenditure in this category since last year. The US and the UK spend approximately one-third of their defence budgets on equipment; Canada slightly less than that. The amount committed to this item by the EU countries is increasing (Fig. 9.5b), and in 2023 it appears more in line with the level of expenditure of other advanced economies (27.8% of GDP). Three of the non-NATO EU countries (Austria, Ireland, and Malta) spend less than 20%in this category. On the contrary, equipment expenditure accounts for more than 40% of total defence expenditure in Luxembourg, Poland, and Hungary in 2023. Given that there is no indication that this category of spending has a detrimental influence on growth among EU and NATO members, the expansion in this category in the majority of the countries can be beneficial in light of the need to increase investments spending and fill strategic capability gaps.

Equipment category corresponds to investment in defence according to the EDA definition, which can be further divided into equipment purchases, and R&D. The equipment component has the largest share of defence investment and accounts for over 90% on average. Defence investment is subject to a target fixed by NATO (2014) and confirmed by the European Council (2017),[22] asking for a "medium-term increase in defence investment expenditure to 20% of total defence spending (collective benchmark)". While at the European level the benchmark is collective, already in 2006, NATO Defence Ministers committed to devote 20% of the defence budget to investment.

Data at the disaggregated level, for 2022, reveal that twenty EU Member States met the 20% target for defence expenditure dedicated to investment (Fig. 9.6a), which marks a significant improvement over the previous five years when only eight Member States achieved that aim. Luxembourg has the largest investment quota (53.5%), while Austria spends the least (9.5%). The aim has been met collectively since 2019. It now accounts for 24.2% of the twenty-seven countries' overall defence expenditure (EDA 2023), which, however, is 0.2% lower than the previous year (24.4%) (Fig. 9.6b).

Looking at the breakdown of defence investments, apart from a positive trend in the equipment component[23] since 2014, we see a negative tendency for R&D until 2017, when it climbed by 26.3% and stabilized at around 17% of total defence investment (Fig. 9.6b). Further rises are projected in the future, at least for one of his two components: defence expenditure on R&T corresponding to the expenditure for basic research, applied research and technology demonstration for defence purposes. This component of the R&D spending is expected to reach 2% of total defence expenditure as a collective benchmark by all the Member States (European Council

22 Council decision (CFSP) 2017/2315 of 11 December 2017.

23 According to the European defence industrial strategy (2024), it is expected that by 2030, EU countries should: buy at least 40% of the defence equipment by working together.

2017). Collectively the percentage spent on this item is equal to 1.5% in 2022 with an improvement of 0.6% compared to 2017 (EDA 2023). In 2021, at country level, three quarters of EU Member States have increased their spending on R&T since 2017 (Fig. 9.7). Only two countries (Germany and France) had reached the 2% target in 2021 individually.

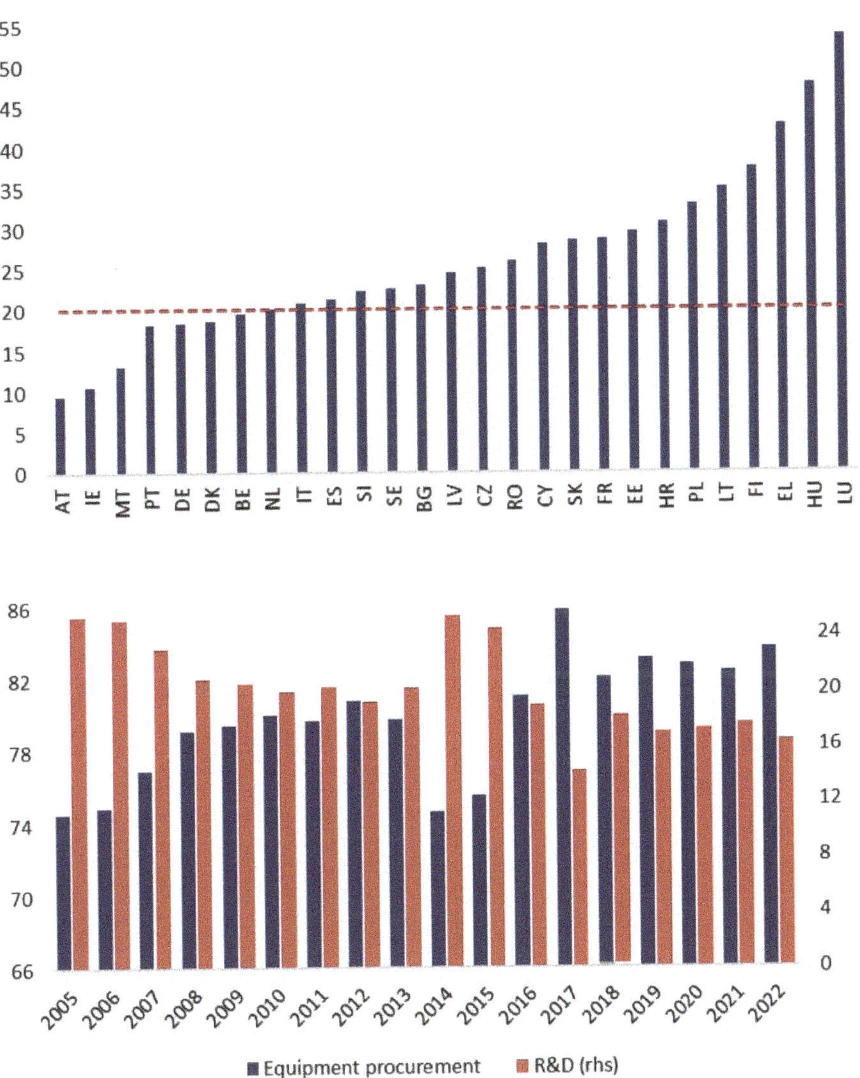

Fig. 9.6 Defence investments. (a) EU countries 2022 (% of total defence expenditure) (above); (b) EU composition evolution (% of defence investments) (below). *Source*: own elaborations on EDA defence data 2022. *Note*: Malta did not commit to any specific target as it is not among the PESCO participating members and not a NATO ally. The data for Denmark comes from the NATO database and reports the percentage spent on equipment.

In terms of defence spending composition and its impact on economic growth, the outlook of additional increases in R&D is quite positive, thanks to the development of new technology (i.e. radar, jet engines, nuclear energy), favouring commercial spin-offs (Pivetti 1992; Dunne et al. 2005). Indeed, due to high-risk environmental and public-good characteristics, certain research projects are unlikely to be carried out by the private sector (Benoit 1978). Thus, there is evidence of crowding-in effects of public defence-related R&D investment on private R&D. Increases in government-funded R&D for an industry or a firm result in significant increases in private sector R&D in that industry or firm, with evidence of international spillovers in the same industry in other countries and positive effects on overall productivity growth (Moretti et al. 2023).

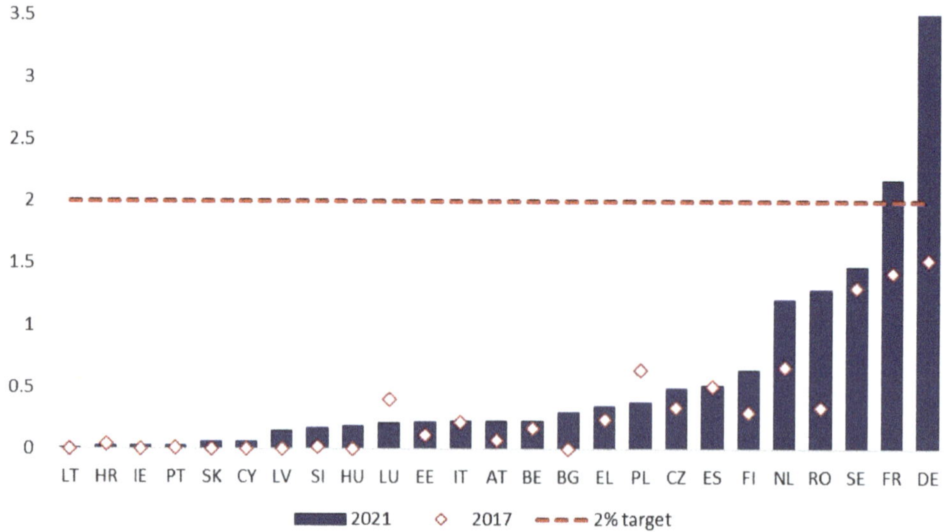

Fig. 9.7 Defence R&T expenditure (2021[24] vs 2017, % of total defence expenditure). *Source*: EDA defence data 2022. *Note*: the data for Latvia and Slovakia are not available for 2017. No data are available for Denmark. Malta is not among the PESCO participating members and so they did not commit to any specific target.

This is consistent with Antolin-Diaz and Surico (2022), who find that in the US the fiscal multiplier for military spending and other government outlays would shift from below one in the short term to above one in the long run, driven by sizeable government R&D expenditure.[25] Also, in a Sraffian supermultiplier model of growth that takes into account the entrepreneurial role of the state (Deleidi and Mazzucato 2019 and 2021) there is evidence of a strong crowd-in impact of government R&D defence expenditures and of their large fiscal multiplier. The impact is larger for policies aimed at producing a structural change—like mission-oriented innovation policies (Mazzucato 2018)—

24 This corresponds to the latest available data in the public dataset provided by EDA.

25 See Ciaffi et al. (2024) for a survey of the macroeconomic effects of public R&D spending.

that boost growth expectations, stimulate private R&D investment, and have a large positive effect on economic growth. Draghi (2024a) recommends to increase and concentrate on common initiatives the European funding for R&D. This could be reached via the dual-use programmes and a proposed European Defence Projects of Common Interest to organize the necessary industrial cooperation.

9.5 Conclusion

This chapter has provided new evidence that almost all EU countries have boosted military spending in recent years and are planning to increase it even further in the future. The trend started after the Russian invasion of Crimea in 2014, and while at that time almost no EU country met NATO's spending target of 2% of GDP in defence, today around ten countries have reached that benchmark. The increase in overall spending is also accompanied by a change in the composition of such expenditure, with a growing share of investment in equipment, which may also be conducive to positive economic spillovers, according to the literature.

The articulation across different budgetary authorities in a multilevel governance system like the EU is of fundamental importance. Not only because of efficiency concerns in terms of public expenditure, but also and mainly for the sake of the effectiveness of the overall defence policy.

In March 2024, the European Commission launched a new strategy to boost defence spending and achieve better readiness. A new fund should also add €1.5 billion to the current common provisions for defence spending in the Multiannual Financial Framework. But most of all, this new strategy calls for a leap forward in integration and joint spending in the next common financial framework.

This chapter has explained the rationale behind stronger integration in defence spending at EU level, but it has also highlighted the reasons why national governments may resist such delegation of power. While, on the one hand, economic arguments suggest potential efficiency gains and improved returns from mutualization of defence spending; on the other hand, the political reality of a multilevel governance system, in which central powers are only delegated by the national level, calls for some caution.

Without convergence of broad geopolitical objectives, budgetary integration in this area may not be fully possible. The institutional evolution of defence policy in the EU attempts to build on a progressive convergence of foreign policy objectives across Member States. The main questions for the future of the EU common defence policy are to what extent this convergence will hold in the new geopolitical context and, if so, to what extent it will be reflected in new common provisions for defence in the common budget.

References

Alptekin, A., and P. Levine (2012) "Military Expenditure and Economic Growth: A Meta-analysis", *European Journal of Political Economy* 28(4): 636–650, https://doi.org/10.1016/j.ejpoleco.2012.07.002

Angelopoulos, K., A. Philippopoulos, and E. Tsionas (2008) "Does Public Sector Efficiency Matter? Revisiting the Relation between Fiscal Size and Economic Growth in a World Sample", *Public Choice* 137: 245–278, https://doi.org/10.1007/s11127-008-9324-8

Antolin-Diaz, J., and P. Surico (2022) "The Long-Run Effects of Government Spending", *CEPR Discussion Paper* 17433.

Benoit, E. (1978) "Growth and Defense in Developing Countries", *Economic Development and Cultural Change* 26(2): 271–280.

Becker, J. (2017) "The Correlates of Transatlantic Burden Sharing: Revising the Agenda for Theoretical and Policy Analysis", *Defense & Security Analysis* 33(2): 131–157, https://doi.org/10.1080/14751798.2017.1311039

Becker, J. (2021) "Rusty Guns and Buttery Soldiers: Unemployment and the Domestic Origins of Defense Spending", *European Political Science Review* 13(3): 307–330, https://doi.org/10.1017/S1755773921000102

Becker, J., and J. P. Dunne (2021) "Military Spending Composition and Economic Growth", *Defence and Peace Economics* 34(3): 259–271.

Becker, J., S. Benson, J. P. Dunne, and E. Malesky (2024) "Disaggregated Defense Spending: Introduction to Data", *Journal of Peace Research*, https://doi.org/10.1177/00223433231215785

Buti, M., and G. Papaconstantinou (2022) "European Public Goods: How Can We Supply More?", *Policy Brief* 3, Luiss School of European Political Economy, https://leap.luiss.it/wp-content/uploads/2022/06/PB3.22-European-Public-Goods.-How-can-we-supply-more.pdf

Cepparulo, A., and P. Pasimeni (2024) "Defence Spending in the European Union" *Discussion Paper* 199, European Commission, https://economy-finance.ec.europa.eu/publications/defence-spending-european-union_en

Churchill, A. S., and S. L. Yew (2018) "The Effect of Military Expenditure on Growth: An Empirical Synthesis", *Empir Econ* 55(3): 1357–1387, https://doi.org/10.1007/s00181-017-1300-z

Ciaffi, G., M. Deleidi, and M. Mazzucato (2024) "Measuring the Macroeconomic Responses to Public Investment in Innovation: Evidence from OECD Countries". *Industrial and Corporate Change* 33(2): 363–382.

Council of the European Union (7371/22) "A Strategic Compass for Security and Defence—For a European Union that Protects its Citizens, Values and Interests and Contributes to International Peace and Security".

Council Decision (CFSP) (2017) "Council Decision 2017/2315 of 11 December 2017", https://eur-lex.europa.eu/legal-content/EN/TXT/PDF/?uri=CELEX:32017D2315&from=EN

Deleidi, M., and M. Mazzucato (2019) "Mission-Oriented Innovation Policies: A Theoretical and Empirical Assessment for the US Economy", *Departmental Working Papers of Economics - University 'Roma Tre'* 0248, Department of Economics - University Roma Tre.

Deleidi, M., and M. Mazzucato (2021) "Directed Innovation Policies and the Supermultiplier: An Empirical Assessment of Mission-oriented Policies in the US Economy", *Research Policy* 50(2), https://doi.org/10.1016/j.respol.2020.104151

Draghi, M. (2024a) *The Future of European Competitiveness. Part A: A Competitiveness Strategy for Europe*. Brussels: European Commission.

Draghi, M. (2024b) *The Future of European Competitiveness. Part B: In-depth Analysis and Recommendations*. Brussels: European Commission.

Dunne, J. P., R. Smith, and D. Willenbockel (2005) "Models of Military Expenditure and Growth: A Critical Review", *Defence and Peace Economics* 16(6): 449–460.

Dunne, J. P., and N. Tian (2016) "Military Expenditure and Economic Growth, 1960–2014", *The Economics of Peace and Security Journal* 11(2), https://doi.org/10.15355/epsj.11.2.50

Dunne, J. P., and R. P. Smith (2020) "Military Expenditure, Investment and Growth", *Defence and Peace Economics* 31(6): 601–614, https://doi.org/10.1080/10242694.2019.1636182

European Commission (2017) *JOIN. 41 Final Improving Military Mobility in the European Union*. Brussels: European Commission.

European Commission (2018) *JOIN. 5 Final On the Action Plan on Military Mobility*. Brussels: European Commission.

European Commission (2022a) *JOIN. 48 Action Plan on Military Mobility 2.0*. Brussels: European Commission.

European Commission (2022b) *JOIN. 24 Final On the Defence Investment Gaps Analysis and Way Forward*. Brussels: European Commission.

European Commission (2024) *JOIN. 10 Final A New European Defence Industrial Strategy: Achieving EU Readiness through a Responsive and Resilient European Defence Industry*. Brussels: European Commission.

European Council (1999a) "Declaration of the European Council on Strengthening the Common European Security and Defence", European Council, Cologne 3–4 June 1999, https://www.europarl.europa.eu/summits/kol1_en.htm

European Council (1999b) "Presidency Conclusions", Helsinki European Council, 10–11 December 1999, https://www.consilium.europa.eu/uedocs/cms_data/docs/pressdata/en/ec/ACFA4C.htm

European Council (March 2024) "Conclusions—21 and 22 March 2024", https://www.consilium.europa.eu/media/70880/euco-conclusions-2122032024.pdf

EDA (2018) *Factsheet: Capability Development Plan*. Brussels: EDA, https://eda.europa.eu/publications-and-data/factsheets/factsheet-capability-development-plan

EDA (2021) *Annual Report*. Brussels: EDA.

EDA (2022) *2022 Coordinated Annual Review on Defence Report*. Brussels: EDA.

EDA (2023) *Annual Report*. Brussels: EDA.

EU (2014) "The Mechanism for Financing Military Operations (Athena). Summaries of EU Legislation", https://eur-lex.europa.eu/EN/legal-content/summary/the-mechanism-for-financing-military-operations-athena.html

Fiott, D. (2023) "In Every Crisis an Opportunity? European Union Integration in Defence and the War on Ukraine", *Journal of European Integration* 45(3): 447–462, https://doi.org/10.1080/07036337.2023.2183395

Fuest, C., and J. Pisani-Ferry (2019) "A Primer on Developing European Public Goods", *EconPol Policy Report* 16(3), https://www.econstor.eu/bitstream/10419/219519/1/econpol-pol-report-16.pdf

Håkansson, C. (2023) "The Ukraine War and the Emergence of the European Commission as a Geopolitical Actor", *Journal of European Integration* 46(1): 25–45, https://doi.org/10.1080/07036337.2023.2239998

Letta, E. (2024) *Much More Than a Market*, https://www.consilium.europa.eu/media/ny3j24sm/much-more-than-a-market-report-by-enrico-letta.pdf

Malizard, J. (2015) "Does Military Expenditure Crowd Out Private Investment? A Disaggregated Perspective for the Case of France", *Economic Modelling* 46: 44–52.

Mazur, S. (2021) "Security and Defence Heading 5 of the 2021–2027 MFF", *Briefing 2021–2027 MFF*, European Parliamentary Research Service, https://www.europarl.europa.eu/RegData/etudes/BRIE/2021/690545/EPRS_BRI(2021)690545_EN.pdf

Mazzucato, M. (2013) *The Entrepreneurial State: Debunking Public vs Private Sector Myths*. London: Anthem Press.

Mazzucato, M. (2018) "Mission-oriented Innovation Policies: Challenges and Opportunities", *Industrial and Corporate Change* 27(5): 803–815.

Moretti, E., C. Steinwender, and J. Van Reenen (2023) "The Intellectual Spoils of War? Defense R&D, Productivity, and International Spillovers", *Review of Economics and Statistics*, 1–46.

Mowery, D. C. (2010) "Military R&D and Innovation", in B. H. Hall and N. Rosenberg (eds), *Handbook of the Economics of Innovation*. North Holland: Elsevier, pp. 1219–1256. https://doi.org/10.1016/S0169-7218(10)02013-7

Musgrave, R. A. (1939) "The Nature of Budgetary Balance and the Case for the Capital Budget", *American Economic Review* 29(2): 260–271.

NATO. (2014). *Wales Summit Declaration Issued by the Heads of State and Government Participating in the Meeting of the North Atlantic Council in Wales*, https://www.nato.int/cps/en/natohq/official_texts_112964.htm

Oates, W. E. (1999) "An Essay on Fiscal Federalism", *Journal of Economic Literature* 37(3): 1120–1149.

Oates, W. E. (2005) "Toward a Second-Generation Theory of Fiscal Federalism", *International Tax and Public Finance* 12: 349–373.

Pivetti, M. (1989) "Military Expenditure and Economic Analysis: A Review Article", *Contributions to Political Economy* 8(1): 55–67.

Pivetti, M. (1992) "Military Spending as a Burden on Growth: an 'Underconsumptionist' Critique", *Cambridge Journal of Economics* 16(4): 373–384.

Smith, R. P., and P. Dunne (1994) "Is Military Spending a Burden? A Marxo-Marginalist Response to Pivetti", *Cambridge Journal of Economics* 18(5): 515–521.

Santamaría, P. G.-T., A. A. García, and A. G. Domonte (2022) "Scientometric Analysis of the Relationship between Expenditure on Defence and Economic Growth: Current Situation and Future Perspectives", *Defence and Peace Economics*, 34(8): 1071–1090, https://doi.org/10.1080/10242694.2022.2091191

Wyplosz, C. (2016) "The Six Flaws of the Eurozone", *Economic Policy* 31(87): 559–606.

Yesilyurt, F., and M. E. Yesilyurt (2019) "Meta-analysis, Military Expenditures and Growth", *Journal of Peace Research* 56: 352–363. https://doi.org/10.1177/0022343318808841

10. Sustainable Mobility and Industrial Policy

Dario Guarascio[1] *and Annamaria Simonazzi*[2]

Focusing on the automotive industry, this chapter addresses the problem of Europe's vulnerability (e.g., import dependency, technological backwardness in key domains) and the hypothesis of the obsolescence of its growth and production model. First, we analyze the evolution of the Sino-German relationships highlighting the emergence of two divergent trajectories: while a well-tailored combination of industrial and trade policies allowed China to become the leader in electric vehicle (EV) production, the German development model, mostly driven by the choices of key carmakers, slowed innovation, fostered fragmentation within the European Union (EU) and created the conditions for the current vulnerability. Second, we identify the key elements—i.e., increasing demand for affordable EVs, investments in infrastructure for the provision of public goods, building-up a European Directorate for Resource Security—of a European industrial policy for sustainable mobility which may help achieve the multiple goals of decarbonizing the economy, increasing resilience, and reducing inequalities between and within countries.

10.1 Introduction

This chapter addresses the problem of Europe's vulnerability and the hypothesis of the obsolescence of its growth and production model in light of the "twin transition" (i.e., green and digital) taking place in a changing international economic and political order. Technological change is causing major transformations in industries and companies alike, contributing to a reallocation of production between countries, regions and macro-areas. Likewise, growing conflicts and ensuing global shocks are encouraging the adoption of de-risking strategies aimed at reducing dependencies along critical value chains (VCs)

1 Sapienza University of Rome.
2 Sapienza University of Rome.

 https://doi.org/10.11647/OBP.0434.11

and eventually resulting in a reshaping of trade/production networks (e.g., reshoring). Yet, the heterogeneous positioning of European Union (EU) Member States concerning their economic and technological capabilities, as well as the key structural characteristics that may affect their degree of resilience/vulnerability (e.g., population aging, skill supply, inequalities), may pave the way for further internal divergence with dangerous implications not only for the periphery but for Europe as a whole.

In this context, a major driver of change that is bound to have a profound impact on the EU and on its internal hierarchies is the acceleration of the green transition, motivated by the twofold need of meeting increasingly ambitious climate targets and reducing the dependency on (fossil) energy imports (Celi et al. 2022). To assess the EU's position and infer its future structural trajectory, it is, first of all, necessary to identify the key peculiarities of the restructuring process brought about by the green transition. The latter differs from the two previous restructuring episodes that shook the European economy in the 1970s and in the first decade of the 2000s. In the 1970s, southern economies (e.g., Italy) were those that paid the highest price as a consequence of the changing composition of demand and of the shock in commodity prices, especially oil. Specialized in more mature products and facing growing competition from newly industrialized nations (NICs), these countries bore the brunt of a deeper change in their productive structure as compared to their northern peers (e.g., Germany). This resulted, in the medium run, in an increasing divide between the core and the periphery of the EU. In the first decade of the 2000s, restructuring was driven by growing competition from China. Again, the burden was asymmetrically distributed with the Southern periphery (SP) bearing the greatest costs. Recently admitted to the World Trade Organization (WTO), China had in fact a medium-tech specialization that, along with comparatively lower labour costs, made it a fearsome competitor for the SP. As Chinese goods flooded European markets, the reorientation of German production chains to Eastern Europe put further pressure on the SP, deepening the core-periphery divide (Celi et al. 2018).

The current situation is rather different, however. The green transition is going to affect the EU's core and periphery in a more symmetric way, as the costs of restructuring depend, among other factors, on two characteristics that the two areas (at least partly) share: relative weight of energy-intensive industries and energy (import) dependency. No less relevant is the fact that today it is above all the core and, in particular, Germany, which is specialized in a technology that we could define as "solid but mature", that is going to suffer the most from Chinese competition. From being a convenient location for foreign direct investments (FDIs) aimed at exploiting low labour costs, China is now becoming a technologically qualified competitor, threatening the EU's core both in its traditional specialization sectors (e.g., automotive and, in particular, the EV segment), as well as in domains where Europe was already lagging behind the US (e.g., digital). In what follows, we analyze the EU's response to these challenges and the potential problems for internal cohesion from the perspective of its core country, Germany, and one of its key industries, the automotive one.

10.2 The Automotive Industry: From Mature, Sleepy Oligopoly to Breakneck Change

The current vicissitudes of the European automotive industry perfectly illustrate the crisis engulfing the German and, hence, the European economy. The sector deserves special attention due to its relevance for the German and European industry: it represents 7% of the European Union's GDP, directly and indirectly employing around 13 million workers, equal to 7% and 11.5% of EU total and manufacturing employment, respectively. It is of crucial relevance to Germany: exports of motor vehicles and parts represent 15–16% of its total exports, with China's share accounting for 12% of exports and 5 to 10% of the total demand of the German automotive industry in 2022.

The car industry is operating on a pan-European value chain and its present structure is the result of two different strategies. The German model specialized in the luxury and sports car segments, whose production in Germany has continued to grow over the years, while production of lower-priced subcompact cars was relocated to the Eastern European countries. The German industry grew closely integrated for inputs or final assembly with the Eastern periphery (EP), where the automotive industry represents from 15% to 23% of manufacturing value added (Pavlinek 2023). At the same time, German companies have also relocated production to China, aiming to seize the economic, technological and cost-related advantages offered by the very rapid expansion of its market. Over the last twenty years, the German automotive companies' presence on the Chinese market has been decisive for their success, with revenues from their Chinese divisions accounting for about 30% of total foreign affiliates (Deutsche Bundesbank 2024: 19, fn. 31). In 2018, Volkswagen built more cars in China than it produced in Germany, making nearly 50% of its profits there. French and Italian companies, on the other hand, have specialized in volume class, medium- and low-quality cars, where for price and cost reasons the "local to local" strategy prevails, i.e. the cars are produced in or close to the final market. The relocation of the entire supply chain to low-cost areas, inside and outside Europe, together with France and Italy's limited presence on the Chinese market, have resulted in the reduction of their production share in the countries of origin (Russo et al. 2023).

Pardi (2022) traces the contrasting fortunes of the German, on the one hand, and of the French and Italian car industries, on the other, linking their divergent trajectories to the peculiar evolution of the EU regulatory framework regarding CO2 emissions (under pressure from the German lobby). The weight-based CO2 standards resulted in a "upmarket regulatory pressure... [that] prevented generalist car manufacturers from going downmarket to meet CO2 targets and to protect their market shares by making more affordable cars" (Pardi 2022: 33). Yet, demand dynamics proved heterogeneous across areas, exacerbating the core-periphery divide: higher prices could be afforded by core countries, where they were countered by generous subsidies, much less so in peripheral ones (Pardi 2022: 47–48). Between 2001 and 2019, the generalist car manufacturers lost market shares, and had to relocate production to low-cost countries. In the EP, the combination of upmarket drift and low wages led to massive second-hand car imports that killed the market for new cars. The stark contrast in the evolution of the two groups of automakers—Pardi concludes—highlights the considerable economic consequences that upmarket drift has had in terms of restructuring and deindustrialization (Pardi 2022: 44).

However, the new stricter regulatory procedures put forth as a consequence of the Dieselgate scandal left the shift to electric cars—both battery electric vehicles (BEVs) and plug-in hybrid electric vehicles (PHEVs)—as the only solution. The "new" principles underlying regulation have meant that electrification has simply substituted "dieselization". Without any change in business models and product architectures, "we are electrifying conventional multipurpose vehicles rather than creating new energy vehicles" (Pardi 2022: 55–56). As previously experienced with diesel cars, the entire production of BEVs and PHEVs moved towards an "upward shift", which is documented by the rapid increase in the average weight and price of vehicles: between 2001 and 2020 the average mass of the new European car increased by 15%, engine power by 43% and price by 60%. In 2019, the average BEV sold in Europe was 52% more expensive than in China and 10% more expensive than in the US.

10.3 How Fast It Goes: Innovation and Competition

Two different but somehow connected challenges are transforming the automotive sector, from a relatively mature oligopolistic industry to a new, aggressively competitive tech industry. The so-called CASE disruption (Connected, Autonomous, Shared, and Electrified) is changing the "car" product itself: its quality is based less and less on mechanical characteristics, such as engine power, and more and more on interconnection and infotainment characteristics. Consequently, the entire industry is facing a process of change concerning its technological, organizational and knowledge-related characteristics: the traditional mechanical skills that characterize the vertically integrated supply chain are no longer sufficient to produce a competitive car. In turn, various complementary specializations that belong to different supply chains (vehicles, batteries, autonomous driving, entertainment) are required. New competitors from inside (China) and outside the industry (Big Tech and software startups) are changing the geography of competitive advantages, blurring the boundaries of the sector (Simonazzi et al. 2022). Continuous, fast innovation in products, inputs, and technologies has decreed the end of the incumbents' traditional strategies, forcing them to chase innovation to survive. China is at the forefront of this process. Far from being purely a cheap manufacturing hub, China is more and more important for costs and technological upgrading, especially in the green and digital domains.

Leaping from infant industry to world champion, in just a few years, China has become the world's leading car manufacturer. It has achieved absolute leadership in electric vehicles thanks to a far-sighted, targeted industrial policy aimed at developing the entire supply chain. Generous subsidies and strictly regulated foreign investments (importing know-how through mandating joint ventures with local companies) have accelerated the learning process; a fully vertically integrated business model, from mining to chip manufacturing to software, has ensured the supply of inputs at stable prices; heavily subsidized consumption has ensured a huge, rapidly expanding market and the achievement of dynamic economies of scale. Unlike Europe, where emissions regulations have pushed the industry towards heavier and more powerful cars, in China, thanks to a different conception of regulation, electrification resulted in BEVs that are significantly cheaper to acquire and to use than equivalent petrol and hybrid vehicles, even without any subsidy. All these factors have given the industry a first-mover advantage, placing competitors at a permanent disadvantage.

Foreign automakers have been eager to gain market access for their "traditional" cars, but have been slow in perceiving the changing context. Tesla stands out as the exception (Hvistendahl et al. 2024). Being the absolute precursor in the EV industry, for Chinese leaders a Tesla factory on domestic soil could bring technology and know-how while serving as a "catfish" that makes other fish swim faster and forcing homegrown brands to innovate. It has also created a huge talent pool which spread to the whole value chain (McMorrow and Li 2024). In exchange, Elon Musk received profuse government subsidies, low-interest loans, cheap and docile labour, and "targeted" new emissions regulations that brought huge profits to the company as Chinese manufacturing took off. Tesla's Shanghai plant became a flagship, accounting for over half of Tesla's global deliveries and the bulk of its profits (McMorrow and Li 2024).

Chinese groups are now moving rapidly into the technologies behind autonomous driving (AD). Tesla is once again leading China's push into the new frontier, partnering with leading Chinese Artificial Intelligence (AI) companies, such as Baidu, and benefiting, once again, from ad-hoc regulations on AD, namely a regulatory approval of data security provisions for more capable autonomous vehicles. EV startups and Big Tech companies such as Xiaomi and Huawei are joining in, developing connected and smart features and AD technology (Li and Campbell 2024). Software developments lead to new sources of revenue, from licensing technologies for enabling digital services to charging infrastructure. Western automakers are scrambling to catch up, partnering with Chinese companies across the entire value chain to access Chinese technology and know-how. Volkswagen's "In China for China" project, which involves massive investments in the industrial centre of Hefei, China's Silicon Valley where companies from various sectors design the "car of the future", is just one (paradigmatic) example.

The change in comparative advantage is starting to show up in trade data. China's share of EV sold in Europe is still quite low, but rising rapidly: formerly 8% in 2022 and is expected to reach 15% in 2025 (De Quant et al. 2024). Until recently, electric car imports from China were dominated by western brands exporting the vehicles from

China to Europe (with Tesla and Renault's Dacia accounting for 50%). But Chinese brands are quickly catching up: Chinese EVs are significantly cheaper, stylish and of high quality. The recent decline in German car exports to China, contrasted by the increase in German luxury car production in China and the reversal of Germany's trade balance with China, suggests that what happened for low-medium quality cars could also occur for the premium segment, where producing locally becomes the only possible strategy.

Yet, success on the Chinese market is no longer guaranteed. The recent decline in the growth rate of Chinese car demand has hit the internal combustion engine (ICE) segment particularly hard (-37% in 2023 compared to 2017), pushing Chinese manufacturers to flood the markets of developing countries with low-cost cars, and thus eroding the market shares of Western competitors (ICE cars still account for 77% of Chinese exports) (White et al. 2024). Despite the shift in demand towards electric cars, the growth rate of this segment has also slowed. Overcapacity across all market segments has sparked a fierce price war that has led to squeezed margins, bankruptcies and industry consolidation.

By relying on a much broader network of local suppliers and benefiting from stable access to low-cost inputs and batteries, vertically integrated Chinese companies can weather the crisis better than foreign manufacturers. Excess capacity and the price war mean that foreign producers, too, could try to export more from their Chinese factories, and thus risk undercutting their own factories in Western markets. If China's price war reverberates in Western markets, warns Stellantis CEO Carlos Tavares, it could end in a bloodbath. In this context, the upmarket regulatory pressure, which prevented the generalist car manufacturers from going downmarket to meet CO2 targets and to protect their market shares by making more affordable cars, leaves the European market for mass EV consumption wide open for Chinese entry.

10.4 The New EU Industrial Policy in Troubled Times

There is no doubt that the EU has drastically revised its position on competition and industrial policy, dropping its long-standing hostility towards public intervention. Bauerle Danzman and Meunier (2024) underline the extent and rapidity of such a policy change, arguing that "the EU has since 2017 created a panoply of innovative policy tools that blend trade and investment with essential security concerns". The deployment of defensive and offensive tools has been made possible "by the confluence of external factors that triggered European leaders' beliefs that change was necessary and internal factors that made such change institutionally and politically possible, a trend reinforced by the pandemic and the Russian invasion of Ukraine". Among these factors, Graf and Schmalz (2023) stress the changed German attitude—including both the government, the BDI, as well as German trade unions—towards selective state intervention and protectionism in the face of the "Chinese threat".

However, assessments of the new EU industrial policy differ concerning its size, quality and, more importantly, expected effectiveness in countering external and internal challenges (Guarascio et al. 2024). Decarbonization and self-sufficiency (i.e., strategic autonomy) have added complexity to industrial policy, traditionally aimed at pursuing production and employment objectives (Andreoni 2024). The problem is now how to de-risk the European economic model, while simultaneously closing the gap in green and digital technologies as well as preserving growth and cohesion in a fragmented union. The European response is aimed, above all, at the external challenge, but in doing so it risks leaving open, or deepening, internal problems. Its strategy is played out on two levels. Internally, the ideology of the market is put aside by rediscovering industrial policy: it has liberalized state aid and is promoting initiatives aimed at creating alliances between European companies in sectors crucial for the green and digital transition. On the international level, it has abandoned the "dogma of free trade" with the introduction of measures aimed at protecting the internal market against (Chinese) imports or subsidized FDIs. With its "open strategic autonomy" approach, the EU wants to secure supply chains and technological sovereignty in an open economy, trying to strike a fine balance between responding to techno-nationalism and protectionism abroad and keeping markets open. However, Europe's ambitious agenda lacks a strategy to ensure its achievement and to address internal conflicts and latent policy dilemmas.

It is now a common opinion that Chinese imports damage domestic production and employment. As a result, protectionist measures are rampant on both sides of the Atlantic. Protection of the American market diverts Chinese exports to Europe. At the same time, it could benefit the EU's exports to the US. By the same token, US subsidies are likely to attract investment in green technologies from European companies. The extraterritorial reach of US-imposed restrictions, which tell European companies what to do and what not to do in their dealings with China, limits their options if they wish to maintain access to the American market. Yet, for many European/German companies, being on the Chinese market is vital: in the words of Siemens CEO Roland Busch, the company "cannot afford not to be [in China]" (Alim and Jones 2024). The attitude of the German industry is heeded by the German government, which wants to "further expand trade with China, taking into account the need to reduce risks and diversify", as a German government official said during the German Chancellor's visit to China at the head of a business delegation (Alim and Jones 2024). A fairly vague statement. In fact, large German companies have continued to invest in the Chinese market, concluding joint venture agreements with Chinese companies for the production of low-cost cars, possibly to be imported into Europe.

If producing in China becomes more profitable (or deemed indispensable for competitiveness), companies' goals may conflict with broader national economic interests. Offshoring production will affect not only the final stage of production, but the entire value chain, as components and parts suppliers will either have to follow their original equipment manufacturers (OEMs) or downsize. This adds to the difficulties the value chain already faces with the transition to electric cars due to the much lower number of components required. Large components companies such as Bosch and ZF Friedrichshafen have already announced significant job cuts in Germany. Decisions about which plants to close and which suppliers to penalize can go beyond the corporate sphere: how to reconcile the conflicting interests between the various national industries (and their governments) becomes a thorny political problem. Protecting domestic production could also clash with countries' broader interests: in the case of imposing import duties on Chinese vehicles, the policy put forth by the EC and supported by France was not welcomed by Berlin and its automotive companies, who are fearful of negative repercussions on Sino-German trade relations.

Furthermore, the political choice of leaving the task of financing the transition to the Member States, liberalizing state aid without providing for a common EU fund, and the parallel choice to leave the direction of change to companies correspond to strongly underestimating the risk that the green transition will result in an increase in inequalities between countries and classes (as demonstrated in the case of the upmarket shift experienced by the industry in past years). State aid liberalization means that countries with fewer budget constraints have more resources to attract investments. In this regard, protectionist measures could further distort the functioning of the single market in the very likely case that the inflow of foreign investments to circumvent the protective wall is directed mainly towards low-cost, more generous or politically friendlier countries. Recent information on Chinese investment projects, mostly directed towards Eastern countries, shows that these concerns are not far-fetched. Additionally, preventing or limiting Chinese FDIs for economic or security reasons, as in the case of electronic devices and connected cars, could put the EC at odds with Member States keen to attract investment and know-how at lower costs, in order to counteract their disadvantage in the race to attract or retain production and plants. In the case of the new Foreign Subsidies Regulation (FSR), operational since July 2023 and already resulting in numerous investigations (Moscoso and Stoyanova 2024), regulatory uncertainty could deter foreign investment and raise the cost of green tech.

The automotive revolution raises serious concerns regarding the core-periphery divide (Celi et al. 2018 2022). Both SP and EP lack national OEMs and Tier1 suppliers. Hence, their industrial fate tends to be decided in the core. Nonetheless, due to their different development paths, the two peripheries differ in the quality of their supplier networks. In the EP, "the low-tier domestic-owned suppliers specialized in ICE-specific manufacturing did not develop enough capabilities and know how to withstand the change and can easily be erased from the market if they fail to adapt and reposition themselves" (Szalavetz 2022). On the other hand, the dependence on the core could shield the EP from the most devastating (short-term) effects of the transition to electromobility. In fact, they will continue to produce internal combustion engine vehicles for a longer time, relying on the competitive advantage resulting from low production costs, especially low labour costs, and from relatively new factories. The division of labour between the core and its EP can allow OEMs to benefit from the full range of products, from increasingly obsolete ICE technologies in the East to full-scale production in dedicated EV factories in the West (Pavlinek 2023). However, a slower transition to electric vehicles and failure to attract the battery sector could undermine the EP's long-term competitive position. Conversely, the SP still retains a network of capable, state-of-the-art parts and components firms that supply German and French OEMs and their first-tier suppliers. Yet, different factories within the same transnational enterprise compete with each other for investments, products and projects (Pardi 2022: 45) relying on a complex of "attractive factors" (labour and energy costs, government subsidies, innovation clusters), making it difficult to predict how the difference in the quality of domestic suppliers in the two peripheries will play out. The inability to retain assembly, coupled with the poor ability to attract battery plants (as proximity to assembly plants is a major cost driver), the risk of scaling back R&D, the weakness of complementary sectors—such as electronics, high technology, software—cast a shadow on the future of the sector in the SP (but the situation in Spain and Italy could be different). Even if a relevant share of components suppliers is not directly affected by the electrical transformation, the entire value chain is in danger if clusters of innovation and economies of agglomeration lead to the reallocation of production.

Summing up, security and de-industrialization concerns may affect the speed and costs of the green transition. Cheap imports from China could reduce the costs of decarbonization and benefit consumers, but risk undermining the industrial base. On the other hand, protecting "European" industry and jobs could become socially unsustainable and politically incendiary if it results in a highly unbalanced reallocation of the automotive value chain. It could also be self-defeating if companies' strategies are not reoriented towards the production of less expensive and polluting cars.

10.5 Conclusion

The new European industrial policy must reconcile conflicting objectives and manage multiple diverging interests between and within countries in an EU that remains highly fragmented. While the previous policy of non-interference with the market, in accordance with the principle that the best industrial policy is the one that does not exist, could play on the fiction of a neutral and non-discriminating market, whereby unfair results could be attributed to inexorable economic laws, the new industrial policy makes clear the choices made, the privileged interests, and the consequent distribution of costs and benefits.

The current fragmentation risks irremediably undermining internal cohesion and further slowing down growth. The task, therefore, is to find a shared strategy that enhances the elements of common interest over those of conflict: a policy that aims to leave no one behind, to reduce the imbalances between regions, countries, and European citizens. In what follows, we stress three points that may be included in a strategy aimed at expanding the market (thus sustaining production and employment), securing resources, and promoting decarbonization.

1. Increase demand for affordable EVs. The European premium car market is too small compared to the production capacity of the German industry. Demand can only grow if the supply of affordable EVs increases, encouraging their adoption in poorer countries/or by poorer consumers. Revised emissions regulations (the phasing out of weight-based CO2 standards), targeted subsidies for less expensive EVs, and the threat of Chinese imports of cheaper electric vehicles could encourage a downward drift by generalist manufacturers. This change would accelerate decarbonization, as larger electric vehicles require a larger battery, more critical raw materials, and consume more energy on the road (Pardi 2022). It could also revive production in the SP, although it is doubtful whether local production would be able to withstand Chinese competition without public support.

2. Investments in infrastructure for the provision of public goods. Regulations and subsidies are not enough. The growth of the EV market can only occur if accompanied by an expansion of supporting infrastructures: charging stations, renewable energy networks, software services, connectivity technologies. This requires a common long-term strategy that coordinates various decisions on planning, financing, material procurement and governance, mobilizes and coordinates public and private investments, and avoids harmful internal competition between states. The green transition is an opportunity for growth: the European market is large enough to offer the benefits ensured by scale and dynamics economics, provided that a shared strategy addresses regional inequalities, helping lagging countries to seize the opportunities offered by the transition while avoiding the low road of competition on labour costs. Investments in green energy production in the SP and a European energy grid could activate a multiplicative process while contributing to reducing the energy cost for the entire European economy. The IPCEI program (Important Projects of Common European Interest), if properly managed to avoid being captured by bigger actors, could offer a possibility of inter-country, inter-firms collaboration.

3. A European Directorate for Resource Security. Resource security requires a coordinated foreign policy to secure global supplies and access to CRMs, avoiding the "cacophony" of multiple national initiatives. Fluctuations in demand for EVs, transmitted through the entire supply chain to CRMs, may result in greater fluctuations in mineral prices that damage the producing country's economy, thus discouraging investment. Simply relying on market-driven private investment falls short of China's long-term strategy of supporting and stabilizing production through subsidized inventory buildup. Competition on different grounds, such as a European policy of cooperation with producing countries, the creation of non-exploitative trade relationships, the provision of financing, the guarantee of non-polluting extraction, and a greater appropriation of value by producing countries, could better guarantee the strategic autonomy sought by the EU.

Finally, collaboration with China on green technologies could reduce the costs of decarbonization. Western automakers are already collaborating with Chinese companies in software technology and core components for electric vehicles to produce cheaper and more attractive electric vehicles. If properly managed and monitored, the adoption of these innovations in European manufacturing could benefit workers, consumers and the environment, and help the EU carve out a place for itself in the trade war between the United States and China.

Decarbonizing the economy while maintaining a thriving European automotive industry will require more than just regulations, subsidies and protection. It will require a delicate balance between conflicting objectives and policy measures to ensure technological progress and social cohesion.

References

Alim, A. N., P. Nilsson, and P. Campbell (2024) "Volkswagen Considers Partnership to Produce Mass Market Electric Vehicles", March 13, *Financial Times*, https://www.ft.com/content/0985f16c-105c-4b62-aa80-3658fa9b629a

Alim, A. M., and S. Jones (2024) "German Companies' Dependence on China Will Last Decades, Warns Siemens", 14 April, *Financial Times*, https://www.ft.com/content/e8634f5c-5a28-4741-a13d-024665456f43?

Autor, D. H, D. Dorn, and G. H. Hanson (2016) "The China Shock: Learning from Labor Market Adjustment to Large Changes in Trade", *BNER* 21906.

Baqaee, D., J. Hinz, B. Moll, M. Schularick, F. A. Teti, J. Wanner, and S. Yang (2024) "What If? The Effects of a Hard Decoupling from China on the German Economy", *Kiel Policy Brief* 170.

Bauerle Danzman, S., and S. Meunier (2024) "The EU's Geoeconomic Turn: From Policy Laggard to Institutional Innovator", *Journal of Common Market Studies* 62(1), https://doi.org/10.1111/jcms.13599

Beattie, A. (2024) "Europe's New Anti-subsidy Weapon Is Powerful but Hard to Control: The EU Foreign Subsidies Regulation Is Looking to Score Some Notable Hits", 9 May, *Financial Times*, https://www.ft.com/content/db880189-6556-427d-9c80-b4af3c8917d2?

Celi, G., A. Ginzburg, D. Guarascio, and A. Simonazzi (2018) *Crisis in the European Monetary Union*. Oxford: Routledge.

Celi, G., D. Guarascio, J. Reljic, A. Simonazzi, and F. Zezza (2022) "The Asymmetric Impact of War: Resilience, Vulnerability and Implications for EU Policy", *Intereconomics* 57(3): 141–147.

De Cecco, M. (1978) "Il sistema monetario internazionale", in M. Carmagnani and A. Vercelli (eds.), *Economia e storia*. Florence: La Nuova Italia, pp. 810–830.

De Quant, S., S. Tordoir, and S. Vallée (2024) "Caught in Geopolitical Fragmentation: How to De-risk Germany's Economic Model", *Working Paper* 02/2024.

Deutsche Bundesbank (2024) "Risks Facing Germany as a Result of its Economic Ties with China", *Monthly Report*, January.

Graf, H., and S. Schmalz (2023) "Avoiding the China Shock: How Chinese State-backed Internationalization Drives Changes in European Economic Governance", *Competition and Change*, https://doi.org/10.1177/10245294231207990

Guarascio, D., J. Reljic, G. Cucignatto, G. Celi, and A. Simonazzi (2024) "Between Scylla and Charybdis. Long-term Drivers of EU Structural Vulnerability, *Review of Keynesian Economics* 12(4): forthcoming.

Hvistendahl, M., J. Ewing, and J. Liu (2024) "A Pivot to China Saved Elon Musk. It also Binds Him to Beijing", 27 March, *New York Times*, https://www.nytimes.com/2024/03/27/world/asia/elon-musk-tesla-china.html

Janeway, W.H. (2024) "Is Techno-Monopoly Inevitable?", 5 April, *Project Syndicate*, https://www.project-syndicate.org/onpoint/us-big-tech-monopolies-market-power-from-key-innovations-by-william-h-janeway-2024-04

Li, G., and P. Campbell (2024) "BYD Loses EV Throne to Tesla as Sales slip", 2 April, *Financial Times*, https://www.ft.com/content/4f1a2188-ced0-4018-998d-5148209a5f5e

Matthes, J. (2023) "Entwicklung des Konkurrenzdrucks durch China auf dem EU-Markt: Update einer Vorläuferstudie" [Evoluzione della pressione competitiva della Cina sul mercato UE], *IW-Report* 39/2023.

McMorrow, R., and G. Li (2024) "The Steve Jobs of China Turns Car Salesman. in Xiaomi's EV Evolution", 5 April, *Financial Times*, https://www.ft.com/content/f0664662-ea9f-4bd6-a5c1-6c76c99b6ccd

Moscoso, L., and I. Stoyanova (2024) "The Foreign Subsidies Regulation—100 Days Since the Start of the Notification Obligation for Concentrations", *Competition FSR Brief* 1, https://competition-policy.ec.europa.eu/document/download/22197012-2036-4b1e-8b02-0eb8b2d6e666_en?filename=kdar24001enn_competition_FSR_brief_1_2024_100-days-of-FSR-notification-obligation.pdf

Nilsson, P. (2024) "German Car Parts Suppliers Plan Job Cuts amid Costly EV Transition", 18 January, *Financial Times*, https://www.ft.com/content/40585c6c-741c-4450-8f06-8d367839594c

Pardi, T. (2022) "Heavier, Faster and Less Affordable Cars: The Consequence of EU Regulations for Car Emissions", *ETUI Research Paper-Report* 7, http://dx.doi.org/10.2139/ssrn.4304165

Pavlinek, P. (2023) "Transition of the Automotive Industry towards Electric Vehicle Production in the East European Integrated Periphery", *Empirica* 50: 35–73.

Russo, M., F. Alboni, J. C. Sanginés, M. De Domenico, G. Mangioni, S. Righi, and A. Simonazzi (2023) "Regionalisation and Cross-region Integration. Twin Dynamics in the Automotive International Trade Networks", *Structural Change and Economic Dynamics* 67: 98–114.

Sandbu, M. (2022) "Europe Is Learning that You Can't Separate Trade and Politics", 6 November, *Financial Times*, https://www.ft.com/content/a1b97de4-b366-4a0e-aa58-93a6b6fa8b2a

Simonazzi, A., J. Carreto Sanginés, and M. Russo (2022) "The World to Come: Key Challenges for the Automotive Industry", *Economia & Lavoro* 56(1): 7–23.

Szalavetz, A. (2022) "Transition to Electric Vehicles in Hungary: A Devastating Crisis or Business as Usual?", *Technological Forecasting and Social Change* 184: 122029.

Weissmann, J. (2016) "Did Donald Trump Win the Election Because of Trade? A New Study Suggests It Helped", 2 December, *Slate*, https://slate.com/business/2016/12/study-suggests-job-losses-to-china-helped-donald-trump-win-the-election.html

White, E., M. Pooler, A. A. Lakshmi, and C. Murray (2024) "China's Plan to Sell Cheap EVs to the Rest of the World", 5 June, *Financial Times*, https://www.ft.com/content/c77fefa3-7f47-429b-8149-50aa60f39498?emailId=edd2675d-ec77-423b-89f1-680005d5b02d&segmentId=22011ee7-%E2%80%A61/16

11. Financing Structural Investment after 2027

Sophie Barbier[1] *and Helmut von Glasenapp*[2]

An investment can be described as structural if it contributes to financing the structural transformation of the economy and thus making it sustainably competitive. Experience shows that private investments alone are not sufficient due to externalities associated with this type of investment. A mixed public and private financing method is essential and it will help to accelerate the transformation. The challenge of the next European Union (EU) Multiannual Financial Framework ("post-2027") will be to promote the development of this financing method. In this respect, the European budget will have to rely on four pillars: prioritize and plan, activate expenditure, decentralize implementation and strengthen steering. It is on this basis that Europe will be able to finance its structural investments and achieve the structural transformation necessary to maintain and develop its long-term competitiveness within the framework of a new European Competitiveness Pact.

11.1 Introduction

The European Union has faced an accumulation of crises (i.e., financial crisis, pandemic crisis, geopolitical crises, energy crisis), partly interconnected, as they are symptomatic of a crisis in the development model at the global and European levels.

To face these crises, the European Union (EU) proves particularly vulnerable due to a chronic investment deficit over the past years: as European savings, although abundant, do not allow for investment in Europe, it is a Europe weakened by years of underinvestment that must now undergo profound transformation. The needs in terms of investment—to face the climate crisis, to increase the continent's strategic independence, to strengthen the competitiveness of the European economy—therefore

1 Caisse des Dépôts (CDC) Group.

2 European Long-Term Investors Association (ELTI).

 https://doi.org/10.11647/OBP.0434.12

appear all the more considerable as they follow years of chronic underinvestment. For instance, the European Commission (EC) estimates that additional investments of over €620 billion annually will be needed to meet the objectives of the Green Deal and REPowerEU.

These sums also appear particularly massive in comparison to the amounts of available resources today—with national and European public budgets under strong constraint and a majority of private savings invested in liquid assets or outside Europe, notably in the United States. The question of how to finance these investments, which are essential for the structural transformation of the European economy and society, is therefore becoming increasingly acute. The next Multiannual Financial Framework (2028–2034), already under preparation, must imperatively provide an answer to this question, in order to enable Europe to develop and preserve its long-term competitiveness. As underlined by Enrico Letta in his recent report (2024: 26), "Addressing this funding dilemma is essential for the EU to advance its aspirations and maintain its leadership role on the global stage, ensuring that its ambitious agenda can be transformed into tangible actions and outcomes".

In this chapter, we will start by revisiting the concept of structural investments and highlighting their main features. From this, we will deduce some major principles on which to build the next multiannual budget: prioritize and plan strategic investments, based on documented assessments of externalities and democratically constructed political choices; activate public expenditure, ensuring that it plays a role in driving and guiding non-budgetary, public and private, financing; decentralize the implementation of this policy in favour of strategic investments in order to adapt them to local, regional, and national needs; manage these investments by their results in order to strengthen their effectiveness and democratic legitimacy. This is the foundation on which we can build the new European Competitiveness Pact which the European Council calls for (2024: 5): "In the face of a new geopolitical reality and increasingly complex challenges, the European Union is committed to acting decisively to ensure its long-term competitiveness, prosperity and leadership on the global stage and to strengthen its strategic sovereignty".

11.2 Revisiting the Concept of Structural Investments

This *European Public Investment Outlook* provides an overview of the investments necessary for the structural transformation of the European economy—as clearly indicated by the title of this year's edition. One way to define "structural investments" is therefore to define them as investments that enable the transformation of the structure of the European economy, to make it greener, more autonomous, more resilient, richer in growth and employment, more inclusive—in short, more competitive, in the sense that the European Union defines competitiveness (a competitive economy is an economy whose sustained rate of productivity is able to drive growth and, consequently, income and welfare). Consequently, structural investments are meant to have long-lasting impacts on the structure of the European economy and to contribute to shape it in the long term—be they green investments to face the challenge of climate change, investments in infrastructure that increase potential growth and economic resilience, investment in defence that ensures that we can live in a peaceful environment, and so on.

These structural investments are the consequence of political choices—we will return to this later in the chapter—but they have one common economic feature: they generate long-term positive externalities for the European economy. Therefore, we can propose a second definition of structural investments, as investments generating high positive externalities in the long term. Usually, externalities are defined as the indirect effect of one agent's activity on the well-being or economic activities of other agents. In the case of structural investments, they may generate private returns, but they also produce additional indirect effects by increasing European competitiveness. In this respect, despite being highly desirable for the whole society, private initiative will not spontaneously achieve the optimal level of structural investments, as amply demonstrated by economic theory (and common sense!), since their private return is lower than their total (private and social) return... When externalities come into play, public intervention is necessary to ensure the proper level of investment, even if such measures alone may not be sufficient. The European Council emphasizes this point (2024: 6): "Investments in key strategic sectors and infrastructures require a combination of both public and private financing working together".

In this conceptual framework, structural investments must therefore be partly financed by public resources—only partly. This is fortunate because, regardless of the exact scope chosen to define them, these investments represent amounts that far exceed the capabilities of public budgets, both at European and national levels, which are placed under severe constraints (creating new resources or increasing public debt are not viable solutions considering the investment needs we are facing). But we want to emphasize here that the transformation challenge attached to these investments makes this mix between public and private resources necessary because what is at stake is a massive redirection of investment flows towards projects for transforming the economy. Far from being just the consequence of a necessity linked to budgetary realities, the use of private financing in addition to public financing is imperative in terms of efficiency: what is the point, for example, of channelling public budgets towards green investments, if private resources continue to invest in polluting projects? The concept of structural investments also carries the idea that it is the very structure of investments as a whole that needs to evolve.

The concept of structural investments having been clarified, we are left to address our initial question: how is it possible to finance these investments that are essential to long-term European competitiveness, and what role can the EU budget play in this funding?

11.3 Prioritizing and Planning

The EU budget should be part of a more general framework of incentives and constraints, that provide the private actors with visibility and clarity as far as long-term objectives are concerned. As underlined by the recent paper by Jacques Attali (2024: 16), "a genuine transformation of our society requires the integration of the long-term into the behaviour of everyone: citizens, financial intermediaries, public authorities". And this change in behaviour requires clear signals from public authorities that help economic agents to adapt to a new context and to make the transformation objectives their own.

As we have seen, the concept of structural investments covers a potentially very large field of sectors and projects and makes prioritization and planning necessary. This prioritization process is the result of technical assessments of externalities, but also the consequence of choices that are, in the last resort, of a political nature—in the sense of collectively constructed democratic choices. The European Union naturally resorts to multi-year strategies, plans, and programs. Therefore, it is not the absence of planning that is an issue at this level, but rather the lack of overall coherence and insufficient selectivity between multiple—sometimes contradictory—priorities and objectives. In this respect, competitiveness could become the key word for the European action of the new institutions that are being established and lead to the adoption of a Competitiveness Pact that could provide the overall framework for the policies that the new Commission will roll out in the five next years and thus, for delimitation of the field of structural investments at the European level.

This framework must reflect collective choices in terms of long-term growth and the European model—which implies both taking into account the opinions of citizens represented by legitimate intermediary bodies, ensuring ownership of these decisions once made, and maintaining ongoing education about the choices and their implications. This issue of sharing is all the more important in today's context of mistrust of institutions and significant uncertainty. Prioritization and planning can offer clear perspectives and guide investment directions, extending beyond public investments directly managed by European authorities.

11.4 Activating Spending

As we have highlighted above, activating spending responds to a dual imperative: to leverage private funding to supplement limited public means; but, above all, to use public means to guide private funding in the service of a structural transformation of the economy. This is why the next multiannual financial budget should prioritize, whenever possible, public spending that plays an incentive role in relation to private funding and, to do so, select instruments that increase the crowding-in effect induced by public spending. This principle is in line with what the European Union has started doing in the current framework (2021–2027), notably with the setting-up of instruments like the InvestEU program or the CEF Blending (AFIF) instrument.

This activation involves three key actions. First, the financing of technical assistance, which supports project owners and thus promotes the emergence of a pipeline of viable projects consistent with identified priorities. Second, the establishment of guarantees: implementing first-loss instruments or equity uses public funds to facilitate risk-taking by investors. Third, the offsetting of externalization: this involves the "internalization of externalities" through "blending" instruments, i.e. targeting subsidies on the part of the return not reflected in prices. The remaining financing would be provided by public and private investors (this could be easily achieved by systematically injecting a blending component into EU-managed grants).

Such tools already exist but deserve to be developed within the scope of the next budget. The current InvestEU program, which already includes a guarantee component and a technical assistance component, could be complemented by a "blending" component, and especially benefit from a larger scope and budget via a shift of envelopes currently spent in the form of "pure" grants—without leverage effect (i.e., no non-budgetary, public, or private associated funding) and without return for the European budget (i.e., no repayment, no remuneration, or valorization of the funds spent).

11.5 Decentralizing Implementation

The prioritization of strategic investments centralized at the European level, when they have a European dimension, must be accompanied by a decentralized implementation in order to reconcile the coherence of the objectives pursued with the consideration of territorial specificities. In other words, competitiveness—a common European good—which determines the choice of strategic investments to be promoted at the European level, involves the selection of projects necessarily rooted in ground realities and adapted to local, regional, and national needs—a guarantee of the social and territorial cohesion that accompanies the competitiveness of the European model.

To do this, the European Union must rely on specialized intermediaries, capable of deploying financial instruments at the different scales of community action, both at the European level (international financial institutions such as the European Investment Bank, the European Bank for Reconstruction and Development, the Council of Europe Bank) and at the national and local level (banks and promotional development institutions such as KfW in Germany, the Caisse des Dépôts Group in France, the Cassa Di Depositi in Italy, etc.). These actors serve as effective intermediaries for the deployment of these instruments because they operate at the frontier between the public and private spheres, in support of public policies but in connection with private funders. This role is already recognized since most of them are implementing partners of the European Commission.

To strengthen their role in the future, the next Multiannual Financial Framework should systematically "open" the programs to this multiplicity of implementation partners. Consequently, any European program in favour of investment should be open to the plurality of implementation partners—either directly, in their capacity as partners, or indirectly, as a financial intermediary. The Commission must, in the future, be able to systematically mobilize the network of partners that now covers the entire territory of the European Union, in a logic of subsidiarity which will provide efficiency and simplification. Against the background of the significant funding needs, all European policy fields should benefit from this approach.

11.6 Strengthening Steering

Finally, to achieve this structural transformation of the European economy, it is essential to compare the selected priority objectives with the concrete achievements. This approach not only fosters democratic control and encourages public debate but also enhances the efficiency of action taken. This steering requires a change of approach in the controls exercised and the reports produced, which must now focus more on the achievement of objectives than on compliance with procedures: it is on this condition that the steering of structural investments will be effective. Such an approach to steering is all the easier to envisage as the Commission relies on implementation partners whose process requirements it has checked ex ante (via the pillar assessment): when implementation is entrusted to entities whose processes have already been audited, it indeed becomes possible to lighten audit and control procedures and to focus monitoring and reporting on results reported to objectives, much more than on processes, making reporting more meaningful. This would be in line with the overall policy goal of the European Commission to simplify EU rules, reduce unnecessary burdens, and rationalize reporting requirements with a view to reducing them by 25%.

References

Attali, B. (2022) "Investing for the Long Term, a Short-term Emergency (Some Food for Thought)", *Eltia*, https://www.eltia.eu/images/20201210_texte_VF_EN_FINAL.pdf

Attali, B. (2024) "Investing in the Future: Putting the Long Term at the Heart of our Decisions", Report of the Commission, May, https://www.caissedesdepots.fr/en/news/investing-future-long-term-heart-decisions

Confrontations Europe (2024) *30 idées pour 2030*. Paris: Descartes et Cie.

European Council (2024) "Conclusions", April 17 and 18, https://www.consilium.europa.eu/media/m5jlwe0p/euco-conclusions-20240417-18-en.pdf

European Long-Term Investors (2024) "Strategic Outlook—Activating the EU Budget for Long-term Needs", *Eltia*, https://www.eltia.eu/images/2024_02_29_Strategic_outlook.pdf

Letta, E. (2024) *Much More Than a Market*, https://www.consilium.europa.eu/media/ny3j24sm/much-more-than-a-market-report-by-enrico-letta.pdf

Meade J. E. (1952) "External Economies and Diseconomies in a Competitive Situation", *The Economic Journal*, 62(245): 54–67.

Contributor Biographies

Karl Aiginger was born in Vienna on October 23, 1948. He is director of the Policy Crossover Center: Vienna—Europe (www.euiopaplattform.at). He is Professor at the Vienna University of Economics and Business and is an Honorary Professor at the University of Linz. He is Editor-in-Chief of the *Journal of Industry, Competition and Trade* (*JICT*). He has been the Director of the Austrian Institute of Economic Research (WIFO) from 2005 to 2016 and Coordinator of the research project "New Dynamics for Europe: Reaping the Benefits of Socio-ecological Transition"—WWWforEurope (http://Synthesis-Report-Part-I.foreurope.eu). He had temporary commitments at Stanford University, MIT, UCLA, and at the University of Changsha (Hunan, China). His research foci are industrial economics, competitiveness, and strategies of firms, regions and countries. The Policy Crossover Center published studies on "More or Less Europe", Europe taking the lead in responsible globalization, and a European partnership policy with the South and the East.

Ignacio Alvarez was the Secretary of State for Social Rights of the Government of Spain between January 2020 and November 2023. He holds a PhD in International Economics from the University Complutense of Madrid. He is currently Associate Professor of Applied Economics at the Autonomous University of Madrid. He has also worked as a Research Associate at the Complutense Institute of International Studies (ICEI), Visiting Professor of Labor Economics at the Spanish National University of Distance Education (UNED) and Assistant Professor at the University of Valladolid. He has been visiting researcher at the University Paris VII-Denis Diderot, at the Lisbon School of Economics and Management and at the University of South-Eastern Norway, and has participated in several European Union research projects ("Inclusive Growth through Wage Coordination"; "Collectively Agreed Wages in the New European Economic Governance"; "Collectively Agreed Wages in Europe"), as well as in several national projects. His research currently focuses on the study of the relationship between income distribution, demand, and economic growth. His academic articles have been published, among other journals, in the *Socio-Economic Review*, *Cambridge Journal of Economics*, *Structural Change and Economic Dynamics*, *Review of Keynesian Economics*, *Work, Employment and Society*, *International Labour Review*, and the *Journal of Post Keynesian Economics*.

Sophie Barbier is the Head of European Affairs at the French Caisse des Dépôts (CDC) Group. She graduated from the National School of Administration (ENA) and completed a Master's degree in Economics from the Ecole Normale Supérieure de Cachan and Nanterre University. Previously, she worked at the Forecasting Department in the French Ministry for Finance and in the Asset-Liability Team in CDC. She is currently involved in the implementation of EU programs within CDC, such as the InvestEU program and the blending instrument under the Connecting Europe Facility.

Giovanni Barbieri is a Research Fellow at CRANEC at Università Cattolica del Sacro Cuore. He holds a PhD in Institutions and Policies (2017, Università Cattolica del Sacro Cuore, Milano). He was previously Adjunct Professor of History of International and Commercial Institutions at the University of Palermo (DEMS) and Visiting Scholar at Scuola Normale's 'Istituto Ciampi' in Florence (2022). His main expertises are International Relations Theory and International Political Economy (IPE).

Andrea Brasili is a Senior Economist at the EIB (Luxembourg) where his research interests are both micro (firm level) data analysis and macroeconomic developments, in particular those related to fiscal policy. He received his PhD in Public Economics from the University of Pavia (Italy). Before joining the EIB, he worked in the private sector (in Italian banks and asset management companies) as a research economist, whilst still collaborating with academia.

Alessandra Cepparulo obtained her PhD in Political Economics at Sapienza University of Roma. She worked, as a post-doctoral researcher, at different universities in Italy and abroad and as a researcher, in several projects involving Italian national authorities and in international context. She is a Public Economist, whose research interests cover a wide set of issues: public finance and fiscal rules, forecast errors, quality of public expenditures, public investments and PPPs. She is currently working at the European Commission, DG ECFIN, in the unit responsible of fiscal policy and fiscal surveillance.

Floriana Cerniglia is a Full Professor of Economics at Università Cattolica del Sacro Cuore (Milan) and Director of CRANEC (Centro di ricerche in analisi economica e sviluppo economico internazionale). She is the Co-Editor-in-Chief of *Economia Politica (Journal of Analytical and Institutional Economics)*. She received her PhD from the University of Warwick (UK) and her research interests are in public economics and in macroeconomic policies. She has published in leading international journals and she has coordinated and participated in a number of peer-reviewed research projects.

Vincent Charlet is the Executive Director of La Fabrique de l'industrie, a think tank he contributed to launch in 2011. Supported by the French manufacturers' associations, co-chaired by Louis Gallois (former president of Stellantis, former CEO of Airbus Group) and Pierre-André de Chalendar (former CEO of Saint-Gobain), La Fabrique de l'industrie publishes robust studies on the performance, transformations, and assets of industrial companies and on the professional trajectories of their employees. After training as an engineer, Vincent Charlet devoted himself to the analysis of public systems and the management of change. He first participated in initiatives aimed at renovating the research and innovation system in France (evaluation, construction of indicators, foresight). He notably led the FutuRIS project, a prospective operation supported equally by major private R&D players, public research establishments. and the State, from 2006 to 2011.

Reda Cherif is a Senior Economist at the International Monetary Fund (IMF), an Affiliated Researcher at the Bennett Institute for Public Policy at the University of Cambridge, a Senior Research Advisor at the Center of Technology and Industrialization for Development (TIDE), University of Oxford, and a Fellow at the Royal Society for the Arts. He joined the IMF in 2008, as part of the Economist Program, and worked in several departments: in the Fiscal Affairs Department, where he was an economist on the Gabon program; in the Middle East and Central Asia Department, where he covered Saudi Arabia, Qatar and Bahrain; and in the African Department, where he worked in the Regional Studies Division, issuing analytical work on trade, competition and oil economies. He has published numerous articles on the energy transition, public debt dynamics, commodity exporters, development, industrial policy, growth, and innovation. His work was published in the Journal of Development Economics and World Development among others, and it was featured in the *Economist*, *Financial Times* and *National Geographic*. He is the co-editor, with Fuad Hasanov and Min Zhu, of *Breaking the Oil Spell*, a book studying economic diversification in oil exporters. Reda holds an MSc in Economics from the London School of Economics and a PhD in Economics from the University of Chicago.

Tuna Dökmeci is a PhD candidate in Economics at European University Institute (Italy), and a trainee at the EIB (Luxembourg). Her research focuses on industrial policy, industrial organization, and competition policy.

Helmut von Glasenapp studied business administration in Germany, after an apprenticeship in banking. He gained his first business experience with Treuhandanstalt, the former privatization agency in the eastern part of Germany. In 1993 he joined KfW in the Berlin office. From 1997 until 2005, he invested on behalf of KfW in Venture Capital and Private Equity Funds and managed a part of the innovation financing division of KfW Frankfurt. In 2005 he was asked to assist the European Commission as a Seconded National Expert notably to prepare an Equity Promotional Programme for SMEs. In 2007 he continued in Brussels as head of the KfW Liaison Office to the European Union before he was appointed as member of the EU Task Force for Greece of the European Commission until 2015. He joined the Brussels based Secretariat General of the European Long Term Investors Association in 2016 and was elected as ELTI Secretary General in October 2016.

Dario Guarascio is Associate Professor of Economic Policy at the Department of Economics and Law—Sapienza University of Rome—and external affiliate of the Sant'Anna School of Advanced Studies in Pisa and of the National Institute for Public Policy Analysis (INAPP). Dario's research covers economics of innovation, digitalization and labour markets, European economy, and industrial policy. He is Associate Editor of the journals *Structural Change and Economic Dynamics*, *Journal of Industrial and Business Economics*, and *Economia & Lavoro* and former member of the Commissions of the Ministry of Labour and Social Policy for the reform of social security.

Paolo Guerrieri is Visiting Professor at PSIA, Paris School of International Affairs, Sciences Po, Paris. He was Professor of Economics at the University of Rome "La Sapienza" and Visiting Professor at the College of Europe, Bruges (Belgium) and the USD Business School, University of San Diego, California.

Fuad Hasanov is a Senior Economist at the International Monetary Fund (IMF), an Adjunct Professor of Economics at Georgetown University, an Affiliated Researcher at the Bennett Institute for Public Policy at the University of Cambridge, and a Senior Research Advisor at the Technology and Industrialization for Development (TIDE) Centre at the University of Oxford. Before joining the IMF in 2007, Fuad was an Assistant Professor of Economics at Oakland University in Rochester, Michigan. His recent research focuses on natural resources, growth and innovation, and industrial policy. He is the co-editor, with Reda Cherif and Min Zhu, of *Breaking the Oil Spell* that examines economic diversification in oil-exporting countries. Fuad received a PhD, MS, and BA in economics from the University of Texas at Austin.

Atanas Kolev is Principal Advisor at the Economics Department of the EIB. He has worked on a wide range of topics related to investment and investment financing at the firm-, sector-, and economy-wide levels. He has been an organiser and contributor to the annual economics conference of the EIB on topics like economic and social cohesion, investment in the energy sector, adaptation to climate change, public investment, and infrastructure investment. Atanas Kolev is currently a coordinator, reviewer, and economics editor for the EIB Annual Investment Report. He holds an Economics PhD from Universitat Autònoma de Barcelona.

Xun Li is a Research Analyst at the International Monetary Fund (IMF). At the IMF, Xun has contributed to surveillance and policy formulation to promote sustainable economic growth in Europe. Xun holds a Master in Public Administration from Columbia University School of International and Public Affairs, specializing in renewable energy financial modeling and energy and environmental economic analysis.

Franco Mosconi is the Jean Monnet Professor of Industrial Economics at the University of Parma. He is a columnist for the *Corriere di Bologna*, the Bologna-based daily newspaper of *Corriere della Sera*. His research areas include European industrial policy and Industrial districts and clusters, topics on which he has extensively published in both national and international literature.

Pier Carlo Padoan who has been Italian Minister of Economy and Finance and Member of the Chamber of Deputies of the Italian Republic, is Chairman of UniCredit since April 2021. He is Full Professor of Economics retired at the La Sapienza University of Rome. He is currently Vice President of Istituto Affari Internazionali, Board member of the Institute of International Finance, a member of the Luiss Institute for European Analysis and Policy, and a member of the BoD and Executive Committee of ABI. In 2021 he was also appointed member of the Board of Istituto Luigi Einaudi and of the Committee for Corporate Governance of Borsa Italiana. He is currently a member of the European Financial Services Round Table, and of the Executive Committee of Assonime. In May 2022 he became Chairperson of the High Level Group on Financing Sustainability Transition, which is part of the High Level Groups on EU Policy and Innovation. He has been Deputy Secretary General and Chief Economist of OECD and Executive Director of the International Monetary Fund. He has held academic positions at the University of Rome, College of Europe (Bruges and Warsaw), Université Libre de Bruxelles, University of Urbino, Universidad de la Plata, Chulalongkorn University and University of Tokyo.

Paolo Pasimeni is Deputy Chief Economist at the European Commission, DG Internal Market and Industry, and Senior Associate Researcher at the Brussels School of Governance of the Vrije Universiteit Brussel (VUB). Specialized in international macroeconomics, his main field of expertise is the macroeconomic analysis of the single market and of the economic and monetary union (EMU). Expert on monetary, fiscal and structural policies, he has been working on the proposals for EMU reform, in particular on the design of a stabilization capacity. He has also worked on labour market analysis, as well as on the conception of the EU multi-annual budget. Personal webpage: https://brussels-school.be/team/paolo-pasimeni

Mathieu Plane is a Deputy Director of the Analysis and Forecasting Department at the OFCE Research Center in Economics, Sciences Po, Paris. He is in charge of economic forecasts for the French economy and works on economic policy issues. He teaches at Sciences Po, Paris and at the University of Paris Pantheon-Sorbonne. He was, in 2013–2014, economic advisor to the Ministers of Economy, Industry, and the Digital Sector. He has recently published, in collaboration with other authors of OFCE, *25 Years of Monetary Union: The Eurozone through Its Crises*; *Growth Up Against Fiscal Recovery: Economic Outlook for the French Economy 2024–2025*, and *French Economy 2025* by Éditions La Découverte, Repères collection.

Debora Revoltella has been Director of the Economics Department of the European Investment Bank since April 2011. The Department comprises thirty economists and provides economic analysis and studies to support the bank in defining its policies and strategies. Before joining the EIB, Debora worked for many years at CESEE, was head of the research department in COMIT, and later worked as Chief Economist for CESEE in UniCredit. Debora holds a PhD in Economics and has also worked as Adjunct Professor at Bocconi University. She is a member of the Steering Committees of the Vienna Initiative and CompNet, an alternate member of the Board of the Joint Vienna Institute, and a member of the boards of SUERF and the Euro 50 Group.

Katja Rietzler is Head of the Unit of Fiscal Policy at the Macroeconomic Policy Institute (IMK), part of the Hans-Böckler Foundation. She holds a PhD from the Freie Universität, Berlin. Among other topics, her research focuses on fiscal issues of the municipalities, the German tax-system, public investment needs, and fiscal rules. In addition, she is a member of the IMK's modelling team. As an expert she regularly participates in parliamentary hearings on issues such as tax legislation, annual budgets, or the debt brake and its implementation.

Francesco Saraceno is Deputy Department Director at OFCE, the research centre in economics at Sciences Po in Paris, and Professor of Practice at LEAP-Luiss, Rome. He holds PhDs in Economics from Columbia University and the Sapienza University of Rome. His research focuses on the relationship between inequality, macroeconomic performance, and European macroeconomic policies. From 2000 to 2002 he was a member of the Council of Economic Advisors for the Italian Prime Minister's Office. He teaches international and European macroeconomics at Sciences Po, where he manages the Economics concentration of the Master's in European Affairs, and in Rome (Luiss). He is Academic Director of the Sciences Po-Northwestern European Affairs Program. He advises the International Labour Organization (ILO) on macroeconomic policies for employment and participates in IMF training programmes on fiscal policy.

Annamaria Simonazzi is Former Professor of Political Economy at La Sapienza University of Rome and Cnel Expert Advisor in the X Council. She is President of the Giacomo Brodolini Foundation, Managing Director of *Economia & Lavoro* and member of the editorial board of the web magazine www.inGenere.it. She has published widely on European macroeconomic issues, industrial policy, employment, welfare, and gender economics.

Annamaria Tueske is an Economist at the Economics Department of the EIB. Her current work focuses on public investment, climate and energy economics and sustainable finance. Prior to joining the EIB, Annamaria worked at the University of Luxembourg, at the OECD and at the Fiscal Council of Hungary. Her academic training focused on industrial organization, networks, and transport economics, she graduated from the Toulouse School of Economics.

Jorge Uxó has a PhD in Economics by the University Complutense of Madrid. He is currently Associate Professor of Applied Economics at the Complutense University of Madrid and Vice-President of the Spanish Productivity Board. He has been visiting researcher at the University of Coimbra (Centre for Social Studies), University of Alcalá and the European Trade Union Institute (ETUI) and has participated in European Union and national research projects, mainly focused on Macroeconomics and Economic Policy in Spain and the EMU and Post Keynesian Economics. His academic articles have been published, among other journals, in Cambridge Journal of Economics, Structural Change and Economic Dynamics, Review of Keynesian Economics, Review of Political Economy, International Labour Review, Journal of Post Keynesian Economics, Applied Economics or Metroeconomica.

Andrew Watt is General Director, European Trade Union Institute (ETUI), and former Head of the Unit of European Economic Policy at the Macroeconomic Policy Institute (IMK), part of the Hans-Böckler Foundation. He holds a PhD from the University of Hamburg. His main research fields are European economic and employment policy and comparative political economy, with a particular interest in the interaction between wage-setting and macroeconomic policy. Recent work has focused on reform of the economic governance of the euro area, emphasizing the need to coordinate monetary, fiscal, and wage policy in order to achieve balanced growth and favourable employment outcomes. He has served as advisor to numerous European and national institutions, including the European.

Wouter Van Der Wielen is an Economist in the Economics Department of the European Investment Bank (EIB). He is responsible for impact studies of public and private sector policy support schemes and contributes macroeconomic analyses to the EIB's flagship publications, such as the EIB Investment Report. Prior to joining the EIB, he worked as an economic analyst at the European Commission's Joint Research Centre, where he was principally responsible for the research developing macro-fiscal models accounting for output and employment effects of fiscal reforms. His main areas of expertise are macroeconomics, fiscal policy and labour economics. He holds a PhD in Economics as well as an MSc of Advanced Studies in Economics from KU Leuven.

About the Team

Alessandra Tosi was the managing editor for this book.

Adèle Kreager and Kayla Brison proof-read this manuscript.

The cover was designed by Jeevanjot Kaur Nagpal, and produced in InDesign using the Fontin and Calibri fonts.

Jeremy Bowman typeset the book in InDesign and produced the paperback, hardback and EPUB editions. The text font is Tex Gyre Pagella; the heading font is Californian FB.

Cameron Craig produced the PDF and HTML editions. The conversion was performed with open-source software and other tools freely available on our GitHub page at https://github.com/OpenBookPublishers.

Raegan Allen was in charge of marketing.

This book was peer-reviewed by two referees. Experts in their field, these readers give their time freely to help ensure the academic rigour of our books. We are grateful for their generous and invaluable contributions.

This book need not end here...

Share

All our books — including the one you have just read — are free to access online so that students, researchers and members of the public who can't afford a printed edition will have access to the same ideas. This title will be accessed online by hundreds of readers each month across the globe: why not share the link so that someone you know is one of them?

This book and additional content is available at
https://doi.org/10.11647/OBP.0434

Donate

Open Book Publishers is an award-winning, scholar-led, not-for-profit press making knowledge freely available one book at a time. We don't charge authors to publish with us: instead, our work is supported by our library members and by donations from people who believe that research shouldn't be locked behind paywalls.

Join the effort to free knowledge by supporting us at
https://www.openbookpublishers.com/support-us

We invite you to connect with us on our socials!

BLUESKY
@openbookpublish
.bsky.social

MASTODON
@OpenBookPublish
@hcommons.social

LINKEDIN
open-book-publishers

Read more at the Open Book Publishers Blog

https://blogs.openbookpublishers.com

You may also be interested in:

Financing Investment in Times of High Public Debt

2023 European Public Investment Outlook

Floriana Cerniglia, Francesco Saraceno & Andrew Watt (eds.)

https://doi.org/10.11647/OBP.0386

Models in Microeconomic Theory

Expanded Second Edition (She)

Martin J. Osborne & Ariel Rubinstein

https://doi.org/10.11647/OBP.0361

The DARPA Model for Transformative Technologies

Perspectives on the U.S. Defense Advanced Research Projects Agency

William Boone Bonvillian, Richard Van Atta & Patrick Windham (eds.)

https://doi.org/10.11647/OBP.0184

Having Too Much

Philosophical Essays on Limitarianism

Ingrid Robeyns (editor)

https://doi.org/10.11647/OBP.0338

www.ingramcontent.com/pod-product-compliance
Lightning Source LLC
Chambersburg PA
CBHW050039220326
41599CB00041B/7214
9781805114383